Arting and Writing to
Transform Education

Frameworks for Writing
Series Editor: Martha C. Pennington, School for Oriental and African Studies
and Birkbeck College, University of London

The *Frameworks for Writing* series offers books focused on writing and the
teaching and learning of writing in educational and real-life contexts. The
hallmark of the series is the application of approaches and techniques to writing
and the teaching of writing that go beyond those of English literature to draw on
and integrate writing with other disciplines, areas of knowledge, and contexts
of everyday life. The series entertains proposals for textbooks as well as books
for teachers, teacher educators, parents, and the general public. The list includes
teacher reference books and student textbooks focused on innovative pedagogy
aiming to prepare teachers and students for the challenges of the 21st century.

Published:
The College Writing Toolkit
Tried and Tested Ideas for Teaching College Writing
Edited by Martha C. Pennington and Pauline Burton

The "Backwards" Research Guide for Writers
Using your Life for Reflection, Connection, and Inspiration
Sonya Huber

Exploring College Writing
Reading, Writing, and Researching across the Curriculum
Dan Melzer

Tend your Garden
Nurturing Motivation in Young Adolescent Writers
Mary Anna Kruch

Writing Poetry through the Eyes of Science
A Teacher's Guide to Scientific Literacy and Poetic Response
Nancy Gorrell, with Erin Colfax

Reflective Writing for Language Teachers
Thomas S. C. Farrell

Creativity and Writing Pedagogy
Linking Creative Writers, Researchers, and Teachers
Edited by Harriet Levin Millan and Martha C. Pennington

Academic Writing Step by Step
A Research-based Approach
Christopher N. Candlin, Peter Crompton, and Basil Hatim

Creativity and Discovery in the University Writing Class
A Teacher's Guide
Edited by Alice Chik, Tracey Costley, and Martha C. Pennington

Understanding the Paragraph and Paragraphing
Iain McGee

Arting and Writing to Transform Education

*An Integrated Approach for
Culturally and Ecologically Responsive Pedagogy*

Meleanna Aluli Meyer, Mikilani Hayes Maeshiro,
and Anna Yoshie Sumida

SHEFFIELD UK   BRISTOL CT

Published by Equinox Publishing Ltd.

UK: Office 415, The Workstation, 15 Paternoster Row, Sheffield, South Yorkshire S1 2BX
USA: ISD, 70 Enterprise Drive, Bristol, CT 06010

www.equinoxpub.com

First published 2018

British Library Cataloguing-in-Publication Data

A catalogue record for this book is available from the British Library.

ISBN   978 1 84553 654 1 (hardback)
       978 1 84553 655 8 (paperback)
       978 1 78179 776 1 (ePDF)

Library of Congress Cataloging-in-Publication Data

Names: Meyer, Meleanna Aluli, author. | Maeshiro, Mikilani Hayes, author. |
   Sumida, Anna Yoshie, author.
Title: Arting and writing to transform education : an integrated approach for
   culturally and ecologically responsive pedagogy / Meleanna Aluli Meyer,
   Mikilani Hayes Maeshiro, and Anna Yoshie Sumida.
Description: Sheffield, UK ; Bristol, CT : Equinox Publishing, Ltd, 2018. |
   Series: Frameworks for writing | Includes bibliographical references and
   index.
Identifiers: LCCN 2018012274 (print) | LCCN 2018028101 (ebook) | ISBN
   9781781797761 (ePDF) | ISBN 9781845536541 (hardback) | ISBN 9781845536558
   (paperback)
Subjects: LCSH: Arts–Study and teaching (Elementary)–Hawaii–Case studies. |
   Composition (Language arts)–Study and teaching
   (Elementary)–Hawaii–Case studies. | Culturally relevant
   pedagogy–Hawaii–Case studies.
Classification: LCC LC1100 (ebook) | LCC LC1100 .M48 2018 (print) | DDC
   372.5/04409969–dc23
LC record available at https://lccn.loc.gov/2018012274

Typeset by S.J.I. Services, New Delhi
Printed and bound by Lightning Source Inc. (La Vergne, TN), Lightning Source UK Ltd. (Milton Keynes), Lightning Source AU Pty. (Scoresby, Victoria).

Contents

Appendices

Foreword by Sir Sidney M. Mead

Children are born with the ability to be creative thinkers, to be curious about the world around them and to be avid learners. Within them is the creative spark ready to be ignited. The challenge for teachers at all levels of education is to engage the creative abilities of the children we teach. The challenge is also about innovation and how to produce innovative and critical thinkers and problem solvers.

Here is a book that provides a way of engaging the creative abilities of students at the beginning of their journey in education. The authors have devised an approach to teaching that is designed to engage the creative spark in the children, ignite it, nurture and develop their creative abilities, and engage those abilities in the activities of the classroom and beyond. Not only will the classroom be transformed into an exciting world of learning, but the children themselves become engaged learners and keen researchers on the way to becoming problem solvers and innovative and creative thinkers.

The authors of this book have explored a way of developing the creative abilities of children and have now set out their philosophy and provided information and teaching materials to assist teachers who might like to try out their approach. The approach is grounded in culture, Hawaiian culture in this case, but it is the principle that needs to be noticed. The culture of the children, of their home and of their ethnic group, is the starting point. For the authors, the culture is foundational and necessary in educational discourse, and I agree with them.

The authors focus on activities associated with art and writing. Doing art is called "arting" and doing written exercises is "writing," and both are creative activities. They say "creativity animates spirit, mind and body." They also say that once the creative spark is energized a child becomes "totally engaged and absorbed" in what they are creating. If I were a classroom teacher, I would support an approach that would make that happen.

The authors combine culture, ecology, arting, and writing into a theory of teaching – in other words, a pedagogy – one which they view as transforming education through the integration of these elements. It is an approach for classroom teaching that is motivating, relevant, and place-based. It generates "opportunities to explore" with an important end point of "liberating creativity." The liberation of creative ability and energy aims at affecting and informing classroom practice and thus the whole curriculum. I support the authors in bringing to the attention of a global audience the creative approach to classroom practice that they have set out in this book.

– Sir Sidney M. Mead
Te Whare Wananga o Awanuiarangi
Whakatane, New Zealand

Foreword by Manulani Aluli Meyer

"The true goal of Education is liberation."
– Hale Makua

You have in your hands a rare opportunity to understand emergent mutuality. It is a spiritual process that includes, expands, and transforms everyday concerns into a whispering potential few acknowledge. It is so subtle that you may think this is only a book, or another pedagogical process to school children differently. Look again. Linger through the pages; touch words like *multiple dimensions*, *arting*, *dynamic complexity*, *creativity*, *liberating thinking.* Explore the imagery. These are not mainstream visuals or ideas for a predictable and standardized schooling structure. They are extra-ordinary facets of true education, and they are birthed because of the needs of our time, and with exquisite excellence found in trusting, stubbornness, and inspiring collaboration. As the authors say:

> Education, in its highest form, liberates human potential through transformational teaching and learning experiences.

Meleanna Aluli Meyer, Mikilani Hayes Maeshiro, and Anna Yoshie Sumida are the cultural creatives of this movement. They are teaching us to link right and left hemispheres of our brain to our pulsing and wise heart. They are educators in the best sense of the word because they *draw forth* what is most vibrant and desirable in students/teachers/community – and that is the *love* of learning. This in turn creates the kind of meaning that transforms and teaches us to know ourselves. Here is the purpose of life, and the point of education that seems to have been misplaced with standardization, uniformity, and the commodification of knowledge.

We here in Hawai'i must help education and society more generally evolve. We can do this with our rich and vibrant understanding of cultural pedagogy, discovered within the cacophony of our intersecting cultures and shared history. There is infinite knowing within Indigenous sensibilities, and in Hawai'i, the root of all this dynamism is *nā mea waiwai* – the massive wealth of Hawaiian wisdom found in our principles, language, stories, and proverbs still vibrating throughout our shorelines.

- Ka waihona o ka na'auao. A wealth of knowledge
  Knowledge is enlightenment of oneself which radiates outward to the greater community.

- Kanu nei au, aia iā 'oe ka ulu.
  I plant and the growth is yours.

- Ahuwale ka po'okela i kāu hana iā ha'i.
  It is through the way you serve others that your greatness will be felt.

Here is a (k)new way of seeing and teaching, collected and expressed in language and imagery for the benefit of your own remembering as a teacher, parent, community member, or administrator. How fortunate you are to be holding this book! It heralds a change that has arrived. We are beginning to articulate tacit knowledge systems that define wholeness in clear, succinct patterns so they can now be seen, recognized, and used. In the authors' words:

> *Traditionally, the visual arts and writing have been taught as separate, stand-alone subjects, when in fact their greatest relevance as educational tools is in their capacity to intersect one another, creatively and constructively. Each form mutually benefits from the many ways in which they overlap and parallel each other. Used together, arting and writing work in tandem to create a dance between the two art forms. What we share in this book enlarges educational experience from one that is flat and linear to one of multiple dimensions and dynamic complexity. Arting and writing empower students to unleash their creativity, to intuit, and to liberate their thinking in transformative ways.*

Our world longs for this kind of transformative tool. So please, take your time. *Arting and Writing to Transform Education: An Integrated Approach for Culturally and Ecologically Responsive Pedagogy* has come to print with a radical intentionality. The authors have answered with their lives the questions that gave it meaning. Feel and experience excellence and *be inspired.* Be changed by the passion of these three educators, and know that they are beside you cheering you on, and trusting that you too are the center of the evolution!

Ulu aʻe ke welina a ke aloha.
Loving is the practice of awake minds.

– Dr. Manulani Aluli Meyer
University of Hawaiʻi, West Oʻahu

Editor's Preface

This book presents an integrated approach to the education of children that teaches them how to see and describe their world – both the natural world around them and their own culture and identity – through linking the media of art and language, considered as parallel creative-expressive processes of *arting* (representation in visual images) and *writing* (representation in words). The work presents conceptual background and practical materials developed in a collaboration by two Hawai'i elementary teachers, one with a doctorate in Education from the University of Hawai'i (Anna Sumida) and one an Education Design Specialist (Miki Maeshiro), and a well-known Hawaiian artist and educator (Meleanna Meyer). This team of three authors, who evolved their curriculum ideas and instructional activities over several years teaching at the Kamehameha Schools in Honolulu and in community education programs throughout the state, merges interests and expertise in literacy and culture, art and science in a pedagogy that is culturally and ecologically responsive and that bridges across different areas of knowledge and skill. Their goal is one of transformative education based on the combined power and synergy of arting and writing processes.

In their introduction to the work, the authors use their own personal stories to illustrate what it is like growing up outside the cultural mainstream and how empowering it is to feel a sense of one's own identity, capabilities, and place in the world. The conceptual background provided in Part I suggests how the learning of bodies of knowledge and practical skills in school can be raised to a higher level of exploration and personalized learning that leads to a situated and empowered sense of self, through arting-and-writing projects which center on local ecology and culture and on students' own lives and interests. Part II describes arting and writing processes in detail, focusing on commonalities and offering what amounts to a series of chapter by chapter mini-tutorials on the stages artists and writers go through in evolving their work, each one culminating in a reflection on how arting and writing processes can work together and be mutually reinforcing. Part III provides two extensive multi-lesson units, complete with objectives, lesson plans, and printable exercise sheets given in appendices. These units illustrate the authors' integrated arting–writing approach as applied in the Hawaiian context and as can be adapted for use in elementary and middle-school classes in other contexts. Hawaiian ecology and stories about the land offer illustrations of how teachers can integrate learning in students' home language and culture with mainstream English language and culture. Further illustrative lesson material shows how students can explore their own cultural identity as connected to family and place through arting and writing activities.

The book is inspirational in content, suggesting an approach to educating children that will be enjoyable to teach and will engage learners in many ways and help them realize their full potential. It is also visually inspirational, richly illustrated in color with examples of student work and the work of artists and teachers, including that of the authors themselves. I believe strongly in its integrated writing–arting and science–literacy approach and find the model of Hawaiian language and culture to be interesting in itself and also a good illustration of the approach that can be adapted to local language and culture anywhere. I believe it would be wonderful if all children were taught in this way, and would no doubt stimulate a lot of learning and unlock a great deal of passion, pride, and energy to create and achieve at a high level.

– Martha C. Pennington
Series Editor, *Frameworks for Writing*

Acknowledgements

'A'ohe hana nui ke alu 'ia
"No task is too big when done together."
– 'Ōlelo No'eau no. 142

Mahalo nui i nā lima he nui i kāko'o mai iā mākou i kēia huaka'i o ka 'imi na'auao.

This book would not have been possible without the brilliant minds and aloha-filled *na'au* (intuition) of the children, parents, teachers, friends, administrators, and organizations we've worked with over the years to realize this book. Their schools, classrooms, and conversations provided a context for inquiry and creativity to flourish. Their counsel and input affirmed and inspired new ideas. Collectively, with our contributors, we have created a work that moves beyond us – with the hope of nurturing creativity and transformative educational experiences for future generations.

First of all, we wish to give our personal *mahalo* (thanks) to all of the young artists and writers who have contributed their beautiful work. They continue to amaze us with their creativity and profound thoughts for a better world. Mahalo to the *po'okumu* (principals) and *kumu* (teachers) of Ke Kula 'o Samuel M. Kamakau and Ke Kula Kaiapuni o Hau'ula, where these arting and writing concepts, ideas, and lessons were actualized through the *kumu* and *keiki* (children). They embraced the messiness of t³, transmediation, and were always willing to explore new ideas. They are the creators of much of the beautiful artwork within these pages. A complete list of contributors appears at the end of the book.

In addition, we thank the Bishop Museum Press for allowing us to quote generously from the following source:

Hawaiian proverbs are from *'Ōlelo No'eau: Hawaiian Proverbs & Poetical Sayings*, collected, translated, and annotated by Mary Kawena Pukui. Copyright © 1983 Bernice Pauahi Bishop Museum. Used with permission from Bishop Museum Press.

Gratitude from Meleanna ...

Mahalo nui to the many brilliant lights in my educational and creative life whose encouragement and mentoring have guided me in innumerable ways. Especially to my earliest art teachers Meg Homestead and Chuck Welborn, who instilled in me a love of beauty, curiosity and joy in all things creative. To my beloved parents Emma and Harry Meyer, who saw that the arts were the most important thing for my well-being. Beloved artist–instructors, Nathan Oliviera, Leo Holub, and Matt Kahn, who made a profound difference in my artistic pursuits. Dr. Royal Fruehling, for never letting me give up on my studies. Dr. Elliot Eisner, for his Educating [my] Artistic Vision by allowing me into his graduate class when I was an overzealous undergraduate. To my kumu, J. Keola Lake, Kalani Meinecke, and Hale Makua, whose deep 'ike Hawai'i and great patience encouraged the best from me as I continue to strive to fully integrate all things cultural and creative. To my family, sons, grandchildren, and partner Laurie for their constant love, support, and boundless encouragement on this incredible adventure.

Gratitude from Miki ...

Mahalo nui to Donald Graves and Ralph Fletcher, whose writing wisdom, guidance, and encouraging words have always inspired me to aspire to become that writing teacher who makes a difference in the lives of my students. Colleague extraordinaire, artist, and teacher Debra Drown, who first showed me, many years ago, the impact on student learning when art and writing sit side-by-side. My cousin Linda Kubota, for generously giving of her time, keen editing eye, and revision suggestions on our early drafts. My husband Brian, for his patience, understanding, and supportive words during the many, many hours and late nights spent on writing this book.

Gratitude from Anna ...

Mahalo nui to distant teachers, Don Murray, Donald Graves, and Ralph Fletcher, whose words I always return to when writer's block creeps in. Special thanks to Lloyd – my personal English teacher – always willing to painstakingly teach and show his younger sister how to improve any piece of writing. We lovingly thank all the students and families we've worked with over the years from whom we've learned so much.

Mahalo, mahalo, mahalo from all of us to our incredible editor, Martha Pennington, for first seeing the potential in our work years ago. We are grateful for her patience, guidance, insight, understanding, persistence, and nudging – always gentle yet intense when needed. Because of Martha, our ideas are now in this world to share with you.

Ideas have been shared and now continue with you, our readers.

– Miki, Meleanna, and Anna

Figure I.1. *Nā Piko ʻEkolu*, The Three Wisdom Centers, which connect one to past, present, and future generations.

Introduction

Our Inspiration

The universe has grand designs – we are convinced! The three of us were brought together by a united purpose, a mutual passion, and great desire to share our exploration of culture and education. Anna researched the intersection of culture, identity, and pedagogy. Meleanna explored the juncture of art and spirituality as concrete expressions of culture. Miki integrated reading and writing within a cultural context as daily classroom practice. Each of us grew to understand *culture* as a way to empower students, positioning them to become producers of knowledge and igniting their potential to become agents of social change. The experiences we share within these pages offer insights into a constellation of transformative processes that integrate arting – that is, all of the activities involved in making art – and writing, grounded in culture.

Hawaiʻi is our educational home. Although this book is grounded in the Hawaiian culture and our experiences with students, it embraces all cultures, as we believe that humanity is truly a family of families. The concepts and ideas shared within these pages can be applied to a diversity of educational contexts. We hope other teachers will consider our experience in Hawaiʻi and the examples we give from our context to illuminate relevant perspectives that are liberating and empowering, and we hope inspiring, for any cultural environment or geographical location. Collectively, the intersection of your lives with ours was not random happenstance but perhaps part of a larger, cosmic design.

Figure I.2. Kūkaniloko, sacred cultural site on the island of Oʻahu, is the historical birthing site of Native Hawaiian chiefs.

Coming Together at Kamehameha

Kamehameha Schools, a private school system in Hawaiʻi with three kindergarten–12th grade campuses, was our nexus. Founded by Princess Bernice Pauahi Bishop,[1] the great-granddaughter of King Kamehameha I, the original school was established in 1887 to educate Native Hawaiian children. Princess Pauahi had witnessed the devastating effects of Western contact on her people: loss of land, depopulation from infectious diseases, illegal overthrow of the Hawaiian monarchy, banning of the Hawaiian language in public schools. As a response to these events, she established the school to remediate the cataclysmic decline of Native Hawaiians.

Hawaiian children constitute 26% of the total enrollment in Hawai'i's statewide public and charter school system. Kamehameha Schools brought the three of us together in a literacy outreach program as a way to extend its educational reach into Native Hawaiian communities. Anna was director of the literacy outreach program, Miki was recruited as a Hawaiian language literacy resource teacher, and Meleanna was recruited as a visual arts and culture specialist. The program goals were to integrate Hawaiian culture-based arting and writing to produce reading materials that would empower students to find their voices through cultural grounding, and to support them to be producers of knowledge by illustrating, writing, and publishing their own original books. Since Native Hawaiian children are essentially absent from mainstream educational texts, the vision was to have students see themselves, their language, their culture, and their unique sense of place represented in printed classroom materials.

Figure I.3. A 1st grader's arting and writing interpretation of the *Kumulipo*, a Hawaiian creation chant.

Teaching to the 4th Power

Anna's doctoral studies focused on curriculum through the lenses of cultural identity and critical theory. As a result, a pedagogical framework, Teaching to the 4th Power, T^4, was envisioned as a transformative educational paradigm involving four dimensions: transmission, transaction, transmediation, and Transformation. When multiplied together to form a constitutive whole – t^1ransmission × t^2ransaction × t^3ransmediation $\rightarrow T^4$ransformation – these dimensions hold a capacity to exponentially elevate teaching and learning experiences, creating the potential for transformation and social change. It is within this pedagogical framework that the relationship between the visual arts and language arts became fertile ground for our partnership and for exploring new ways of deepening educational experiences.

Culture

Culture is the critical component that grounds the work we do on all levels of our teaching and learning. As social beings, how we interact and are in relationship with one another is critically important for the success and flourishing of our species, and for broadening an appreciation of worldviews that may be different from our own. Understanding that *culture* originates from the Latin root *cultus*, meaning "to care for" and "to cultivate," inspires the desire to awaken within our students their culture: their connection to the land from which they come, their ancestral genealogies and roots, and the unique gifts found within them. Through this mindset, we share nested interrelationships framed as Home, Host/Indigenous, Local, and Global cultures. This idea of cultures envisions an educational center that is not dominated by any one group; instead, it is held open, a place where discussion is invited and where all are asked to participate.

Arting

Meleanna developed the concept of "arting" as a verb, a process. The inspiration for arting is derived from a Hawaiian worldview of animating energy as a dynamic and creative process, breathing life, or *hā*, into thoughts, words, colors, and actions. *Hā* enlivens the soul of any artistic experience, allowing for creative endeavors to become transformative. When teaching the visual arts, she uses arting as a way for students to explore, find, and work with their intrinsic motivations and passions. As a result, students become more fully present and engaged as learners, making their educational experiences relevant, authentic, useful, and rigorous. Arting awakens creativity as a parallel process to writing.

Figure I.4. This example from an artist–writer's notebook shows how the two art forms sit side-by-side.

Writing

In a Hawaiian worldview, words have *mana*, or power. As Mary Kawena Pukui puts it, "Words can heal; words can destroy" (Pukui, 1983; #1191). Because words have *mana*, they have the ability to heal and empower. We use writing as a vehicle for students to tell and share their stories of home, family, community, and things they care about. The act of writing empowers students to discover meaning by bringing voice to their thoughts, feelings, and lives. Writing allows students to record, express, explore, discover, define, and reflect upon what matters most in their lives. Writing calls ideas into being. As a creative and literary process, writers carefully select and arrange words, craft sentences, and complete compositions that communicate across time and space.

Arting and Writing

We believe artists and writers move through similar stages when creating. The mark-making of a visual artist is similar to the mark-making of a writer. Understanding arting and writing as complementary processes of expression and communication, one through image and the other through word, enables teachers to incorporate the visual arts in tandem with the literary arts in meaningful ways across the curriculum. They bring together visual and print literacies in ways that recognize their increasing interrelationship in the modern world of multimedia and digital culture, thus preparing learners with the skills and the ways of seeing and thinking they will need in the 21st century. Visual and literary art when used as an ensemble provide a dynamic and layered learning experience resulting in deeper understanding from one's whole being.

Traditionally, the visual arts and writing have been taught as separate, stand-alone subjects, when in fact their greatest relevance as educational tools is in their capacity to intersect one another, creatively and constructively. Each form mutually benefits from the many ways in which they overlap and parallel each other. Used together, arting and writing work in tandem to create a dance between the two art forms. What we share in this book enlarges educational experience from one that is flat and linear to one of multiple dimensions and dynamic complexity. Arting and writing empower students to unleash their creativity, to intuit, and to liberate their thinking in transformative ways.

Figure I.5. *Po'e Kānaka* (Hawaiian People): A section of an acrylic painting by Hawaiian artist, Solomon Enos.

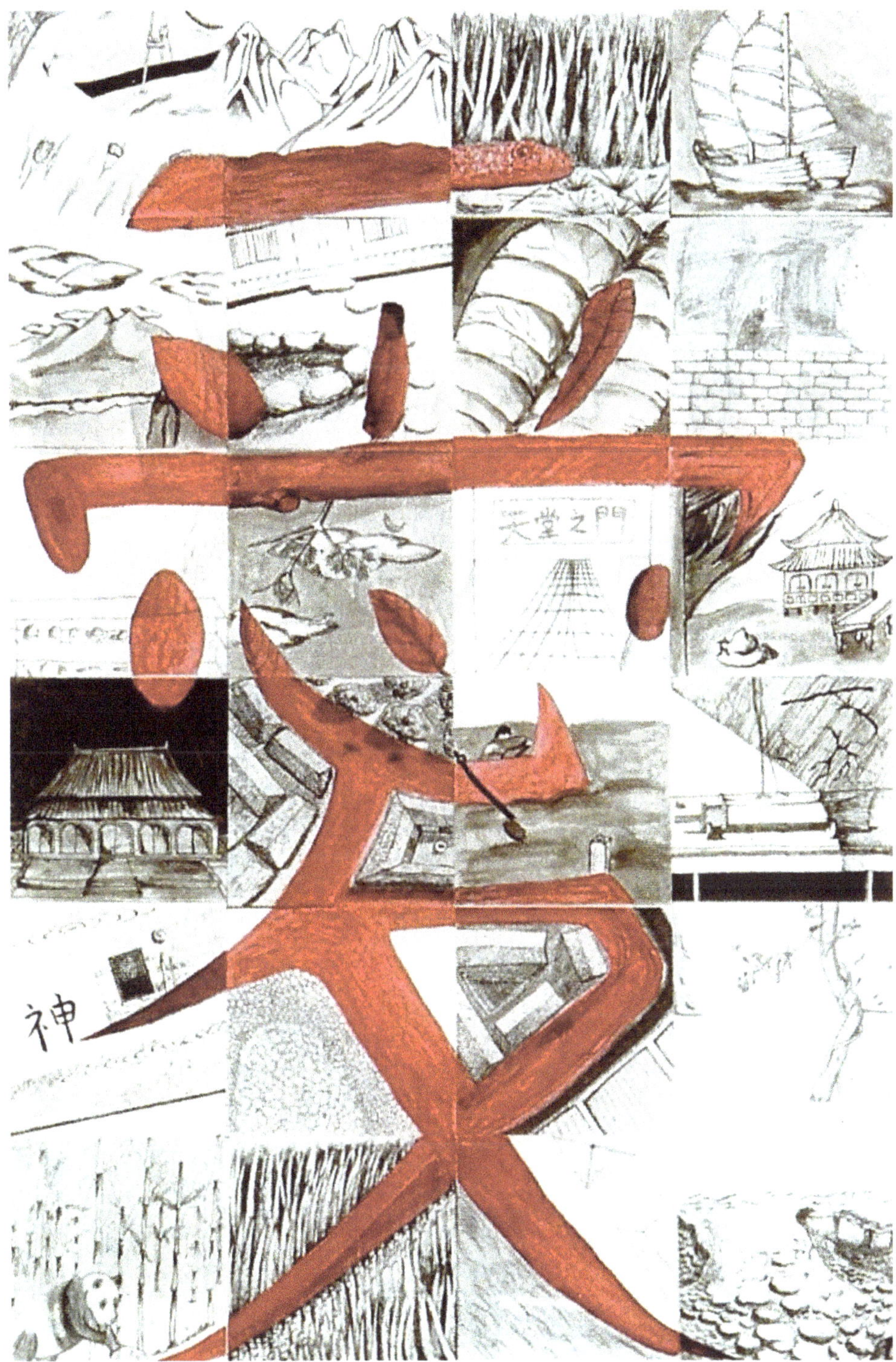

Figure I.6. Through the arting and writing processes, high school students explore connections to their Chinese cultural heritage. In this mural, the red *hànzi* character for "love" is written as an integral part of the overall composition. The smaller drawings represent important aspects of place and culture.

Meet the Authors

Figure I.7. The authors: Meleanna Meyer, Mikilani Maeshiro, and Anna Sumida.

Meleanna Meyer

I am *hapa*, of mixed racial descent, Hawaiian and a mixture of Chinese, German, and English, the second child of seven. In the United States, in 1954, couples were not legally allowed to marry out of their race. But in Hawai'i, these kinds of marriages were more readily accepted – as the mores of this island nation were influenced by a Polynesian worldview that was more accepting of difference. My mother was of Hawaiian–Chinese ancestry, born and raised in Hawai'i; my father, from Illinois, of German–English heritage. Thus, my family values and practices were a rich mix of Hawaiian, Asian, and European traditions. Being of many cultures allowed me to appreciate the richness of my own identity and that of others.

Whenever my parents entertained guests from abroad, they were treated to a variety of local foods and traditions. Our extended family gatherings, however, were more Hawaiian, filled with prayer, story, music, song, and dance. Whenever the aunties made requests of us *keiki* (children), the expectation was that we would share our gifts and talents such as singing Hawaiian songs, playing the *'ukulele*, or dancing a *hula*. And for my father, it was reciting poetry or sharing a story. Whatever was offered was always one's best effort.

Figure I.8. Treasures from the sea.

My parents believed that my six siblings and I could accomplish anything in life as long as we had a good education and worked hard. The values of hard work, respect, proper manners, and cleanliness were instilled in us from an early age. We learned that who we were in the world was dependent upon how we acted and how we cared for and treated others.

My family lived in Kailua, within walking distance of the ocean in an area known as Mōkapu. This extended family consisted of four smaller families, including my mom, dad, aunts, uncles, and 24 cousins. From an early age, I felt a great comfort and sense of belonging because my large extended family lived in close proximity to one another. My cousins and I ran as a pack, ate dinner and slept over at each other's houses. We were free to roam with abandon. This was a childhood of ease and safety which gave me a strong sense of belonging. I developed a deep kin relationship with my extended family and my *one hānau*, my birth sands, my home.

As an innately curious child, nature and the elements became my best friends. Exquisite beauty surrounded me in the ocean waves, twigs and seeds, clouds, and fragrant ginger blossoms. I felt an awe and wonder in all things. Vibrant flowers, gentle winds, pounding waves, warm rains, and passing showers crowded my daydreams and sparked my imagination; perhaps this is how the arts found me. When I was five years old, I discovered that I could create with my hands, turning raw materials into something beautiful. I spent my days observing, drawing with pencil and crayon, painting, building with papier-mache and clay, working with power tools, and anything else I could get my hands on. Creativity captured me and awakened my being, igniting a passion and a curiosity, while also instilling confidence and joy within me.

Academic learning was a challenge. I was not a fast reader, nor was I good with numbers. But the arts gifted me with confidence to express myself, visually, grounding me with a sense that I could participate academically in meaningful ways. I created drawings and models to support my writing, presentations, and projects.

Without mediating through creativity and the arts, I probably would never have had the access nor the success I had in my academic learning. The arts were my saving grace: they provided me with a sense of independence. Realizing that I was good at something was the boost I needed to feel and experience a sense of accomplishment and self-worth. This attitude stood me in good stead my whole life because I have always been able to offer and share something of myself – a very Hawaiian value that has been invaluable.

The arts were the lens through which I experienced my world and the rich cultures of others throughout my life. My parents and just a handful of intuitive teachers knew how to tap into my creative strengths and passion for the visual arts. They nurtured my growth and development as an artist. By encouraging me to develop my strengths, they helped me to overcome my early academic challenges. The visual arts became my entry point into learning by giving me a comfortable way to participate. For example, I drew pictures to make sense of mathematical word problems and created mental images to understand historical timelines and events. For this reason, I have always believed in capitalizing on multiple modalities as a way for students to access academic learning. In my view, the arts, sports, music, and other forms of creativity should be seen as essential to the school curriculum.

Through my work in the visual arts in schools, I am able to identify children who have a facility and acumen in the arts, but may themselves have had little or no success in other school subjects. The arts may be their entry point into learning as they were for me. Students with artistic ability have keen observational skills; vivid imaginations; a strong intuition; and an attention to detail: to colors, textures, light, and form. It is my hope to provide these *keiki* (children) – and indeed all students – successful learning experiences that will allow them to tap into their visual sense to create a unique "visual voice," to recognize and use their other learning modalities, and to build productive habits of mind: to become curious, persevering, engaged, and excited about learning.

Figure I.9. Waimānalo Beach, a favorite place.

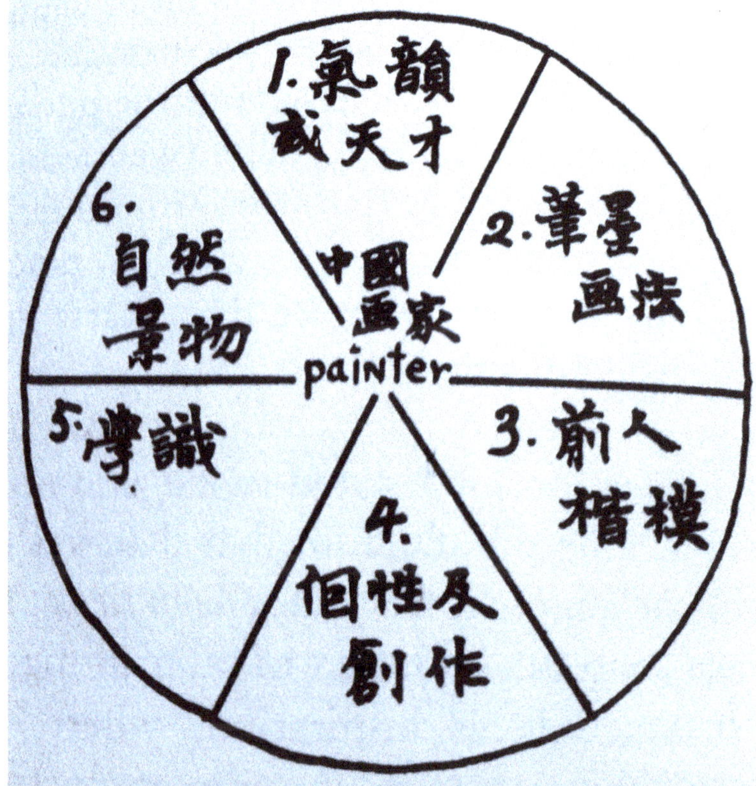

Figure I.10. Tseng Yu-Ho, a Chinese artist, uses this model to orient her artwork. The model includes six components: inspiration, practice of techniques, study of old masters, personality and creation, knowledge (culture), and nature.

Anna Sumida

I was always confused about my identity growing up in the 1960s. I was born in Hawai'i, a Japanese-American. The advent of television made an impressionable impact on my desired self-identity, particularly, the episodes of *Leave it to Beaver* that I watched every day after school. I distinctly remember wanting to live in a house and neighborhood like Beaver Cleaver and wanting my mother to look like Mrs. Cleaver, with her waisted dresses and thin patent leather belts. I knew that I didn't want to look Japanese or act Japanese. Why did I eat out of a *chawan* (rice bowl) when Beaver's family ate on dinner plates? They used forks and knives; we used chopsticks. I felt alien in many ways.

I also grew up with the *Dick and Jane* basal reader series. My heart's desire was to look like Jane and have blonde hair. As early as first grade, although I went to Japanese language school and saw pictures of Japanese children in our *hon* (reader), I did not want to have small and upwardly slanting eyes, straight black hair, and a razor-edged line of bangs running horizontally across my forehead. I wanted to look "American," which meant I wanted to look *haole* (Caucasian).

Figure I.11. Heart speaks.

Our family lived with my paternal grandparents, who arrived from Japan circa 1910 to work on the Hawai'i sugar plantations. My grandparents could speak only Japanese. My parents were bilingual and conversed in Japanese and English. As a child, the predominance of spoken Japanese in the household created a handicap for me. I remember not feeling confident to articulate my thoughts and opinions in English. As a result, I was quiet and shy, and I barely said a word in school. My parents were always told during parent–teacher conferences that "Anna needs to speak up more often." But I didn't have the words to be able to pop them out of my mouth.

Our next door neighbor, Mrs. Richards, was Caucasian, and I marveled at her eloquence in a conversation. She sounded intelligent and knew so many big words. Why couldn't my parents speak like her? Why couldn't I speak like her children? I secretly wished to be *haole*. Mrs. Richards' children loved the Nancy Drew and Hardy Boys mystery series. They loved *The Sound of Music* and memorized all the songs from that movie. The books they read at school and the library books in their home were all about Euro-American children and families.

Why didn't I see myself reflected in the stories I read, the movies I saw, or the TV programs I watched? I felt invisible. This feeling fueled a sense of inferiority and voicelessness; hence, I remained silent and mainly an observer. But it was a bewildered silence, an asphyxiation, a psychological muzzling of sorts that I was subconsciously aware of but unable to consciously name.

In the outside world, I was uncomfortable in my own skin and lived an unvoiced sense of displacement. But at home in my "nest," I felt deeply secure, loved, nurtured, and safe to be and feel Japanese within my nuclear family, consisting of paternal grandparents, mother, father, brother, and sister. What provided that deep sense of unshakable grounding?

It was my home culture. I was rooted in family and all of the traditions that came with my cultural heritage. On New Year's Eve, my father displayed branches of bamboo, pine, and plum blossoms on both sides of our front door. Dad conveyed that we must be like bamboo: flexible, able to bend in the wind but never break. The pine and bamboo remained green and strong during the cold winter months. We too must stand strong and resilient through stormy weather in life. The plum blossom revealed its greatest beauty and flowered during the winter. We too must bring out the best of our character even in the toughest of times. Each cultural symbol was a metaphor for mental fortitude, strength, and living a forthright life even during times of adversity. Also, it was ingrained in us from a very young age that the worst thing we could ever do in life was to bring shame to our parents. These cultural values became the core of what my father and mother wanted us to express and to become.

Just before the clock struck midnight on New Year's Eve, Mom and Dad sat us around the dinner table to eat *soba* (buckwheat noodles) as a family. Slurping noodles in the midst of transitioning from one year into the next symbolized the continuation of life and the blessedness of a long life.

Figure I.12. Coming into being.

The very next morning, our first meal was *ozoni*, a traditional Japanese soup made with *mochi* (sticky rice cake), so the family would stick together and be close. My sense of identity as Japanese was molded and shaped from these and many other cultural practices and "funds of knowledge" (González, Moll, and Amanti, 2005). Within my deepest core, I had a sense of who I was and where I came from that grounded me. However, a mysterious dissonance surfaced when I watched television and read books, where I could feel myself dissolve, unrepresented in the world outside my home and family.

It was not until taking graduate level college courses in postmodernism and postcolonial theory that I began to demystify and deconstruct the cultural perspectives and hegemonic oppression I unwittingly placed upon my self-image as a child. As an obedient Japanese 5-year-old girl, I unconsciously subsumed and negated my own genetic, cultural, and individual identity, marginalizing myself to dominant Euro-American culture as seen through mass media, school curriculum and textbooks, and Western literature. I started to think about what happens to those in the margins – silenced, socialized in a lower stratum, oppressed, and unrepresented.

Gayatri Spivak asked the question, "Can the subaltern speak?" (Spivak, 1988), referring to underrepresented social groups that feel excluded by the dominant or established groups. At one time, I was a subaltern who could not speak. I was muzzled but never knew why. At that time, I had no idea why those in the margins – those silenced, those socialized as if in a lower stratum, those oppressed, and those unrepresented (like me) – felt subordinate. And what about young children, like myself, who could not speak, or could not speak adequately, in the dominant language?

The evolutionary journey of understanding the self has brought me here, to the writing of this book. I now know that I had my home culture to hold me secure. But what about children whose home culture suffers from the historical trauma of their colonial

Figure I.13. *Ke ānuenue* (Rainbow) Koʻolau, Oʻahu.

past or racial discrimination? Like rubbing black permanent marker off one's skin, the stains of cultural domination and racial discrimination are hard to remove entirely and painfully slow to fade.

Miki Maeshiro

I am the oldest child of a mixed marriage. My father, Caucasian with some Cherokee blood, grew up in the hills of Kentucky. My mother was born and raised in Puʻunēnē, Maui, the daughter of Japanese immigrants, and grew up in a sugar cane plantation camp, company housing segregated by ethnic background. My younger brother and I grew up in a predominantly white suburb of Portland, Oregon, during our elementary school years. My home culture was principally local (Hawaiʻi) Japanese. We wore rubber slippers ("flip-flops"), called phlegm ("snot") *hanabata* (literally, "nose butter"), and ate raw egg over hot rice with *shoyu* (soy sauce). It was not until I began school, first grade, at the age of six that I understood that I was "different" from my neighborhood friends, as stares and derogatory names greeted me in the classroom and on the playground. My difference and "otherness" multiplied in second grade, when I met my best friend, who remained as such through childhood. She was Chinese; her family had immigrated to the United States from Taiwan. Adults frequently stared and stopped us to ask, "What are you?" At first, we were unsure how to respond. What did they mean? Wasn't it obvious we were girls? Eventually, our uncertainty grew into annoyance. At the early age of seven, I understood that I was different from most of those around me, that is, "other." These early childhood experiences nurtured a rebelliousness and a desire to right what I saw as unfair or prejudicial behavior. They heavily influenced decisions and choices which I made as a child, such as choosing to side with a child being bullied on the playground, and the decisions and choices which I continue to make today as an adult.

Moving to my mother's home, Hawaiʻi, in my early teens was a homecoming for me. Here there were people who looked like me. There was even a word for us, *hapa* (literally, "half"), meaning "of mixed ancestry." Even though I was initially seen as "other," a mainlander not from Hawaiʻi, I soon blended into the local culture and the multicultural diversity of this place. Everyone wore rubber slippers, knew what *hanabata* was, and raw egg over hot rice with shoyu was not strange. I was not in fact "other."

The spirit of the land and Hawaiian culture surrounded me. I learned Hawaiian cultural traditions from a friend's family and soaked up the stories of my new home. I roamed the mountain paths with my dogs, raided the patches of white and yellow ginger to make *lei*, and watched the rain crawl across the Koʻolau Mountains every afternoon. I collected and prepared seaweed from the ocean, picked breadfruit from the tree next to our garage, and gathered young fern shoots from the patch near my home. I learned the Hawaiian language.

It was through my studies of Hawaiian language and culture at the University of Hawaiʻi that I met my mentor and greatest teacher, Uncle Harry Mitchell. Uncle Harry, from Keʻanae, Maui – taro farmer, Hawaiian *kupuna* (respected elder), activist, and mentor – is much of the inspiration behind the person I have become and the work I do as a teacher. Uncle Harry's experiences growing up Hawaiian in a Hawaiʻi that had undergone vast and culturally traumatic changes since his birth shaped his beliefs, and in turn mine, about the historical disempowerment of the Hawaiian people. Uncle Harry helped me come to understand that the empowerment of young Hawaiians was in culturally grounding them.

Uncle Harry was raised by his *kūpuna* (elders) in the old ways, grounded in his native language and culture with deep connections to the land and place. He always said, "*Hauhili ka manaʻo*" (The mind is tangled.). "The problem is that our *ʻōpio Hawaiʻi* (Hawaiian youth) are not grounded in their culture." He said, "If you are grounded in your own culture, then you can navigate the white man's world. You need to know who you are, where you come from." He understood that our *keiki* (children) first need to understand who they are as Hawaiians, to be grounded in their own culture, place, and language so they have the knowledge and tools that will allow them to navigate this world, beyond these tiny islands, as their ancestors did. Polynesians are reputed to be the greatest navigators on earth, traveling thousands of miles across open ocean using their intimate knowledge of nature: the stars, the ocean currents, the clouds, the winds, the sun, the moon, and the flight patterns of birds.

Since my formative years as a young teacher to the present day, my goal to realize Uncle Harry's vision inspires decisions I make in the classroom. I continually strive to design culturally relevant curricula that provide an opportunity for my students, both Hawaiian and non-Hawaiian, to learn about their cultures and to explore what it means to be Hawaiian or from this place, Hawaiʻi. I aspire for my students to develop a strong sense of identity, grounded in their culture and place, an understanding that was so absent in my own education. I hope to nurture and strengthen their voices to wonder, to question, to generate new understandings, and to shape the world.

Figure I.14. Lanihuli: My back yard.

This collaborative work with Anna and Meleanna around arting, writing, and culture as transformative pedagogy has forever changed the way I teach. My goal for students is always transformational learning, a deep sense of having been changed by an experience. I am always striving to sequence lessons or scaffold a unit to lead students toward important learning and insights – toward their transformation. I am now more intentional in planning for transformative learning experiences, rather than hoping and waiting for them to happen. As a result, the learning in my classroom has a lasting effect and empowers students to take risks, to explore their creative potential, to put their voice out into the world, to take a stand, and to know that they make a difference.

Mahalo (Thank you) to Anna and Meleanna for inviting me into this exploration, for all of the hard questions, and for the opportunity to grow. This book has been a true collaboration, a journey we traveled together. None of us could have arrived at our current understanding without the knowledge and influence of the others. I will always be striving to provide transformational learning experiences for my students – not an easy task. As I continue on this journey, I hope to amplify my capacity to teach and learn from a transformative space that empowers me as a teacher and my students as Hawaiians, strengthening their voices and identity. I hope that you, too, will be encouraged to begin your own journey of discovery into arting, writing, and culture – and be forever changed by that journey.

'A'ohe hana nui ke alu 'ia.
"No task is too big when done by all."
– 'Ōlelo No'eau no. 142

Note to Introduction

1   Bernice Pauahi Bishop was the great-granddaughter of King Kamehameha I, who united the Hawaiian Islands under one kingdom in 1810.

Part I

New Ideas of Transformation and Culture

Chapter 1

Pedagogy of Transformation

Lawe i ka maʻalea a kūʻonoʻono
"Take wisdom and make it deep."
– ʻŌlelo Noʻeau no. 1957

Teaching to Transform

Education, in its highest form, liberates human potential through transformational teaching and learning experiences. According to the 4th edition of *Webster's New World College Dictionary* (1999), *educate* originates from the Roman and Latin root of the word *edos,* meaning to educe, draw out, to raise and support. Transformational education maximizes the possibilities for educing, drawing out, raising, and supporting the potential in all learners. Learning opportunities are meant to assist students to successfully negotiate their place and to have a voice in the world. This is what education is meant to be.

Figure 1.1. Seeding the world: This mural detail was created by students and community members for the Kaiao Community Garden Mural in Hilo, on the island of Hawaiʻi.

The pedagogy of transformation in Paulo Freire's work (e.g. Freire, 1970) connects the classroom to the political, economic, historical, cultural, ecological, and social issues of *real life*, meaning life outside the classroom. Freire's ideas demand that multiple voices and worldviews enter into the educational arena in order to deconstruct stereotypes, awaken intellectual strengths, and work toward social justice for the greater good. In a Freirean view of education, learners "read the world," think critically, see from multiple perspectives, ask questions, seek out answers, and develop a sense of agency to effect change.

As a catalyst to transform education, insights into Hawaiian epistemology inspire us to think radically about how we teach. Manulani Meyer's insights on Hawaiian ways of knowing and being in the world (Meyer, 2003) inform us as educators to think more critically and challenge the status quo of what constitutes education in the classroom and what it means to educate our *keiki* (children) in Hawai'i today.

As an emancipatory opportunity, why we teach, what we teach, and how students learn inspires us as literacy and art educators toward a pedagogy of transformation. We share this journey with you, the reader.

Figure 1.2. *Kua Ke Ahu*, Camp Mokulē'ia community mural in Waiālua, O'ahu.

Figure 1.3. Young artists work on the Camp Mokulēʻia community mural transforming this gathering space.

Our Story

In Hawaiʻi, there has always been a lack of culturally relevant, place-based education to transform and liberate the human potential of students. A Native Hawaiian perspective and voice continues to be largely absent from mainstream literature and education. Native Hawaiian and local children of mixed ancestry are virtually invisible in school curriculum and educational resources, making it difficult for them to build meaningful connections and to fully engage with stories and content. Cultural knowledge of native insects, farming and fishing practices linked to the moon phases, and the origins of place names have not been written into books or school curriculum materials, particularly for the youngest learners. This absence of relevant cultural learning materials compels us and our colleagues to search for ways to fill the gap in order to remedy the disparity, just as a similar absence of culturally relevant materials in many other locations leads teachers there to seek ways to fill their own cultural gaps in educational materials and practices.

Our journey through arting and writing begins with the realization that when students illustrate and write their own books, those activities affirm their identity, story, and voice in the world. The sharing of stories empowers students and their families by recognizing and honoring their knowledge, history, traditions, and cultures. Through publication, both informal and formal, students send their voices out into the world to be seen, read, and heard by others.

Illustrating, writing, and publishing books for classroom, school, and home libraries increases students' motivation for learning by strengthening their sense of being, cultural identity, language, and sense of place. Students' home, host/indigenous, local, and

Figure 1.4. This mural created by 1st and 2nd graders at Ke Kula ʻo Samuel M. Kamakau represents the very first *kalo* (taro) plant, Hāloanakalaukapalili, the elder sibling of the first Hawaiian man and ancestor of the Hawaiian people.

Figure 1.5. Culturally relevant learning: Students express their Hawaiian cultural understanding of the natural elements as alive and possessing energy.

Figure 1.6. Students from Kamehameha Elementary School, Kapālama, Oʻahu, share their student-authored books.

global cultural experiences grow into stories that enable them to learn about each other: their strengths and challenges, their family memories, their favorite activities, their fears, their fantasies, and their aspirations. These student-authored books are the most well-loved, well-read, and frequently borrowed materials in our young students' educational experience (see Figure 1.6).

The sharing of stories and the publishing of books gives students an authentic purpose to express their opinions and thoughts, to exchange ideas, and, as a result, to learn more about themselves, each other, and their shared culture and place in the world. Building students' capacities to have something to say makes room for real participation and freedom for creative expression. Educational experiences in which there is a high degree of relationship, relevance, and rigor, like the publishing of books, elevates learning by engaging students in creative processes, inciting a very different kind of learning – one of inquiry and creativity, of educing or drawing out. This educational experience is comprehensive and transformational, becoming one of journey and discovery.

The telling and publishing of stories is one pathway we have chosen toward actualizing a pedagogy of transformation that honors children's

Figure 1.7. Hawaiian immersion 6th graders at Waiau Elementary School work on illustrations for their soon to be published book, Ke *Kiʻowai ʻO Honokawailani* (Honokawailani Pond).

Table 1.1. Teaching to the 4th Power: Multidimensional Teaching and Learning.

T^4 → TEACHING TO THE FOURTH POWER
Multi-dimensional Teaching and Learning

$t^1 \times t^2 \times t^3$ → T^4	t^1RANSMISSION	t^2RANSACTION	t^3RANSMEDIATION	T^4RANSFORMATION
LEARNERS as . . .	*Consumers of information*	*Users of information*	*Synthesizers and creators of information*	*Producers of knowledge Agents of social change*
TEACHING AND LEARNING PROCESSES	• Facts • Information • Basals, textbooks, teacher guides • Workbooks and worksheets • Algorithms	• Collaborative • Interactive dialogue • Application • Inquiry • Goal setting • Capacity building • Lifelong learning • Problem solving	• Interdisciplinary study (cross content) • Multiple intelligences • Multiliteracies • Multiple ways of knowing • Multiple learning styles • Experimenting • Risk-taking • Authentic	• Real-life application • Place-based learning • Culturally relevant content • Critique (critical literacy, Freire's "reading the world") • Service learning and stewardship • Problem-based learning • Challenge-based learning
TEACHING AND LEARNING STYLES	• Teacher as expert • Student as receiver • Training • Apprenticeship • Explicit • Skill and drill • Memorization • Repetition and practice • Behaviorist	• Teacher as facilitator • Student as participant • Process oriented • Inquiry-based • Social • Interactive • Constructivist	• Teacher as mediator • Student as meaning maker • Involves multiple sign systems and perspectives • Interpretive • Metaphoric or Symbolic • Creative • Negotiated meaning-making with others • Intuitive/Instinctive • Spiritual	• Teacher and student as co-learners • Critique (political, social, economic, religious, etc.) • Dialogic (multiple perspectives and voices) • Transcendent • Empowering • Liberating
TEACHING AND LEARNING CONTEXTS	• Classroom-based • Whole class • Differentiated homogeneous groups (age, ability, skill level, etc.) • Individualized • Formal	• Multi-contextual • Social • Inclusive of student, family, and community funds of knowledge (Moll, 1992) • Heterogeneous • Multiage • Formal and Informal	• Workshop-based • Mediated • Personal and relational • Open • Fluid • Informal • Complex	• Transformational • Beyond the classroom • Based on real world issues • Impactful • About improving social conditions • Cross-age • Inter-generational
ASSESSMENTS AND EVALUATION	QUANTITATIVE • Mastery learning • Timed tests • Chapter tests • Multiple choice tests • Letter grades or percentage scores • Norm-referenced	QUALITATIVE • Open ended • Student generated criteria and rubrics • Observations and anecdotal notes • Narrative • Learning logs • Portfolios • Reflective • Criterion referenced	QUALITATIVE cont'd • Based on student strengths and interests • Performance-based • Presentation-based (exhibitions and displays) • Triangulated data	• Based on real world impact • Based on contributions made to society • Based on production of new ideas/knowledge • Innovative and inventive • Creates change

home, host/indigenous, local, and global experiences and also their creative capabilities. It is a meaningful framework to teach a constellation of skills, concepts, and processes that will take students through multiple dimensions of learning: transmission (t^1), transaction (t^2), and transmediation (t^3), in order to maximize the potential for Transformative (T^4) learning.[1] When designing learning experiences, all three dimensions are necessary in order to exponentially increase the potential for teaching and learning to become truly transformational.

Our multidimensional teaching and learning framework (see Table 1.1) is intended to give teachers a new way to think about teaching and learning, with transformation as the goal. Think in terms of an apex (see Figure 1.8) where one arrives at a pinnacle, T^4, the dimension of Transformation, and learners are changed by the journey in reaching that pinnacle.

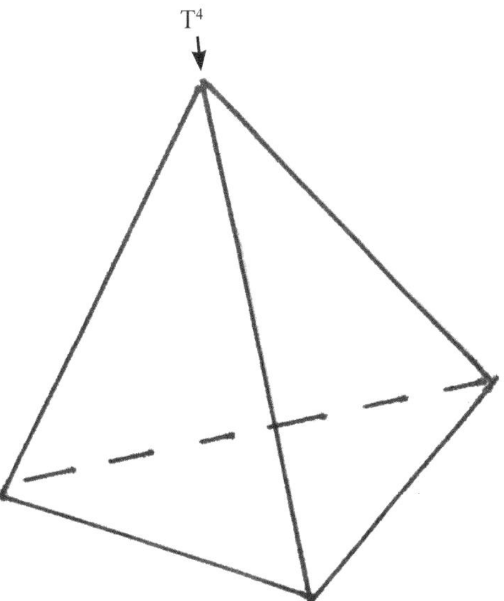

Figure 1.8. Tetrahedron: Multidimensional Teaching and Learning.

We use the tetrahedron as a metaphor and visual representation of multidimensional teaching and learning, borrowing from Buckminster Fuller's works, *Synergetics* (Fuller, 1975) and *Synergetics 2* (Fuller, 1979). As a mathematician, an architect, a systems theorist, and an inventor-designer, Fuller always worked in three dimensions, never two. He viewed the tetrahedron, with its ability to transform and become a larger, more complex shape, as the most stable geometric building block.[2]

We believe T^4 teaching and learning acts as the tetrahedron does, a building block that is stable yet has the ability to transform and become something more. Education as a journey is an adventure of varied dimensions, experiences, and stories. This multidimensional framework illustrates going beyond the flat, two-dimensionality of the printed page, literally and metaphorically, to strive for educational learning which is about life experiences that are relational, relevant, innovative, creative, and real (see Figures 1.9 and 1.10).

Figure 1.9. As part of an inquiry on native sea creatures, this Hauʻula Elementary School student identifies and observes *ʻaʻama* crabs in their natural habitat.

Figure 1.10. *Kumu* (Teacher) Meleanna and 5th grade students from Kalihi Waena Elementary School study a masterwork to learn arting techniques.

T¹ = Transmission: Learners as Consumers of Information

Transmission (Barnes and Shemilt, 1974), t¹, represents the "what" of teaching and learning. This dimension focuses on *transmitting* skills and information from teacher or text to student. Transmission of skills and information is like a one-directional arrow in which information moves from the outside in, involving primarily the left brain consuming, or taking in, and storing information.

Teacher / Text → Student

From the t¹ perspective, curricular content is broken down into a scope and sequence of discrete learning objectives so that learners can accumulate and master information and skills. Memorizing the names of the 50 states, practicing the multiplication tables, and repeating vocabulary items and grammatical rules of a language are examples of learning transmitted information. Learning to tie different kinds of knots, using an index to locate information, doing long division, and graphing linear equations are skills learned through transmission. Texts such as basal readers, dictionaries, reference materials, documentary films, and the Internet are types of tools used to transmit information that can be learned. The quantifiable and measurable nature of this type of learning makes it easy for the teacher to assess and evaluate students. Performance can be observed or measured on an individual basis as determined by the mastery of specific information or skills.

Explicit instruction, repetition, memorization, practice, worksheets, and drills are the primary instructional modes of t¹. Students are positioned as receivers or consumers of information. Learning in the dimension of transmission is valuable and necessary, *but not sufficient* as an end unto itself.

Figure 1.11. *Kumu* (Teacher) Miki teaches 1ˢᵗ and 2ⁿᵈ grade students about native Hawaiian insects at Ke Kula ʻo Samuel M. Kamakau.

T² = Transaction: Learners as Users of Information

Transaction, t^2, contextualizes t^1, transmitted information, making it relevant and useful. Transaction involves a two-way or multidirectional interaction (see Figure 1.12) in which an exchange and use of information creates a foundational understanding on the part of the learner.

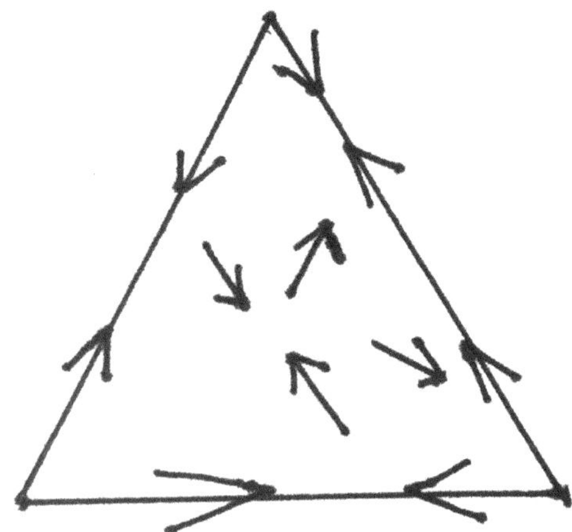

Figure 1.12. Transaction, t^2.

We borrow the term "transaction" from Louise Rosenblatt's Transactional Theory (Rosenblatt, 1978). Rosenblatt believed that any reading event is a back-and-forth transaction between a reader and a literary text. She believed that this type of transaction allows individual readers to create their own unique meaning based on their individual background knowledge, beliefs, and context.

We expand on Rosenblatt's notion of literary text to include visual images, multimedia, and the "real world" as text. One learns from transactional experiences with others, experts more knowledgeable than oneself (Vygotsky, 1978), and from resources like books and the Internet. Beyond Rosenblatt, we also believe that one learns from interactional experiences with tools, raw materials, and the environment that construct knowledge.

Teaching and learning happens in almost any transactional or interactional context. A transactional context for learning is one that engages learners in constructing knowledge in relationship with others and/or interacting with the environment. Learning to season and grill hamburgers with an adult family member is transactional as the adult shares personal information and stories, passing on knowledge about building the perfect fire, when to flip the burger at just the right time, and how to skillfully use the spatula. On each occasion, the learner is able to perform the tasks more independently with confidence. Surfing is an interaction where one shifts and adjusts as a result of a dynamic interplay of one's weight, the surfboard, and the ocean as information to successfully ride a wave and develop expertise as a surfer. Throwing clay on a wheel is an interaction between the wheel, the medium of clay, and the artist. The experience becomes transactional when the artist responds to the weight, texture, and composition of the clay. The clay in turn responds to the artist and the wheel as the object is formed and created.

Figure 1.13. Hauʻula Elementary School 2nd and 3rd graders view visual images, discuss, and wonder about traditional Hawaiian fishing methods as a way to connect their prior knowledge, generate interest, and spur curiosity about their upcoming inquiry project.

In a school context, examples of transaction include literature circles (Peterson and Eeds, 1990; Short and Pierce, 1990) in which students discuss multiple perspectives and differing opinions about characters, events, and interpretations of a story. Making sense of disparate points of view allows students' voices to emerge, converge, and inform one another to broaden understandings they might not have arrived at independently.

Another example of transaction is a writing conference. In writing workshop (Graves, 1983), students learn to dialogue and interact, to give and receive feedback, and to use feedback to improve their writing. Enriched detail, carefully selected vocabulary and punctuation, and the use of crafting techniques enhance the overall quality and coherence of writing for readers to understand. The intentional use of vocabulary and punctuation demonstrates the relationship of transmitted information nested within transactional exchanges that begin to deepen learning.

A third example of particular relevance is arting workshop. When sketching, drawing, painting, or photographing, many of the same attributes and vocabulary are used as in writing workshop: learning to dialogue and interact, giving and receiving feedback, talking story[3] to improve visual image, and articulating and demonstrating techniques to add detail and refine composition.

Transactional learning is wide-ranging and may include activities such as performing a class play, drawing and painting a mural, preparing and eating vegetables from a class garden, or interviewing elders for a community oral history project. Through inquiry and interacting with others to problem-solve, learners access communities and networks that open pathways for creative and collaborative innovation.

Observation, hands-on learning, social engagement, and dialogue allow students to take in information and begin to make meaning through interactions with others and the environment. As social beings, our need to interact with and to be in relationship with one another and our environment is critically important, not only to the success and flourishing of our species, but to a broadening appreciation of worldviews that may be different from one's own. Transaction (t^2) teaching and learning makes t^1 information relevant and useful. It builds a foundation for t^3, transmediative teaching and learning, to happen. For these reasons, we maintain that in a 21st century education, transmission and transaction are necessary, *but not sufficient*, as the ultimate educational goal.

T^3 = Transmediation: Learners as Synthesizers and Creators of Information

The transmissional (t^1) dimension takes learning only so far because the learner takes in the information as is, without changing it in any way. In this first dimension, information only moves from the outside in. In the transactional (t^2) dimension, information is utilized by the learner for certain goals or purposes; learning is responsive as shown by the earlier t^2 example of the surfer using information from the surfboard and the ocean to ride a wave.

Transmediation, t^3, creates a dynamic space for inquiry and active internal synthesis. Learners draw from the inert information of t^1 and an expanded understanding of t^2 to reshape, innovate, and create new knowledge. The synthesized information as new knowledge emerges from the inside out. Figure 1.14 and 1.15 demonstrate the potential for a different kind of educational experience, one of dimensionality that takes "shape" when going beyond the confines of transmission (t^1) and transaction (t^2) classrooms.

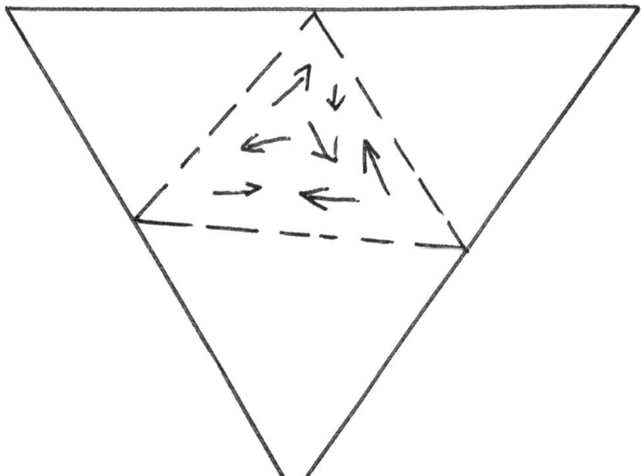

Figure 1.14. Transaction, t^2, as seen within the potential of t^3, transmediation.

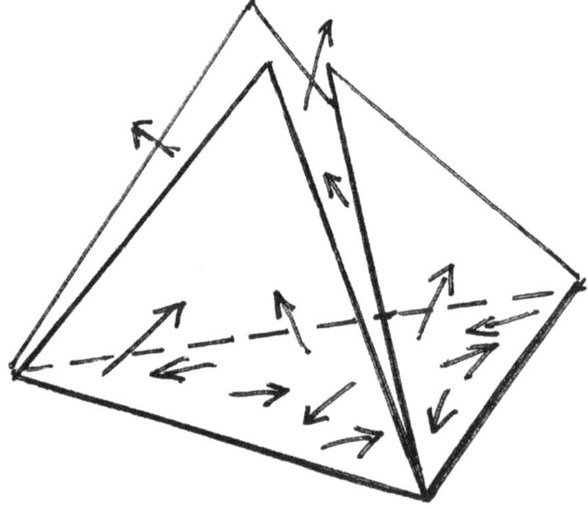

Figure 1.15 Transmediation, t^3, creates a dynamic space.

Transmediation is translating and interpreting meaning from one sign system to another (Leland and Harste, 1994; Siegel, 1995), such as thought to speech, spoken or written language into thought or visual image, or visual image into spoken or written language.

Transmediation is that space where the self works to understand through exploration and creative doing, with the potential to be transformed by the process and its outcome. Transmediation (t^3) is a dimension of healthy struggle, creative incubation, experimentation, and following one's intuition wherever it may lead. It is the realm where learners find their own direction, as they wrestle with, digest, and synthesize information in new ways, creatively and personally reinterpreting and reformulating it.

Learners take risks to use their newfound knowledge in new contexts, for new purposes, and, ultimately, for new understandings. Transmediation (t^3) allows different aspects of perception and cognition, the left and the right brain, to work together to integrate and process information and experiences from different perspectives. It is a space in which holistic perception and reasoning, largely controlled by the right hemisphere, can lead learning. Transmediation enables personal meaning-making, as an active internal synthesis, creating the potential for new and deepened understandings. In such a space, learning can open new frontiers and, in so doing, can get messy or chaotic.

Transmediation, t^3, is the realm of formulating and not being in full control, trusting and acting upon one's intuition. When given creative space and time, the t^3 dimension allows the learner to become a channel or conduit – a medium – in service to the work. Csikszentmilhalyi (1990) describes this state of being fully immersed and engaged in the process of personal problem-solving and creativity as *flow*. Transmediation is an intuitive dimension of the *na'au* (the gut, or intuition), a place with its own mode of communication and expression. It is a dimension of instinct, intuition, and, ultimately, of discovery and connection.

Transmediation requires time for learners to ruminate about and work through creative chaos to discover their own way. Transmediation (t^3) is the dimension educators tend to avoid because it requires the educator to release control, handing over the learning process, and trusting the learners to create meaning for themselves. In Transformational teaching, it is essential to allow students to spend time in t^3 activity, intentionally making room and planning for this critical time and space to gather, process, experience, and find their way through their accumulated information and skills in order to create personal meaning. Answers to life's questions and pressing issues are not generally to be found in a school lesson or a textbook: they are apprehended only slowly, through an internal process of interpreting meaning in relation to the self.

The potential of t^3 teaching and learning is to reunite the Cartesian mind-body split and to move beyond it, adding a powerful attribute – that of spirit, energy, or breath. Spirituality, not to be confused with religion, is unacknowledged in the context of Eurocentric educational systems. Transmediation, t^3, is the dimension where art and sacred rituals have arisen, awakening human imagination, evident in all cultures from the earliest ages and with all indigenous peoples (James, 2001). Indigenous cultures the world over have a profound reverence and respect for nature and spirit that speaks to and inspires the *na'au* (intuition) to guide and give voice and direction to people collectively and personally.

Figure 1.16. Hawaiʻi Kākou Mural Project artists bring together individual ideas and visions into a complex, yet cohesive composition displayed at the Hawaiʻi Convention Center, Honolulu.

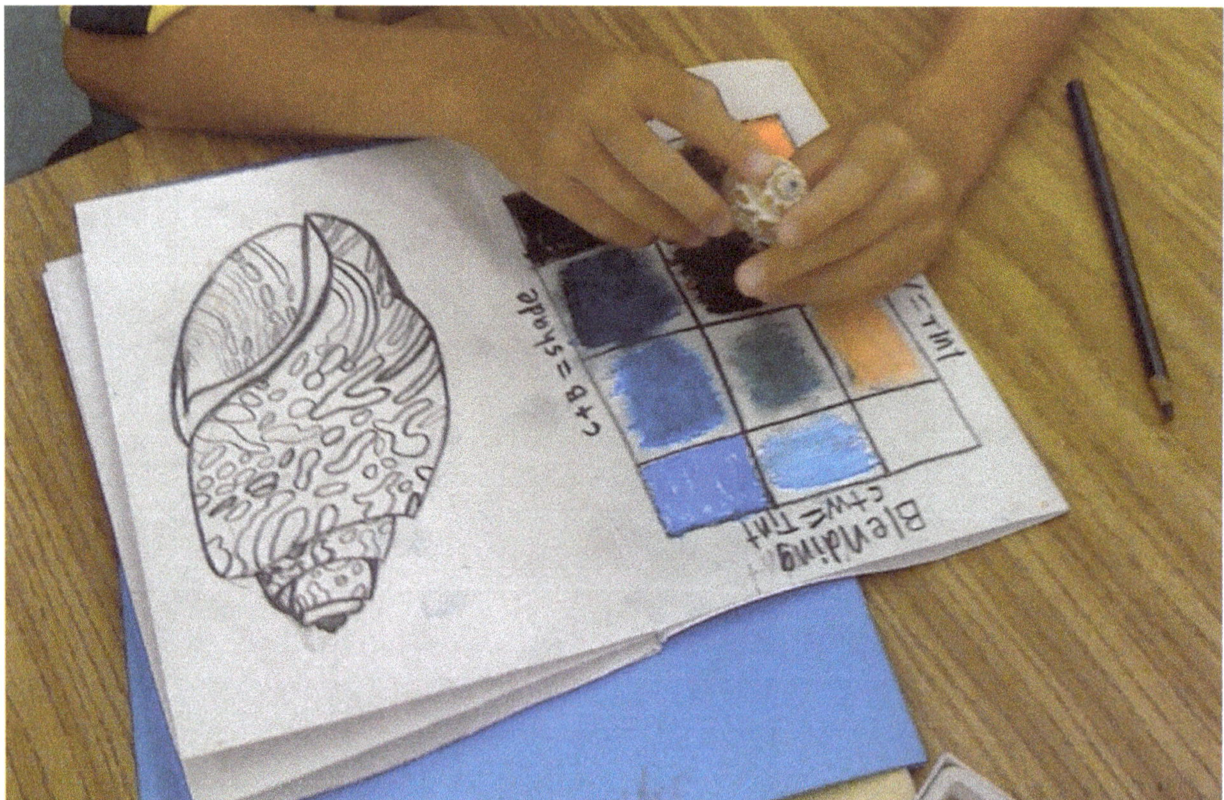

Figure 1.17. An exploration of color: tints, tones, and shades.

Transmediation (t^3) is not wholly visible or tangible, nor easy to measure like transmission (t^1) and transaction (t^2). Transmediation, t^3, teaching and learning, is more powerful than numbers and words can quantify or articulate. Without t^3, the possibility of ever arriving at Transformation, T^4, is not feasible. Many current educational environments are constrained and limited by notions of learning equated with standardized tests, percentiles, stanines, and predictable outcomes. This is clearly too restrictive a focus. Transformational education compels and demands that educators include t^3, transmediated learning, allowing space and time for students to discover and work through the messiness and uncertainty of learning without rigid controls or boundaries (see Figures 1.7 and 1.16). As Michael Fullan states in *Leading in a Culture of Change*: "The paradox is that transformation would not be possible without accompanying messiness. Understanding the change process is less about innovation and more about innovativeness" (Fullan, 2001: 31).

T^4 = Transformation: Learners as Producers of Knowledge and Agents of Social Change

Transformation, T^4, becomes possible when learners move beyond transmission and transaction into transmediation. It is in this t^3 space of mediated learning where the capacity and potential to arrive at T^4 is made possible. Transformation (T^4), as illustrated in Figure 1.18, is the pinnacle of the personal and collective learning experience (Freire, 1970), where an individual or group is changed by the journey of learning, creating, and knowing. Learners experience a shift in awareness when they realize that a fourth – an exponentially elevated space of revelation – has been attained, becoming producers of knowledge and agents of social change. We conceptualize T^4 as a pinnacle in the sense that it is the cumulative effect of t^1, t^2, and t^3 teaching and learning experiences that transforms learners.

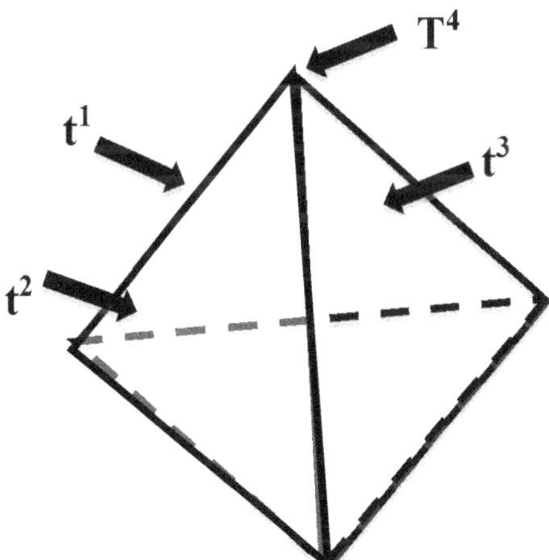

Figure 1.18. T^4=Transformation.

Transmission (t^1) is one directional; transaction (t^2) is an exchange of information: both are two dimensional. Transmediation (t^3), on the other hand, moves beyond two dimensions to become a three-dimensional tetrahedron. Like Fuller's tetrahedron, the most stable geometric building block, transmediation has the ability to propel learners through the messiness of t^3 toward transformation, to become producers of knowledge and agents of social change.

Each plane of the tetrahedron represents a different dimension of pedagogy, viewed as forming an integrated, dynamic system, one where transformational teaching and learning is accessed through multiple entryways. T^4, Transformation, is the result of teaching and learning that is a cumulative experience of t^1, t^2, and t^3, and is responsive to the individual learners, to the content being taught, and to the specific learning context. Learners may enter a learning experience via t^1, t^2, or t^3 dimensions. Yet all three dimensions are necessary to generate meaning and relevance that propels learners toward an "aha" moment of transformation, the pinnacle where t^1, t^2, and t^3 converge in T^4.

Expressing thoughts by creating an original poem that makes others laugh or cry, blending ingredients to create a new recipe enjoyed by friends and family, choreographing a unique dance that moves an audience, sculpting a one-of-a-kind vase that Mom displays proudly, solving a mathematical problem that enables the problem or the math to be seen in a new and different way, inventing a way to recycle without waste that the school or community adopts – all of these are transforming experiences. The T^4 dimension is the creative space where new understandings and creations become meaningful outcomes that can be used to make a difference in the world.

The convergence of t^1, t^2, and t^3, combined with focused intention, can ultimately lead to T^4, the "aha" moment when the synthesis of information and experience becomes an internal sense of having arrived at something altogether different and fresh. In this "aha" moment, new understandings of concepts, processes, and insights about the self in relationship to the world and others are registered and internalized as personalized knowledge. This "aha" experience is a great moment of humility, a realization of deep resonance, authenticity, and reverence, when one becomes part of, not separate from, that which has been understood or created.

Transmediation, t^3, in concert with t^1 and t^2, moves learning towards a transformational experience in which learners are empowered to find their voices, create new insights, and become agents of social change. Teachers and learners who experience and understand the interplay of these three dimensions can work to interface and participate with others to generate new visions and stories that contribute meaningful knowledge to the world. Our nature as humans is to attempt to make meaning of the seeming chaos of information and ideas. This can ultimately lead to Transformation, T^4, the place of deepest revelation and insight, a place of profound personal change. As producers of knowledge, students can then share and utilize their transformational experiences in the world. This is because when one is transformed and able to see from a new vantage point or vista, one is empowered to contribute in a way that affects others, often for the greater good. Every day transformational events and ideas, large and small, effect change in the world.

Transformational teaching and learning as an ultimate goal of education therefore aims to contribute to the greater good of society and humanity. As Freire (1970) so eloquently relates, in its most powerful form, it extends beyond the four walls of the classroom and out into the world at large. In T^4 teaching and learning, educators actively listen to and seek out the ideas of their students. They co-construct learning experiences, empowering students to discover their own intrinsic motivation – what they are

Figure 1.19. Kindergarten students are immersed in creating their World of Butterflies mural as they learn about butterflies, its life-cycle, and environment.

passionate about, absorbed in, questioning, or challenged by – and then allow them to follow their own process leading them to be transformed by all the different kinds of learning in which they may engage.

This is what we envision for our students. Far beyond test scores and commercial programs, transformational pedagogy is not a minimalist standard for educational attainment, but one of exponential and limitless potential. Clearly, this is a more meaningful and higher goal for education that goes beyond "college and career readiness" (Common Core State Standards Initiative, 2010). T^4 nurtures learning with passion in an environment of creativity and innovation. Transformation empowers learners to go beyond what can currently be imagined.

Transformational (T^4) teaching and learning results in high engagement and ownership of learning because it is relevant to learners' lives: it is teaching and learning that *matters*. Transformation is why we teach; it is the heartbeat of all our efforts in the classroom.

Figure 1.20. A 1st grader at Ke Kula ʻo Samuel M. Kamakau selected the Hawaiian flag for the background of her self-portrait to represent her cultural identity.

Notes to Chapter 1

1   John Miller, in his book on *The Holistic Curriculum* (Miller, 2007), considers education in terms of transmission, transaction, and transformation, and both Paolo Freire (Freire, 1970) and Michael Fullan (Fullan, 2001) have spoken of transformative education. The concept of transmediation is adapted from Leland and Harste (1994). Other sources for use of these terms in education are described in the text of this chapter. The multidimensional model, its details, and particularly its parallel application to arting and writing, is our own original contribution.

2   Buckminster Fuller (1895–1983) was also a futurist. He is well known for his geodesic dome, Spaceship Earth, which is the iconic centerpiece of Epcot Center in Orlando, Florida.

3   *Talk story*, meaning to chat informally or have a casual conversation, is a common expression in Hawaiʻi. It can be used as a verb or a noun.

Chapter 2

Pedagogy of Culture

Ua lehulehu a manomano ka ʻikena a ka Hawaiʻi
"Great and numerous is the knowledge of Hawaiians."
– ʻŌlelo Noʻeau no. 2814

The Importance of Culture in Education

Figure 2.1. Gratitude to our ancestors.

Historically, culture was the medium through which traditions, protocols, and life ways were taught by elders and the community to children and newcomers. Today, educational institutions have replaced many of the once influential and important cultural elders and leaders who were the knowledge keepers in communities. Formal education, media, and technology have become the leading vehicles for the dissemination of information, values, norms, perspectives, and worldviews of the dominant culture. The ubiquity of a Western orientation has dominated educational discourse, crowding out room for more diverse, inclusive, and open educational conversations. An American worldview often promotes capitalism and consumerism, where profit is the bottom line. This short-sighted and non-sustainable orientation wreaks havoc on relationships with others, resources, and the natural world. We suggest taking a long view following the wisdom of indigenous cultures.

We invite educators to become more engaged in teaching and learning practices that embrace culture as foundational, creating a more meaningful, relevant, and authentic educational experience for all. What will be vital in this century is a broader and deeper defining of culture as being unique to people, place, and time (Demmert and Towner, 2003; Kana'iaupuni, Ledward, and Jensen, 2010; Meyer, 2003).

Figure 2.2. Family members learn to make a *pū'olo* (gift bundle) for Grandma's 90th birthday.

Culture Shapes Us

Culture is foundational to education because cultures determine the lenses by which individuals and communities view, interpret, and act upon the world. Although educational institutions have taken on the role as the primary disseminators of knowledge and culture, the environment, media, political and world events, economics, and our life circumstances also constantly and continually shape our lives.

> *How can we be free to look and learn when our minds, from the moment we are born to the moment we die, are shaped by a particular culture in the narrow pattern of "me"? For centuries we have been conditioned by nationality, caste, class, tradition, religion, language, education, literature, art, custom, convention, propaganda of all kinds, economic pressure, the food we eat, the climate we live in, our family and friends, our experience – every influence you can think of – and therefore our responses to every problem are conditioned.*
>
> *Are you aware that you are conditioned?* (Krishnamurti, 1969: 25)

Figure 2.3. A mural detail from San Francisco's Mission District community mural.

To answer Krishnamurti, we know that we are conditioned. Culture shapes us; human response and perception are conditioned by culture – the places, conventions, and stories of our lives. In the broadest sense, cultures are mediated realms where conditioned behaviors and all learned and accumulated experiences are socially transmitted.

That one is conditioned is potentially both unsettling and empowering. Yet understanding how and why conditioning happens empowers conscious choice, a sense of agency; and it challenges one to acknowledge and consider other points of view. Acknowledging and considering other perspectives leads to the realization for each individual that not everyone sees the world as I do.

There is often a perception within educational systems that culture is monolithic. However, there is no one, fixed, homogeneous cultural group accurately representing the diversity of students today. Embracing cultures as foundational and necessary in educational discourse, we invite educators to engage in more open-minded, equitable teaching practices where diversity matters.

With this in mind, we have created a framework to explain and clarify a new orientation that considers the nuances, vantage points, and complexities of culture to give educators a new perspective from which to promote teaching and learning.

Figure 2.4. A detail from Kahalu'u Elementary School's mural.

Four Realms of Culture

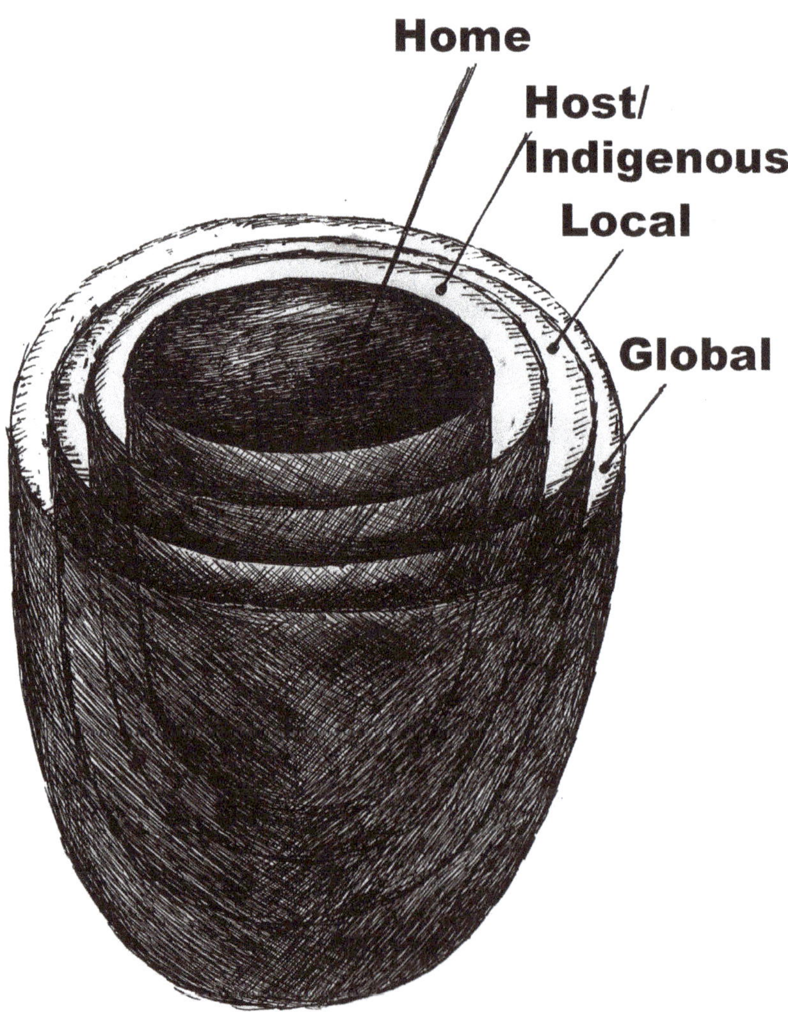

Figure 2.5. The nested nature of culture.

Culture is dynamic and living. It is a vibrant interplay of small and large social systems and markers that shape identity in the context of place. In this cultural framework, four realms define individuals, families, and larger social groups as they interact with and live in the world. They define the individual and the collective within a spectrum – that of relationships. We describe each realm separately, but educators should understand that all four are interrelated and nested. Home is viewed as the center with the other three realms expanding around and beyond this core (see Figure 2.5).

Home Culture

Home is a place of familial and ancestral relationships. If you ask anyone about the importance of home, you will find a wealth of responses that underscores the importance of one's early learning experiences and memories. Home is a place where identity is formed and shaped, where a person becomes rooted to a place. A family's homeland is associated with a people's place of origin and speaks to what individuals and the community as a whole feel about that place – its connections to family, culture, and tradition. Metaphorically, the term *family tree* seems especially apt, as symbolic of generations grounded or rooted and originating from a specific geographical locale.

Home cultures set an emotional and psychological barometer for relationships long before children arrive at the doorway of a classroom. The culture of home is the essential beginning, a place where people are from and often return to. Home is a place where there is a deep sense of belonging. And for most, home is where one feels safe. It is a sovereign space completely defined by self.

Home cultures are where learning is first nurtured. Parents and family are a child's first teachers. Bridging home culture with school culture opens the door to learning. Home culture honors that students enter the classroom completely able to participate. Students are never viewed as deficient. It is essential to acknowledge that children come to school "fully loaded" with their cultural and ethnic identities, religious affiliations, home languages, genealogy, family backgrounds, social class affiliations, interests, curiosities, talents, and learning styles (González, Moll, and Amanti, 2005). Through the lens of this cultural framework, teachers actively seek to make vital connections to the home cultures of students, valuing the diverse perspectives, points of view, and voices which they bring to the learning environment and school experience.

Teaching from and through the home culture connects what learners know, their stories, to new learning in a way that affirms their interests, identities, and cultural resources. Knowledge tilled from the intimate context of home elicits the telling of stories, a complex interweaving of the cultural with the personal. Teaching from the students' home cultures, as a way of making connections, creates relevance and makes learning meaningful. Students are able to access learning from a familiar space where they are heard, seen, and valued for who they are.

Figure 2.6. A child expresses pure joy in the safe place of home.

Figure 2.7. This section of a class collage depicts family portraits and writings by 3rd and 4th grade students at Ke Kula ʻo Samuel M. Kamakau.

Host/Indigenous Culture

The notion of homeland for many indigenous peoples (Native Americans of North America, First Nations peoples of Canada, Hawaiians of Hawaiʻi, Maori of New Zealand, Aboriginals of Australia, etc.) is one of the most profound cultural markers for those who value land not as commodity, but as kin. An indigenous identity and responsibility to the land grows from a relationship to one's place of origin. Understanding the land, the place where one lives and especially where one's ancestors originated, not only as home but also as family, provides an internal compass from which indigenous people orient to the world, in an ecological and holistic way.

The Latin root of the word *culture* means "to care" or "to cultivate," as in the land, nature. Reciprocally, the word *indigenous* derives from Indo-European roots meaning "to be born, begotten, produced of nature." All of nature is animate, living, and possesses energy. Nature is organic, as are human beings. Human beings are in fact a part of nature, not separate from it. From an animist point of view, people are viewed as being part of the land, part of the ocean, or as belonging to the skies, reflecting the sun. Nature is the core of one's being. Nature is mother and father. Nature is humanity. Nature as being alive and as permeating the human being is a foundational indigenous concept.

The land, water, sea, and sky shape a people's social, political, economic, and spiritual relationships. These social relationships are practiced in the form of values, beliefs, medicine, land-use, education, cosmologies, protocols, ceremonies, arts, and traditions. All indigenous cultures exist in unique interdependency with a specific place and its resources. From an indigenous worldview, the act of naming nature – its landforms, rains, winds, oceans, mountains, valleys – acknowledges an intimate relationship with the world that is subjective and personal.

Figure 2.8. The cliffs of Koʻolau Poko on the island of Oʻahu.

Every place around the world has a host or indigenous culture, which positions new-comers as guests in someone else's homeland. The host/indigenous culture of Hawaiʻi is that of the Native Hawaiian people. The host/indigenous cultures within the Americas are those of Native American tribes. This relationship between *host* and *guest* is an important concept. Respecting and acknowledging the existence of a host/indigenous culture in relation to others sets in motion a more mutually defined relationship of respect, care, and appreciation for the cultures of a place.

Figure 2.9. Native American carving in wood, Helendale, California.

Historically, colonizers and settlers did not maintain equitable and just relationships with either nature or the host/indigenous cultures who were the original inhabitants of a place. Consider, for example, these observations by Luther Standing Bear:

The white man does not understand the Indian for the reason that he does not understand America. He is too far removed. The roots of the tree of his life have not yet grasped the rock and soil.... Men must be born and reborn to belong. Their bodies must be formed of the dust of their forefathers' bones. (Standing Bear, 2006: 148)

The white man has come to be the symbol of extinction for all things natural to this continent. Between him and the animal there is no rapport and they have learned to flee from his approach, for they cannot live on the same ground. (ibid.: 166)

Understanding relationships from a perspective of mutuality establishes respect, care, and appreciation of others. Had colonizers and settlers understood their relationship as "guests" of those who already lived in the lands they came to, perhaps a more equitable and sustainable rapport with host/indigenous cultures and the environment could have been maintained, rather than leading to their degradation or extinction.

Indigenous knowing and understanding enabled sustainable practices and ways of being in the world that were harmonious with land and community. The Aboriginal peoples of Australia have lived continuously on their lands for at least 40,000 years (Caruana, 2003). Indigenous people the world over who have not been displaced from their native land still maintain their intimate connection to place. On the other hand, Western cultures have altered their relationships with the land by objectifying natural resources as commodities for the purpose of economic profit and gain.

These postmodern times have removed humankind from the rootedness of place, of being close to nature, close to home, and close to one another. Hegemonic influences of commercialization and globalization have

Figure 2.10. Totems in Skagway, Alaska.

uprooted us from Mother Earth, fragmented homes, and made us strangers, even to our neighbors. Dislocation and separation from the very life sources that sustain us have alienated our children, our families, and whole communities.

Detachment from Mother Earth has allowed destruction of the planet in unprecedented ways. It is evident on all levels that "planetary boundaries" (Rockstrom, 2010) have been breached, such as through ozone depletion, ocean acidification, soil nitrification, climate change, and other effects on the natural world. There is a pressing need to turn to indigenous practices and ways of knowing that balance the needs of humankind with those of Earth, our home planet.

Many indigenous cultures have continued traditional practices, evolving and shaping them to meet today's challenges. Practicing more sustainable lifestyles is imperative, guided by indigenous perspectives of relationship with place and a balanced utilization of resources. Such a worldview and its attendant practices could counter and reduce the exponential pace of the rapid depletion of Earth's natural resources that is taking place today. Indigenous culture-based education holds a key to educating children to live in harmony with the Earth and all of its people. Such education represents an important counterweight to education focused on material success, which has been so much the focus in the current era.

Integrating a host/indigenous cultural perspective into the school curriculum invites students into a dynamic and intimate relationship with nature, place, and each other. It positions them as part of their world, not separate from it, offering an interaction with natural elements that is personal, a physical grounding that is real, and a reverence for life that is profound. Understanding that human beings have a relationship with nature directs students in how to be, or live, and how to act in the world. Nature as family obliges a sense of mutual respect and *kuleana* (responsibility) to care for one another and all living things for the long term. From an indigenous standpoint, responsibility promotes an understanding of place and a commitment to care for and to maintain a balance between human

Figure 2.11. This contemporary totem was completed by students during a summer art session at Linekona Art Center at the Honolulu Museum of Art.

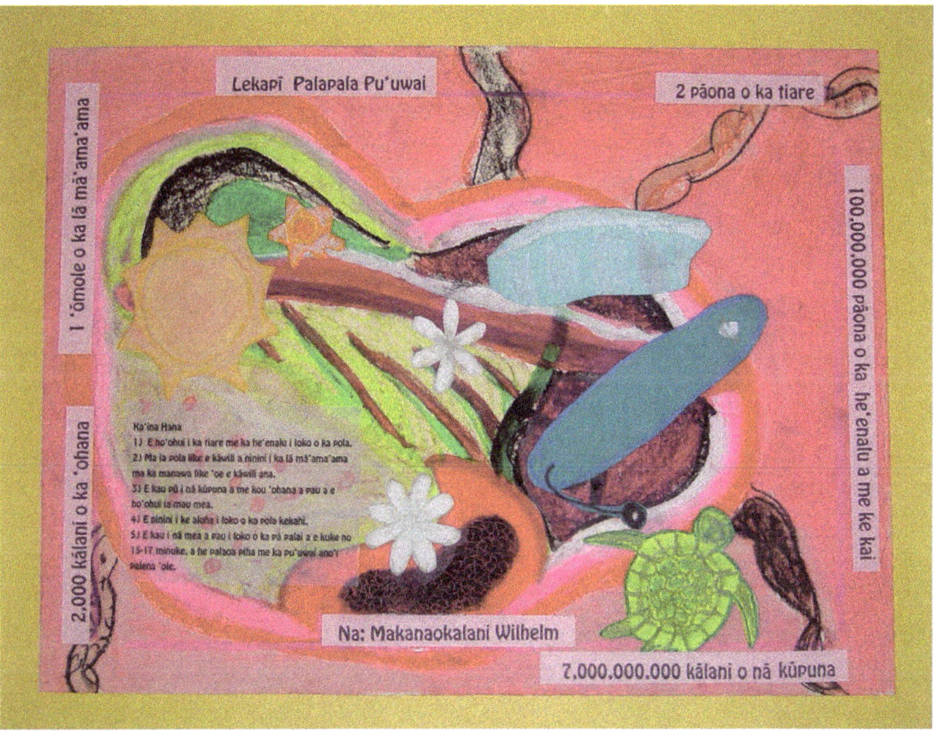

Figure 2.12. This Heart Map and "Recipe of Me" Project allows students to reflect on and express their cultural and personal orientation to nature and the world. (See "Possible Portrait Variations" at the end of Chapter 11 for more examples and a description of the project.)

Translation (clockwise): Heart Map Recipe; 2 pounds of tiare flowers; 100,000,000 pounds of surfing and the ocean; 7,000,000,000 gallons of my ancestors; 2,000 gallons of my family; 1 jar of sunshine. Recipe: 1) Combine the tiare flowers and surfing in a bowl; 2) In this same bowl pour the sunshine in at the same time you are mixing; 3) Place in your ancestors and all of your family and combine; 4) Pour your love into the bowl too; 5) Place everything into a frying pan and cook for 15–17 minutes, and you have bread filled with limitless amounts of your heart's desire.

Figure 2.13. *Pōhaku Aloha ʻĀina* (Stone Representing Love for the Land): This stone is one of many brought from each of the Hawaiian islands to create an *ahu* (altar) symbolizing the unification of Hawaiians from all islands at a 1993 gathering on the grounds of ʻIolani Palace in Honolulu.

needs and nature. Teaching and learning indigenous ways of being can help to develop a deeper social consciousness. An indigenous understanding of the world positions teachers and students to become agents of change, affecting the world for the better.

An indigenous cultural lens is critical to our work in Hawaiʻi, as Hawaiians are the host/indigenous culture of these islands. Our educational orientation and how we teach is predicated upon many of the pedagogical methodologies that stem from Hawaiian culture, which are unique and different from mainstream educational pedagogy. In this book, we explain and illustrate methodologies rooted in the indigenous culture of Hawaiʻi in hopes of inspiring teachers in other contexts by providing models and activities that they can use or adapt to the cultures in their own teaching environments.

Local Cultures

Local cultures are defined by specific, though diversified and shifting, groups of people. These groups are fluid and malleable, forming constellations of relationships with others. You can get a sense of your own local culture by considering: who your neighbors are; who you go to school with; who you work with; and the clubs, groups, or other social networks you belong to.

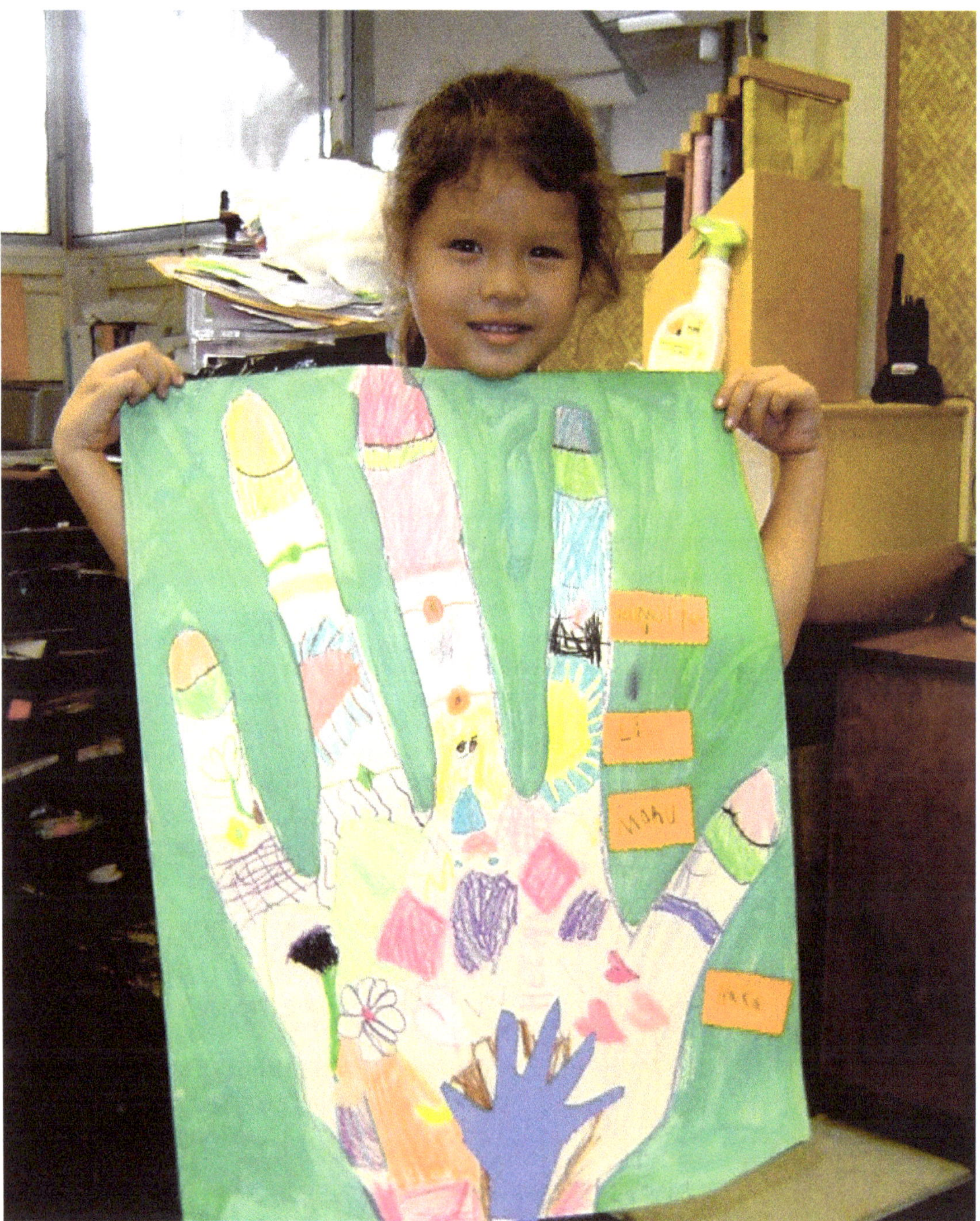

Figure 2.14. This kindergarten project at Ke Kula ʻo Samuel M. Kamakau engaged students in an exploration of identity and their personal vision for the future.

Figure 2.15. A section from the KAUPA *(Kalihi Ahupua'a Ulu Pono 'Ahahui)* Mauka Makai Mural Project.

These days, local cultures are not uniform, but are sites of hybridity and diversity. They involve people of varied ethnicities and/or associations interacting with and getting to know one another. They are made up of multi-faceted groups within larger diverse communities within a specific geographic region, city, state, continent, or island (as Hawai'i). They also encompass smaller settings such as schools, neighborhoods, work places, interest groups, electronic social networks, learning teams, churches, clubs, and other places or spaces where people interact. Significantly, local cultures are the context for understanding relationships beyond home and host/indigenous cultures. They are about interdependence, where a mindset of respect, compromise, and exchange provides an opportunity for learning about a diversity of opinions, interactions, mores, and worldviews.

Educationally, local cultures consist of a rich amalgamation of people within a community. They hold the unique stories and histories of a particular cultural mix of traditions and people, but must not be assumed to represent all other locales where similar groups gather. In the realm of Hawai'i's local cultures, diversity is embraced by integrating a hybrid of traditions and cultural practices such as: Hawaiian *lei* giving for graduations and birthdays, which signifies a rite of passage; celebrating Chinese New Year by popping firecrackers to ward off evil spirits; and all-cultures potlucking with a welcome and dizzying array of foods from a wide range of ethnicities.

Educators need to consider how they will include and give voice to a community's local cultures. Connecting local cultures to school culture creates a relevant platform for students to view themselves as participatory citizens within their community. Even when using national standards or mainstream textbook-driven curricula, it is important for educators to localize curriculum and tap into community resources because each local community holds common, yet unique cultural strengths and resources that can be made equally meaningful and relevant for students (see KAUPA community mural, Figure 2.15, and 'Umeke Writings, Figures 2.16 and 2.17).

Figure 2.16. *'Umeke Writings: An Anthology* (Luke and Meyer, 2008; Nā Kamalei Ko'olauloa Early Education Program) was published as a result of the workshop conducted in Ko'olauloa, on the north shore of O'ahu.

Figure 2.17. An arting and writing piece from *'Umeke Writings: An Anthology* (Luke and Meyer, 2008: 46–47), created by community member, Kawehi Kammerer.

Global Culture

Global culture is the largest possible grouping that encompasses everyone as a member of the culture of humanity. The notion of a global culture sets us all in an inter- and intra-dependent relationship with one another, orchestrated on the largest cultural scale. Every culture has a specific, place-based knowledge reservoir with inherent, unique, and diverse capacities. No one culture or people should presume to have all of the answers to human needs, wants, and problems. Honoring each distinct ethnic group as having value, neither more nor less than any other, allows for deeper appreciation of what each culture contributes to the rich tapestry of humanity the world over. Global culture is a relatively new phenomenon in that technologies have greatly facilitated economic, political, and social connectedness; and technologies now direct and shape human interactions on a scale unknown in earlier history. Recognizing the limits of resources and space, an indigenous worldview recognizes Earth as finite, an island. This perspective demands attention to the limits of resources, which necessitates sustainable environmental management. It acknowledges that humankind is indigenous to the planet and is a *part* of nature, not *dominant over* it. Accepting both a diversity of systems and a diversity of worldviews as the true condition of globalization, rather than the dominance of one culture, strengthens and benefits all.

Figure 2.18. This mural detail representing the sky, land, and seas was created by students at Ke Kula ʻo Samuel M. Kamakau.

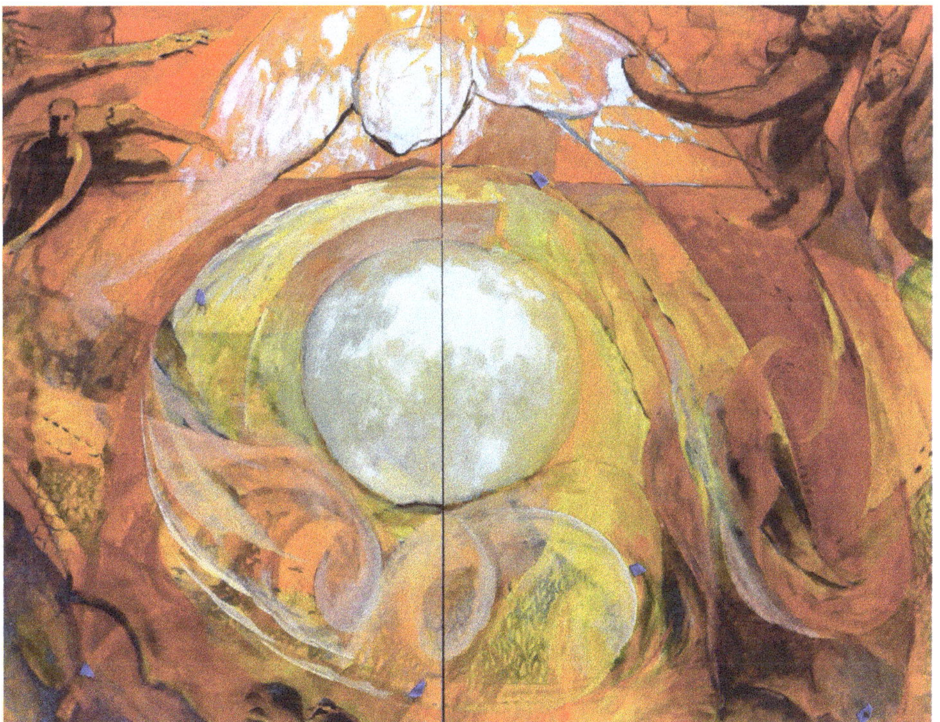

Figure 2.19. This spirit figure represents indigenous wisdom from a Hawaiian perspective; mural detail from the Hawaiʻi Kākou Mural Project at the Hawaiʻi Convention Center in Honolulu.

Valuing Culture

Home culture offers a relevant point of entry for each child and begins the critical interface with school cultures. Grounding education in a host/indigenous worldview provides a common ground for students to understand their connection to the particular place where they live and to value specific knowledge of the indigenous people of that geographical locale. Local cultures build on relationships with others and how various groups intersect and come together in exchanges and interactions, creating a continually evolving social dynamic. Finally, home, host/indigenous, and local cultures coalesce to create the largest grouping of peoples and ideas, shaping global culture.

Figure 2.20. We Are Family, a sticker found in Chinatown San Francisco, California.

Figure 2.21. A Native American hand drum created by Joe Seymour and painted by Meleanna Meyer at a gathering of indigenous artists.

It is essential that educators value and include the realms of culture in teaching and learning: promoting, cultivating, and providing the space for divergent ideas and diverse voices (e.g. see Ladson-Billings, 2009; Gay, 2010; Taylor and Sobel, 2011). This wider lens of home, host/indigenous, local, and global perspectives framing culture invites a broad discussion that is not dominated by any one group, but is rather held open so that all are asked to participate and all points of view are honored. This wide-open perspective ultimately will be what saves humanity, rather than a monocultural homogeneity or uniformity of thought.

Figure 2.22. This symbolic sketch, by Hawaiian artist Harinani Orme, represents human connections in a global context.

Valuing and incorporating the different realms of culture compels teachers to create a more inclusive and open classroom environment. The transformational dimensions of Teaching to the 4th Power demand that teachers get off the page, that is, move away from the exclusive use of static textbooks and set curriculum in the classroom, and create intrinsically motivating, relevant, place-based, and student-generated opportunities to explore and ignite their passions, liberating creativity.

Figure 2.23. This young student learns about herself and her Hawaiian culture through experiential interactions in the environment, in this context the *kumu* (teacher) explains her familial connection to the *kalo* plant.

Part II
Arting and Writing in Parallel:
Catalysts for Transformation
FEB10 2012

Chapter 3

Arting and Writing as Parallel Processes

He pūko'a kani 'āina
"A coral reef that grows into an island."
A person beginning in a small way gains steadily until he becomes firmly established.
– 'Ōlelo No'eau no. 932

An Indigenous Perspective on Creativity

From an indigenous perspective, all things in nature are organic, possessing and emanating energy. This perspective is very different from a Western worldview in which sky, water, rocks, and earth are non-living things. Indigenous people throughout the world put themselves into their work by investing their spirits and transferring their energy into created objects and compositions. This notion of investment of one's spirit and energy can be seen in the Hawaiian understanding of the breathing of life or transfer of breath, *hā,* into an object or form that gives it *mana,* energy or power. This is creativity at its deepest and most profound level, where the dancer becomes the dance (Tangaro, 2009) or the painting becomes an extension of the painter. As a generative force, creativity brings the unseen, the unformed, and the imagined to life.

Creativity is energy. Creativity animates spirit, mind, and body. In its fullest manifestation, it allows one to be connected to all other energies, as in being in the same flow. Flow (Csikszentmihalyi, 1990) is a state of energized focus in which mind and body are totally engaged in and absorbed by what is being created.

When in flow, from an indigenous perspective, all artists (painters, writers, engineers, dancers, musicians, landscapers, teachers, and architects) tap into and channel energy, through the *na'au,* the gut or instinct. From a Hawaiian worldview, creativity and intelligence are centered in the *na'au.* They make up the sixth sense, the most prized of all the senses for creative people. Intuition and instinct are the *na'au*'s way of knowing, thinking, creating, and relating. Beyond *nānā,* to see, there is *'ike,* active seeing, as in observing and working in order to know and understand that which is being studied. We call creativity, *'ike na'au,*[1] knowing intuitively and instinctively – a "gut instinct."

Non-linear and fluid, creativity finds organization in a seeming chaos. When creativity is activated, the whole mind, both hemispheres of the brain, are engaged in the production of new ideas, processes, and formulations (McGilchrist, 2009). Kent and Steward (2008) theorize that the intuitive mind makes sense of the world and through creativity organizes disparate perceptions into a coherent picture, whereas the analytical mind deconstructs the whole into its parts. These two acts are mutually exclusive and cannot be done at the same time. The formative nature of the arts is that they represent what is seen and felt, making visible what the mind and intuition perceive and want to represent in a concrete form (Arnheim, 1969). The arts are a manifestation of culture and foundational to education because they are a demonstrable expression of the way in which people see, interact with, and interpret the world.

The Origin of Arting

Ho'o- is an animating prefix in the Hawaiian language that transforms the meaning of words by making them causative and active, as in *ho'ōla*, "to give life to"; *ho'oulu*, "to cause to grow"; *ho'olohe*, "to actively listen," not just to hear. We equate *ho'o-* with the English suffix *-ing*. This suffix animates by changing nouns to verbs: *canoe* becomes *canoeing, paint* becomes *painting*, *art* becomes *arting*, the act of creating art.

Arting is a new term conceived by Meleanna to explain the creative process an artist goes through when drawing, painting, sculpting, and creating, or breathing life, into any of the visual arts. Her "aha" moment was the realization that visual artists move through a process, arting, that parallels writing, the creative process of writers. Arting, as an aspect of visual thinking, is a kind of knowing, from an intuitive, sensorial orientation.

As a new concept, arting is a way for educators to think differently about teaching, learning, and creating art. For the artist, it is the process through which s/he works to arrive at a concrete expression of an idea or thought. All art forms are comprehensive, each with its own protocols, techniques, and degrees of rigor specific to the discipline. Each has its own mechanics, vocabulary, criteria, refining points, and platforms of presentation. We theorize that arting, as concept and process, can be applied to any art form; in this book, we apply it specifically to the visual arts.

Figure 3.1. Elegance of a seed pod: This organic form, resembling a double-helix, inspires a mediation between nature and science.

The Hawaiian Literacy Tradition

I ka 'ōlelo no ke ola; i ka 'ōlelo no ka make.
"In language there is life; in language there is death"[2]
Words can heal; words can destroy.
– 'Ōlelo No'eau no. 1191

The Hawaiian language, before contact with the Western world, was an oral language. Various forms of oral tradition (stories, prayers, and chants) were vehicles used to transmit and pass on cultural knowledge from one generation to the next. Eloquence in orality, the ability to

Figure 3.2. Meleanna chants to honor the last Hawaiian monarch, Queen Lili'uokalani, in a celebration of the late queen's birthday at 'Iolani Palace.

Figure 3.3. Hawaiian language newspaper, *Ke Aloha Aina*, 1912.

express and articulate fluently in speech, oration, and formal discourse was, and still is, considered to be the highest art form of cultural expression.

After 1820, with the introduction of the written word, Hawaiian literacy broadened beyond an oral tradition to include the written language (see Figure 3.3). Hawaiians eagerly embraced this new form of expression. Since Hawaiians are prodigious storytellers, writing became a critical medium for recounting, sharing, and recording traditional knowledge and current events. At one time there were 100 different Hawaiian language newspapers throughout the islands (Benham and Heck, 1998). The kingdom had one of the highest literacy rates in the world as Hawaiians voraciously absorbed all manner of reading and wrote prolifically to document their traditions and the stories of their lives. Hawaiian language literacy was nearly universal (Nogelmeier, 2010).[3]

From a Hawaiian worldview, all of nature is imbued with energy. Even thoughts and words hold *mana* (power). The voice is one vehicle for transferring energy and spirit, breathing life or *hā*, and invoking *mana* to honor an event, a place, or a person. The words of a chant, a song, a prayer, or a story are animated when chanted, sung, prayed, or spoken. The words combine with the intent and *na'au* (spiritual center) of the chanter, singer, storyteller, or orator, to commune with the natural world, invoking spirit and energy.

Hawaiian thought and language conveys an intimate relationship with nature; a deep reverence for and connection to the environment and place engenders a familiarity expressed through the naming of specific locales, events, persons, and phenomena. The winds, rains, moon phases, oceans, and reefs are still known by their first names: Moa'e, the name of the wind of Punalu'u, O'ahu; Kanilehua, the name of the rain in Hilo, Hawai'i; Mahealani, the name of the full moon. The act of naming invokes these elements and calls them into being, recognizing them as animate, alive, and significant.

Figure 3.4. As above, so below: As a poetic expression, the sky is reflected upon the ocean where the land protrudes from the water.

Traditionally, what was created through the voice of a composer or at the hands of an artisan was imbued with the spirit of the natural material and its creator. These compositions and objects served a function, were given names, revered, and passed on. Even today, what is composed and hand-crafted – chants and songs, canoes, surfboards, and homes – continue to be named, honored, and cherished. The traditional practice of imbuing with spirit continues. Compositions, events, and created objects are still infused with *hā* (breath) and *mana* (energy) through the act of creating: naming a child, braiding a *lei*, carving an image, composing in arting and writing.

Arting and Writing as *Haku*, or *Lei* Making

Figure 3.5. *Lei haku.*

In order to understand the interrelationship of arting and writing, we use a particular form of *lei* making, *haku*, as a cultural and visual metaphor (see Figure 3.5). The Hawaiian word *haku* – to braid as a *lei* (garland) or plait as feathers – likens the act of braiding with physical materials to composing, weaving with images, words, and sound. *Haku* is the act of a *lei* maker, weaving or braiding plants or feathers together to form a *lei*. *Haku* is also used to describe the act of an artist, speaker, or writer weaving images, sounds, and words together into a visual, oral, or written composition. *Haku mele* means "to compose a song"; *haku mo'olelo*, "to compose a story"; and *haku ki'i*,[4] "to compose an image."

A *lei* maker journeys into the forest to gather plants essential to the composition, the *lei*. Specific flowers, ferns, and greenery are sought out, depending on who will wear the lei and its purpose. Will it be worn by the *lei* maker in a ceremony or hula performance, or presented as a gift to honor another? Just enough of the finest greenery is selected from the many plants available to fashion a *lei* of great beauty imbued with the *aloha* (spirit) of the *lei* maker.

Similar to a *lei* maker seeking out and collecting raw materials – feathers, flowers, or greenery – an artist and a writer seek out and collect their raw materials: feelings, images, stories, words, and inspiration. Like a *lei* maker collecting greenery in a basket, an artist and a writer have a place to keep and store raw materials for future use. We use and recommend keeping an artist–writer's notebook; when ready to compose, the raw materials, the images and words, are readily available within the pages of this kind of book. In composing, a *lei* maker carefully selects just the right greenery to braid into the *lei*. A *lei* maker also considers the recipient: her/his favorite flowers or colors; how the *lei* will be worn, open or closed around the head or neck; and its purpose – for a birthday, *hula* performance, or other special occasion.

The act of composing is an act of creating, of bringing something new into existence. For the artist and writer, it is thoughtful work as well as play, purposeful play with images, ideas, and words. A visual artist arranges and weaves color, line, and other visual conventions together with ideas, into a composition, whether a painting, a sculpture, a photograph, or a print. A writer arranges and weaves words and sentences to create a poem, a letter, an essay, or a memoir. Composing is the careful selection of just the right colors or words to convey an image or thought to an audience or reader. The artist intentionally plays with the combination of textures, colors, and space to create a compelling composition. The writer plays with the cadence and sounds of words, arranging them in a way that creates emotion or a reaction within the audience and reader. When successful, there is nothing more powerful than the reaction and satisfaction of an audience or reader, or the personal satisfaction of the artist or writer with what was created and composed.

Figure 3.6. Master *lei* maker, Paulette Kahalepuna, of *Nā Lima Mili Hulu Noʻeau* displays a variety of *lei hulu* (feather lei).

Arting and Writing

[T]he aim of education ought to be conceived of as the preparation of artists.... [W]e mean the individuals who have developed the ideas, the sensibilities, the skills, and the imagination to create work that is well proportioned, skillfully executed, and imaginative, regardless of the domain in which an individual works. The highest accolade we can confer on someone is to say that he or she is an artist whether as a carpenter or surgeon, a cook or an engineer, a physicist or a teacher. The fine arts have no monopoly on the artistic.
(Eisner, 2002)

In the context of arting and writing, visual art and literary art complement each other. There is a relationship between the processes of the artist and the writer when creating story. Both artists and writers make marks; both of them use and create forms. The visual artist's simple shapes, three-dimensional forms, and visual representations of objects are like the letters, words, and sentences of a writer. When a visual representation of an object, such as the moon, is given a context in space and time, for example fishing at He'eia Pier on a moonlit night; it creates a story in images like that which a writer creates with words (see Figure 3.7 and Table 3.1).

Figure 3.7. Illustration as story.

Table 3.1. Dimensionality Creates "Story."

Dimensions	Attributes	Visual Representation
One dimension	Length	Line
Two dimensions	Length and Width (Shape)	Square, Circle, Triangle
Three dimensions	Length, Width, and Depth (Object)	Cube, Sphere, Pyramid
Four dimensions	Length, Width, and Depth in Time (Form)	Naming of the Form in Time (Moon)
Five dimensions	Length, Width, and Depth in Time and Space-time (Context)	Story (Fishing on a Moonlit Beach in Hawai'i)

Arting and writing are parallel processes with like structures. Visual artists and writers move through similar (though not identical) stages, which we term: *prearting/ prewriting, envisioning, composing, revisioning, critiquing and editing, exhibiting and publishing.* Juxtaposing both art forms demonstrates the parallel nature of these two processes (see Table 3.2).

Table 3.2. Parallel Stages of the Arting and Writing Processes.

Arting Process	Writing Process
Prearting	Prewriting
Envisioning	Envisioning
Composing	Composing
Conferring and Revisioning	Conferring and Revisioning
Critiquing and Editing	Critiquing and Editing
Exhibiting and Publishing	Exhibiting and Publishing

Understanding arting and writing as parallel and complementary processes of expression and communication, one through image and the other through word, enables teachers to incorporate the visual arts in tandem with the literary arts in meaningful ways across content areas. Arting is, as writing is, a way of deepening one's own understanding, and of demonstrating and sharing what has been learned, internalized, and understood with others. The aspirations of an artist and a writer are to express and to be heard, to share opinions and passions, to provoke thought, to incite reaction, to inform, to tell a story.

As a visual thinker, an artist draws pictures or shapes physical forms to express thoughts, emotions, and perceptions of the world. Through reference to images, the artist is more readily able to recall and retell a story in words, spoken and written. The spoken or written words then further inform and refine the artist's drawing with visual elements: details, color, texture, light, shadow, and scale.

Figure 3.8. Close observations of the *pak lan* flower appear in both visual image and text in this artist–writer's notebook.

Similarly, when telling or writing a story, a storyteller or writer embellishes with sensory details and nuance, creating and conjuring image through words. A writer is able to generate a visual image that further informs the telling of a story.

Visual literacy, reading the world through images, is one's first symbolic language. Most young children choose to draw as a primary means of expression. As they develop in literacy, they usually acquire a fluency in one over the other. A child's visual or written preference indicates the reason why a child orients from either image or word. Integrating arting and writing into instruction supports the development and activation of the whole brain, both right and left hemispheres, synchronously. As facets of creativity, arting and writing are both essential to a sound educational foundation that encourages the development and activation of the whole brain enriched by multisensory experiences.

The interplay between arting and writing creates a dynamic interface through which these two processes, together, go beyond the boundaries of either one of them to converge as a compelling and enduring learning experience. The ensemble of the two modalities mutually support and build upon one another. When used together, the back and forth interplay between these two processes builds and informs a more integrated construction of knowledge, creating a more sophisticated outcome and a more in-depth process and product of learning than would otherwise have been realized. Rather than working solely in one area or the other, in either art or literacy, the intention of the authors is to develop children's capacities in both arting and writing. As generative acts, arting and writing exponentially engage learners in the three dimensions of learning, maximizing the potential for a transformational learning experience, $t^1 \times t^2 \times t^3 = T^4$.

Figure 3.9. In 2nd grade, a science inquiry on sea creatures was used as a platform for an arting and writing unit on seeing from multiple perspectives and writing informational text. This piece is on *puhi* (eel).

Translation: The Eel It has black eyes[.] It has sharp teeth[.] It is spotted[.] It has a long dorsal fin.

We also view arting and writing as vehicles that provide a cultural ground for expressing story, demonstrating understanding, and communicating knowledge through image and word. Arting and writing asks the creating person to reach within, to find her/his voice, visual and/or textual. Culture (home, host/indigenous, local, global), as the ground for arting and writing, creates relevant, authentic, and engaged experiences for the learner and invites the expression and consideration of other perspectives, points of view, and cultural contexts beyond one's own. The transmediating between arting and writing helps to articulate unique ideas that are often universal. When used together, arting and writing can move the learner beyond the representational and the literal to think through complexity and mediated space, thus arriving at new understandings, deeper interpretations, and unique insights – Transformation (T^4).

Arting and writing workshop in a classroom setting provides the mediating space for young artists and writers to generate ideas, tell stories, demonstrate understanding, and create new insights and visions. This inquiry, culture-based workshop is meant to inspire wonder and curiosity, engaging learners in challenging and relevant study.

This workshop approach is transdisciplinary, teaching and learning applied across content areas, thus providing a more comprehensive and in-depth learning experience. Moreover, it brings together visual and print literacy in ways that recognize their increasing interrelationship in the modern world of multimedia and digital culture, thus preparing learners with the skills and the ways of seeing and thinking they will need in the 21st century.

Note to Reader: The Chapters to Come

The arting and writing processes (see Figure 3.10), as detailed in the following chapters of Part II, Chapters 4–9, are organized sequentially for the reader. Each of these chapters begins with a brief definition of one of the stages of these creative–expressive processes, followed by a section on arting and then a section on writing to bring attention to their parallel and complementary natures.

Within each of the arting and writing sections, we begin with an explanation to orient the reader to the specific stage of the processes. We follow with inner thoughts from "An Artist's Perspective" and "A Writer's Perspective" to illuminate the inner workings of an artist's and writer's mind. Discussions on "Nurturing the Artist" and "Nurturing the Writer" then offer educators suggestions to inform classroom practice. For purposes of gender equity, we use the pronoun *she* in discussing arting and *he* in discussing writing. Each chapter in the remainder of Part II concludes with an explanation and examples of the ways in which arting and writing complement and influence each other at that stage of the processes.

Please keep in mind that these stages do not necessarily proceed sequentially when one is engaged in the processes. Arting and writing can be done independently from the other to engage students in creative expression and in-depth study. However, using these two processes together, interwoven or side-by-side, intentionally moves a student beyond t^1 and t^2, through t^3, transmediation, increasing the likelihood of a T^4, Transformative, learning experience.

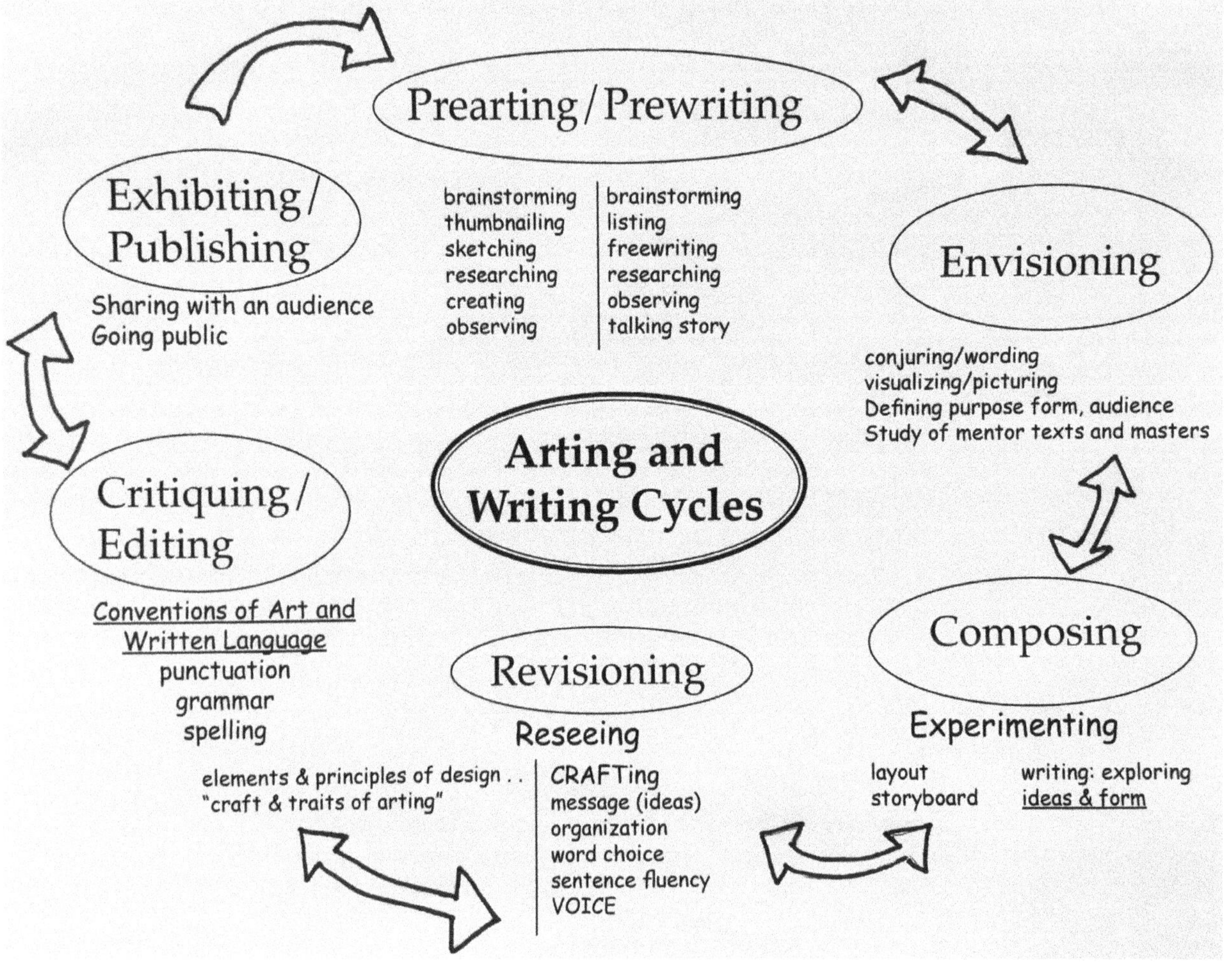

Figure 3.10. Arting and writing processes.

Notes to Chapter 3

1   The expression *'ike na'au* was created by the authors to explain the concept of creativity, as there is no Hawaiian word that expresses a Western notion of creativity.

2   This is the authors' translation of the original Hawaiian proverb. The original Pukui (1983) text reads "Life is in speech; death is in speech."

3   The decline of Hawaiian literacy can be attributed to multiple events that compounded the alienation of Hawaiians in their own land. The Hawaiian language was the language of government, commerce, and education until 1893. As a result of the illegal overthrow of the Hawaiian monarchy by a group of businessmen, predominantly from the United States, English became the language of government and commerce. In 1896, educational policy, *Act 57*, section 30 (Republic of Hawai'i, 1896), mandated English-only as the medium of instruction in all public and private schools. Americanization policies institutionalized the repression of language and culture by imposing assimilation to Western thought and language upon Hawaiians and large numbers of immigrant laborers in the islands.

4   The expression *haku ki'i* was created by the authors to explain composing in the visual arts, as there is no Hawaiian word for composing an image.

Chapter 4

Prearting and Prewriting

'O ke kahua mamua, mahope ke kūkulu.
"The foundation first, and then the building."
Learn all you can, then practice.
– 'Ōlelo No'eau no. 2459

Stage 1: Prearting and Prewriting

Prearting and prewriting are the initial stages of the arting and writing processes in which ideas are generated, researched, and explored. Prearting is more commonly known as "frontloading" in the visual arts.

Figure 4.1. This class chart (in the Hawaiian language) records academic vocabulary and student learning about the Earth, supporting 1st and 2nd graders to draw and write about what they know.

Prearting

Prearting is the first stage that a visual artist goes through in the arting process. The main task of prearting is to more fully understand what one is studying by researching: by gathering information, ideas, and questions, to thoroughly explore a topic. It is a stage that invites sketching, doodling, thumbnail sketching,[1] and conjuring initial images and words. It is taking and collecting photos, as well as noting sensory details and minutiae of objects and their environment in preparation for further creative work. Recording thoughts, words, and expressions is also part of the gathering of ideas.

As a collector, a visual artist needs a place to keep ideas: a shoebox, a computer memory stick, a journal, a cookie tin – a place to store, to treasure, to return to, and to be inspired by. A large part of a visual artist's time is spent in this initial stage, sorting out and exploring these objects, ideas, and feelings.

Prearting often begins with a disparate collection of questions, thoughts, images, and additional kinds of inspiration collected from a range of sources. Ruminating follows. Looking through collections of seemingly dissimilar things encourages an artist to see connections between ideas, intuitions, events, and objects. These ideas, thoughts, and images become the foundation for creative acts and provide direction for what will ultimately be created.

Prearting includes:

- **Observing:** watching, noticing;
- **Researching:** reading, note-taking, sorting images;
- **Sensing:** opening all six senses to inspiration;
- **Sketching:** drawing, doodling, thumbnail sketching, storyboarding;
- **Inquiring:** questioning, analyzing, wondering;
- **Brainstorming:** listing, webbing, juxtaposing images and words;
- **Collecting:** creating a reservoir of resources to fuel future thinking;
- **Collaging:** putting disparate things and ideas together;
- **Remembering:** actively recalling, embellishing and clarifying ideas;
- **Exploring:** tinkering, journeying to bring an idea or image to realization.

Figure 4.2. A kindergarten student from Hauʻula Elementary School uses arting to record observations of Hawaiian fish as part of his research.

Although these practices are typical ones that artists use, they are rarely taught in school to the depth and degree that they should be taught. This initial stage invites creativity into the learning process and requires time, which is always in short supply in the school day. Supporting this type of inquiry, research, and initial exploration is critical to creating a more relevant and meaningful arting experience. Shortchanging this foundational stage is detrimental to creating a meaningful, transformative learning opportunity for students.

Prearting: An Artist's Perspective

An artist is an inveterate observer of nature, people, events, and details. She is a person who, by definition, lives a wide-awake life as she is often captivated by the smallest of details and nuances of the tiniest things. A visual artist notices what others may have missed. Actively seeing is part of being an artist; being an artist means cultivating this kind of sight, sensing and intuiting. A visual artist often begins her work with questions. She is curious and delves into her unexplored ideas through further, deeper investigation.

A visual artist often searches for what is unique and interesting in terms of how things fit together visually. She is in the habit of noticing and remembering specific details of people, places, events, and things. She contemplates the arrangement of objects or the way the light is at a certain time of the day. An artist gathers and collects images and ideas that inform and inspire her. These images and ideas can be personal, critical, conversational, or a candid commentary on life. She weaves them together to create a visual story of image, sign, and symbol which, when translated, interpreted, and assembled, can become paintings, films, and portfolios of work that begin to tell stories.

Figure 4.3. A young artist–writer carefully examines a *pāua* (abalone) shell before beginning her drawing.

Living an artistic life is many things: it is being present and in the moment, paying attention with all one's senses, and documenting what may be insignificant to others but is meaningful, aesthetic, and resonant to the artist.

In the initial stage of the arting process, play and unconstructed time to create without pressure is critical, as in thumbnail sketching and drawing without the need to have anything look finished, complete, or fully rendered. Work in prearting is preliminary. It is a lot like scribbling or setting up a skeletal form of something, when further researching, reading, and exploring are necessary to fashion an idea, concept, or goal worthy of the time, energy, and focus to complete a project.

The image of a bulldozer, scooping up materials to be used in building something, is a good visual and conceptual representation of what prearting is. This process allows an artist to explore and become familiar with a certain area of creative interest, such as learning details of one's home, host/indigenous, local, global cultural context; its history or geography; or its back-story. Without this initial delving into material, a substantive beginning is difficult to envision, develop, engage in, and complete.

Figure 4.4. A bulldozer as a prearting metaphor symbolizes frontloading, the gathering and researching of information.

Figure 4.5. A student at Koko Head Elementary School practices active seeing by sketching shells during prearting.

Prearting: Nurturing the Artist

Educators have the opportunity and obligation to nurture and inspire the living of an artistic life by recognizing and encouraging the creative potential in each and every child. The belief that all children are born artists is a premise upon which arting is founded. Mentoring, coaching, and cultivating the talents of young learners obliges teachers to learn about and incorporate the visual arts into the school curriculum and their lives. Teachers profoundly affect the creative development of children and youth during these pivotal years. Nurturing the budding talents, interests, and curiosities of a young creative – as inventor, musician, dancer, composer, poet, singer, writer, or photographer – is critical to the formational development of any artist. It can be as simple as the teacher providing time daily in the classroom for quiet sketching and directed introspection, similar to the sustained silent reading encouraged in classrooms, or time for exploration and inquiry into areas of personal interest.

Prearting is an early stage of creative work when students are taught to actively see. The teacher can encourage students to slow down in order to pay greater attention to the subtleties within the detail of things: the texture of a surface, the grain of wood, the pattern of a fabric, an aroma or fragrance, a kind of lighting or color, or the size and shape of an object. It is a stage when curiosity is cultivated, when wonder and awe find their initial grounding. It is at this beginning stage that teachers foster a love of color, line, and shape, encouraging students to imagine, invent, and experiment to find their own personal style and visual voice.

Prearting primarily works within the t^1 and t^2 dimensions where students dive into, investigate, and research an idea that has merit. It is also important for young artists to understand how experienced artists use brainstorming and doodling in their own creative processes. Concrete examples and models of what prearting looks and feels like to other artists assists the novice in understanding and developing their own process and thinking.

Figure 4.6. A student's prearting sketch generates ideas for the *Kua Ke Ahu* community mural in Camp Mokulē‘ia, O‘ahu.

Prewriting

Prewriting is the initial stage in which a writer enters into the writing process, when seed ideas for future writing compositions are gathered, nurtured, and sown. These seed ideas may include rambling thoughts, incomplete stories, images, sketches, bits of conversation, messy jottings on the pages of notebooks, napkins, or computers which incubate in the mind of the writer and on the pages of his folder or notebook. Seeds of ideas within the pages of a writer's folder or notebook are read, reread, added to, developed, and nurtured. Ideas that intrigue, spark an interest, or inspire are tried out and explored. Some seeds sprout. These ideas gather strength and form over time, and might grow into a story, a rap, or a song. But more often than not, seed ideas do not sprout beyond these early explorations. Most remain dormant for another day. A writer is almost always prewriting, collecting and gathering ideas, with the intention that they will cultivate and inspire future writing.

Prewriting includes:

- **Talking:** telling stories, discussing, and interviewing;
- **Arting:** sketching, drawing, thumbnail sketching, and storyboarding;
- **Inquiring:** observing, questioning, analyzing, wondering, reading, notetaking, and researching;
- **Brainstorming:** listing, webbing, and outlining;
- **Collecting:** jotting incomplete thoughts and favorite quotes, clipping favorite passages and images, collaging photos and other memorabilia to create a bank of resources to fuel future thinking about an idea or subject;
- **Remembering:** reliving sights, sounds, smells, and emotions;
- **Discovering:** thinking on the page, seeing new perspectives and ideas;
- **Freewriting:** raw writing – writing continuously for a short period of time without censorship of thought and regard for spelling or grammar;
- **Journaling:** the regular practice of recording events, experiences, ideas, and reflections for personal use.

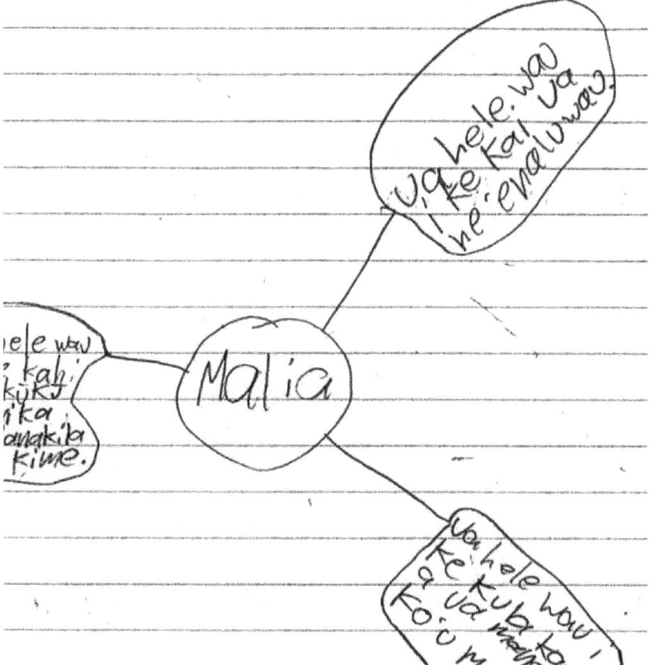

Figure 4.7. A student brainstorms topics for writing in her artist–writer's notebook.

Translation (clockwise): (1) I went to the ocean and surfed. (2) I went to summer school. I loved my classes. (3) I went to a tennis tournament and my team won.

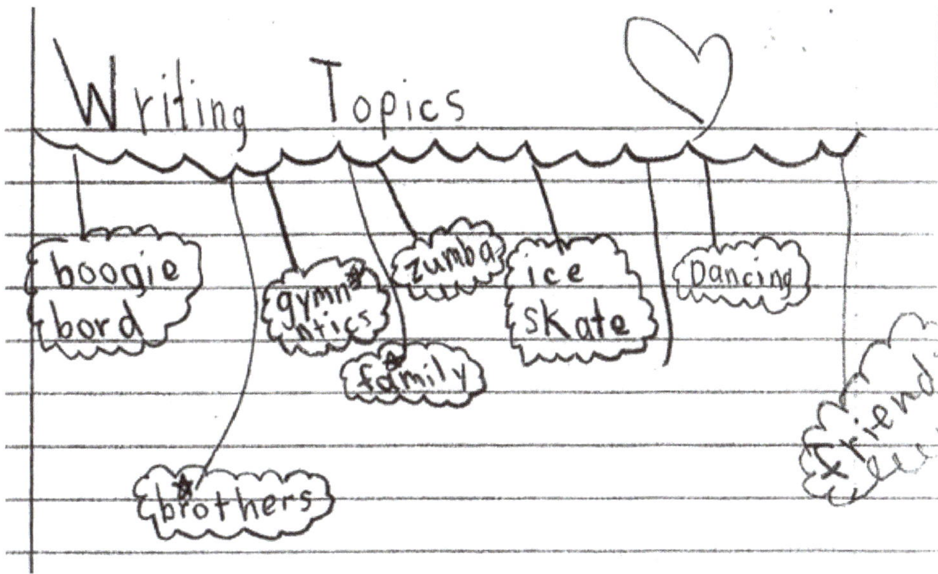

Figure 4.8. A list of possible writing topics is generated early in the year in this 2nd grader's artist–writer's notebook.

Prewriting: A Writer's Perspective

A writer is a consummate observer, living a wide-awake life, captivated by the small details and nuances of the everyday. He notices what others may not. This is the nature of a writer. He is curious, seeing wonder in the ordinary.

A writer pays attention to and is fascinated by words and the ways in which words are woven together to create sentences, sentences to create paragraphs, and paragraphs to communicate ideas. A writer is on the lookout for unique and interesting ways words are used and put together to create indelible images and unforgettable stories that linger in the minds of readers.

Figure 4.9. Ke Kula ʻo Samuel M. Kamakau 3rd and 4th graders discuss and brainstorm project ideas during the prewriting stage.

Always prewriting – observing, remembering, thinking, recording – a writer is a gatherer of words, sentences, quotes, photographs, sketches, and images that interest, intrigue, and inspire. He saves and treasures these seed ideas within the pages of his notebook with the hope that some will develop and grow into stories, poems, articles, or books. As a collector, a writer needs a place to keep that collection – to treasure it, to peruse it, and to be inspired by it. It may be a file, a folder, a notebook, a laptop, or other type of electronic device such as a smart phone. Having a place to store seed ideas gives them a place to incubate (Calkins and Harwayne, 1990; Fletcher, 1996).

Writing is generative: the more one writes, the more one has to write about. A writer requires time and space for regular writing. The prewriting stage of the process offers a writer the space to freely write, without censure, to explore, through his *na'au* (intuition), what is on his mind and in his heart.

A writer's perspective is shaped by his culture, with home, host/indigenous, local, or global aspects of culture defining his orientation. The pages of his notebook are filled with ideas, quotes, remembrances, and wonderings that move and inspire him. His writing seeds are typically grounded in home and local cultures. Writing can also take a global perspective, moving beyond the personal to include informational and/ or other cultural perspectives. Wondering, researching, and collecting are essential during prewriting.

Figure 4.10. Ke Kula 'o Samuel M. Kamakau 1st and 2nd grade students learn about native insects by recording visual and written observations during prearting and prewriting.

Prewriting: Nurturing the Writer

Writers spend much of their time in the prewriting stage; yet this is the stage which is given the least amount of time in formal instruction. Intentionally teaching students about prewriting, how favorite authors go about prewriting, and providing a variety of prewriting experiences throughout the school day and the school year nurtures and inspires the writer within each child. Studying the different ways experienced writers prewrite opens up new approaches and ways of thinking about prewriting for young writers, deepening an understanding of their own processes.

Figure 4.11. A 3rd grader finds a quiet space for prewriting.

The goal is for students to experience what it means to be writers, real writers, and to practice living a writerly life. This means regularly scheduled writing time, daily or as often as possible. Because writing is generative, writers need to be writing. When students say, "I don't know what to write about," they are not writing often enough. Providing time to prewrite – to tell, to draw, and to write their own stories – enables them to see themselves as writers.

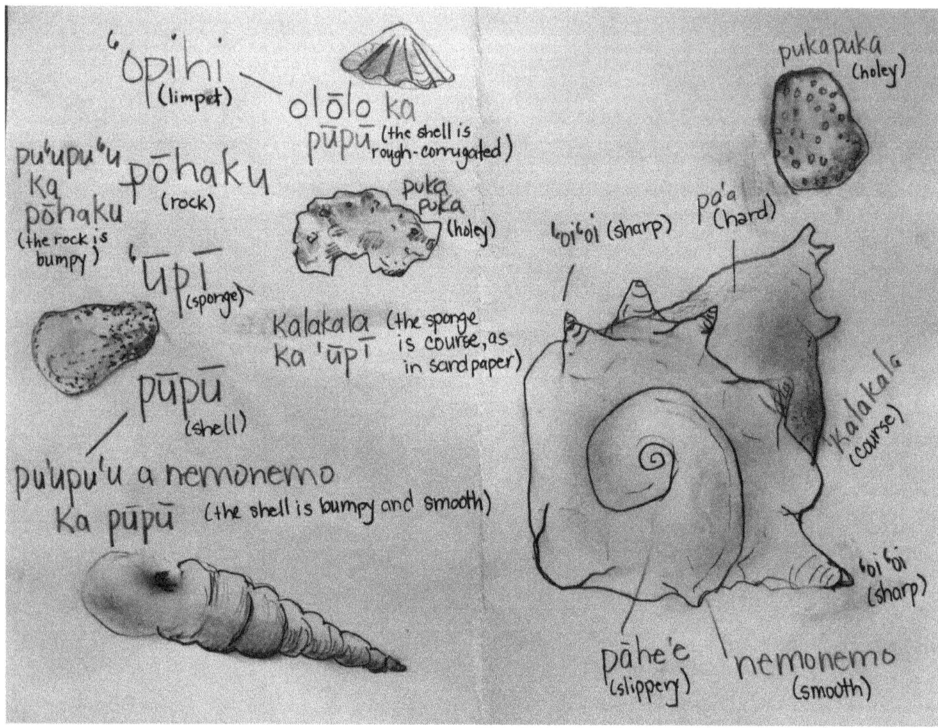

Figure 4.12. A mini notebook (in the Hawaiian language) is used to record descriptive vocabulary and observations of sea life.

Living a writerly life is also about noticing, paying attention to, and capturing important details with all of the senses. It is creating images with words and recording unforgettable moments. It is about describing with precision and using compelling language (see Figures 4.12 and 4.13). It is about paying attention to the way words sound and flow together to create rhythm, resonance, silence, and space. Through prewriting, teachers foster a love of words, encouraging students to word-play – to experiment with, invent, and use words in new and interesting ways.

Prewriting, like prearting, primarily works within the t^1 and t^2 dimensions. Students also practice collecting as a form of prewriting. Photographs, cut-out images, sketches, lists of words, quotes, quickwrites, observations, incomplete stories, interesting information, thoughts, and memories fill the pages of their notebooks, a special box, or folders on their computers.

In order to become proficient, young writers need regular prewriting practice to gain fluidity of thought and become comfortable experimenting and risk-taking. Through prewriting, writers discover an idea or topic that speaks to them and calls them to explore in more depth. Cultural context determines how writers orient to their story. They get curious about or are inspired by a photo of grandma they collected and write about her. They find a story that begs to be told. When a seed idea begins to sprout, writers may be ready to move into envisioning and composing.

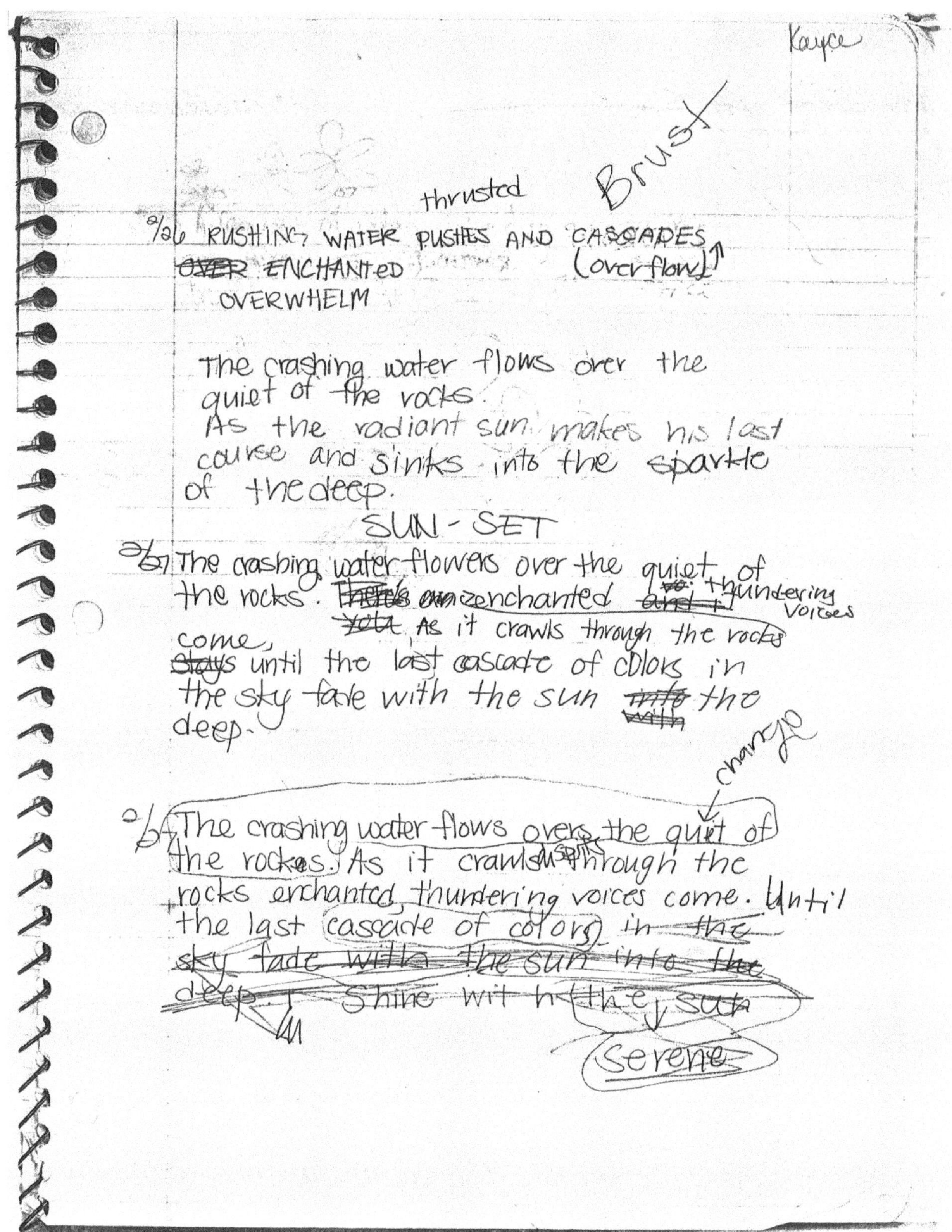

Figure 4.13. A 6th grader's ideas gather strength over time as she freewrites in her notebook.

Figure 4.14. Prearting and prewriting ideas are gathered as part of a planning meeting for the Hawai'i Kākou Mural Project at the Hawai'i Convention Center in Honolulu.

Prearting and Prewriting in Arting and Writing

Prearting and prewriting play a crucial role in starting the processes of researching and collecting ideas, observing and recording information, that are the basis for integrated arting and writing. In our classrooms, the artist–writer's notebook is an essential tool for our students as they practice living a creative–expressive, artistic and writerly life, collecting and making a record of their observations as a first step of artistic and written creation and expression. In this first step, Ralph Fletcher's description of a writer can readily be expanded to include the artist:

> *Writers [and artists] are like other people, except for at least one important difference. Other people have daily thoughts and feelings, notice this sky or that smell, but they don't do much about it. All those thoughts, feelings, sensations, and opinions pass through them like the air they breathe.*
>
> *Not writers [and not artists]. Writers [and artists] react. And writers [and artists] need a place to record those reactions.*
>
> *That's what a writer's [and artist's] notebook is for….*
>
> *A writer's [and an artist's] notebook gives you a place to live like a writer [and an artist], not just in school during writing [and arting] time, but wherever you are at any time of day.* (Fletcher, 1996: 3)

Figure 4.15. Artist Kahi Ching experiments with ideas during the prearting stage.

The artist–writer reacts and records from a place of wonder. Wondering invites a desire to know more about what one is interested in or moved by. Students learn how to observe, to actively see what is there, not what they think is there. Through observation, they learn to notice the subtleties in things and are motivated to acquire the specific descriptive and expressive skills to represent them.

Artists and writers orient from their own knowledge, background, and cultural context in exploring and developing their written and artistic works. For this reason, a first attempt to represent something on paper in arting or writing often shows a person's preconceptions or lack of knowledge. For example, the initial illustration of a lobster in Figure 4.16 lacks detail and specificity, suggesting little or no familiarity with any specific crustacean. It is what we call an "any-kind" drawing.[2] However, after studying the Kona lobster, which is found only in Hawaiian waters – observing live Kona lobsters, studying photos, and reading about the lobster – this artist cultivated the ability to '*ike* (to know through experience) what is seen, heard, tasted, smelled, touched, and intuited. The second drawing, shown in Figure 4.17, became a more accurate, lifelike, and detailed representation of the creature. There is no such thing as a generic lobster. Particularity is quintessential to the artist and the writer in accurately representing or capturing the essence of a person, place, or thing.

Figure 4.16. Before: An "any-kind" image of a lobster.

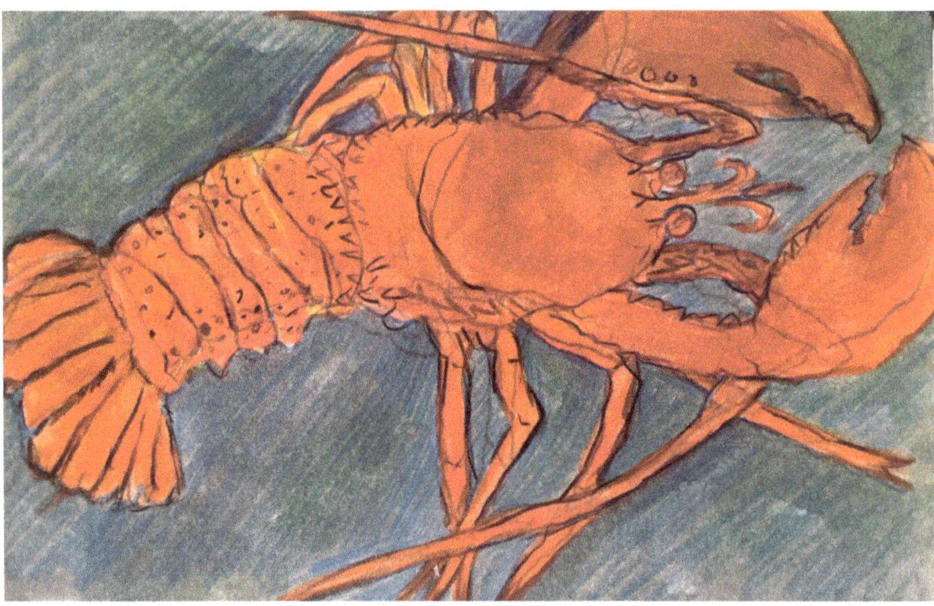

Figure 4.17. After: A fully rendered Kona lobster.

Note to the Reader: Keeping and Sharing Your Own Notebooks

As artists and writers, we keep our own notebooks in our personal and teaching lives. These notebooks become models for students, examples of how artists and writers use notebooks. We share our notebooks with students to teach them how the prearting and prewriting steps are foundational to the arting and writing processes (see Figures 4.18 and 4.19). Students are then able to use their own notebooks in creative ways (see Figures 4.20 and 4.21).

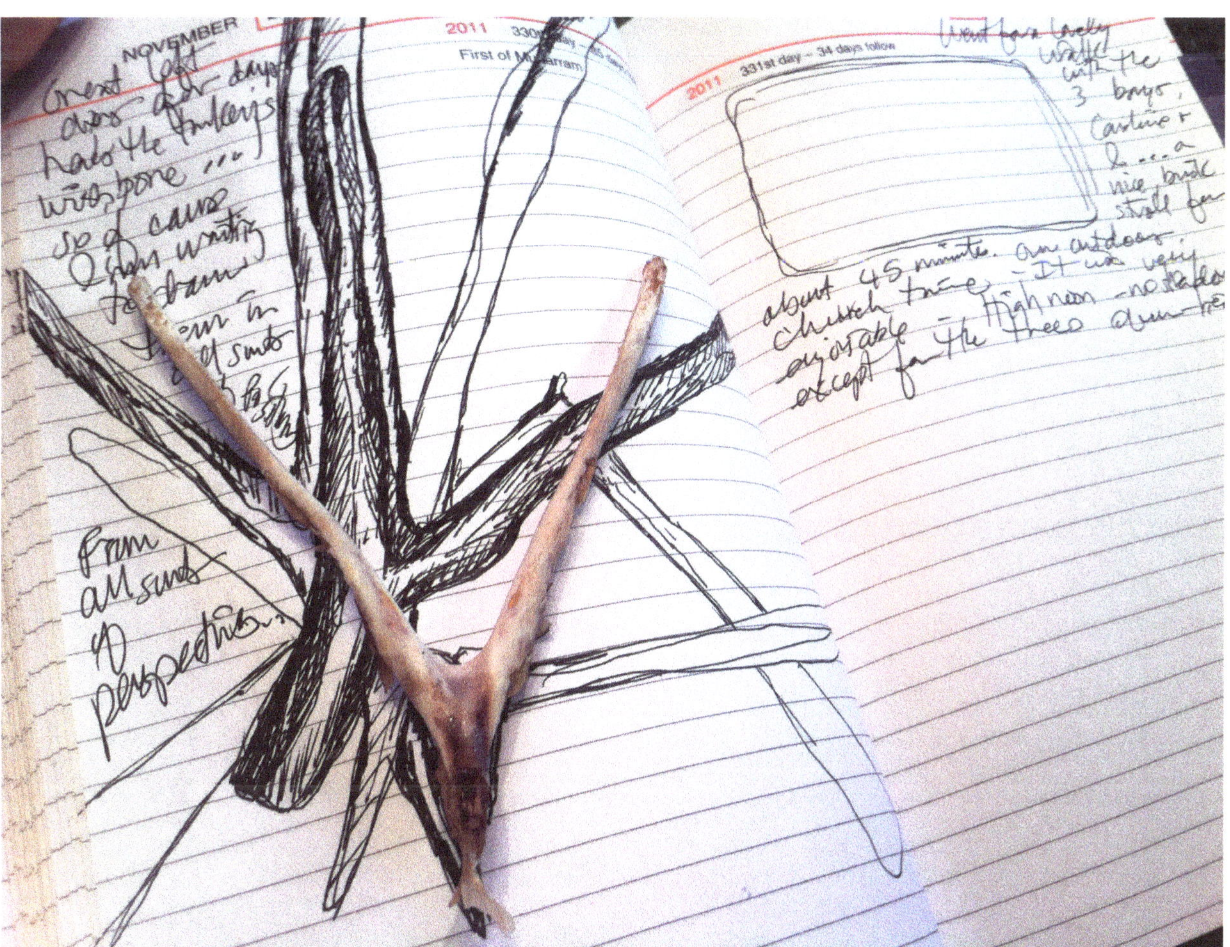

Figure 4.18. This teacher's notebook entry is a drawing and written contemplation of a turkey wishbone.

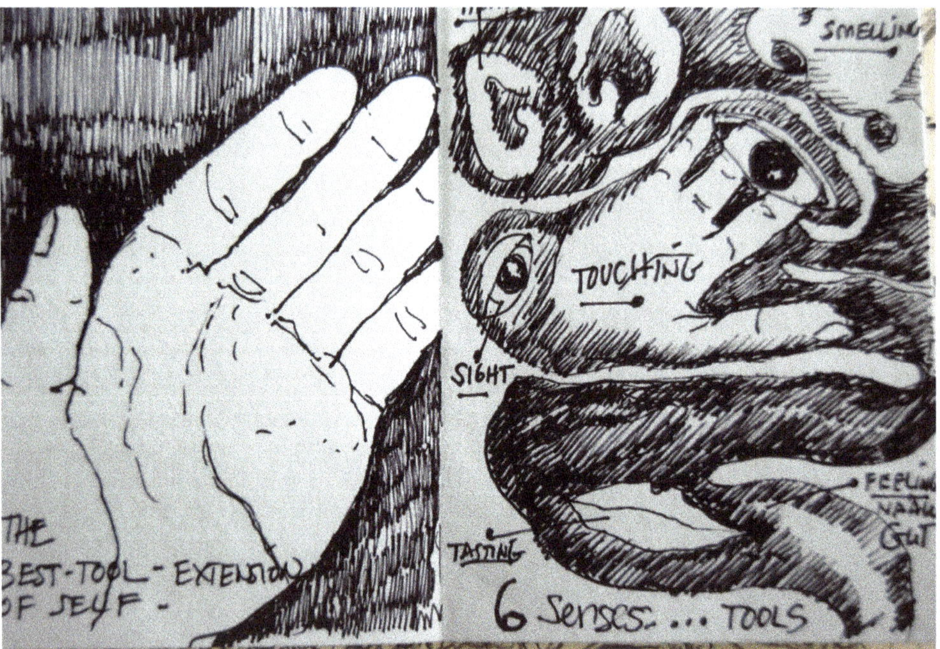

Figure 4.19. This teacher-created artist–writer's mini notebook entry explores and documents her understanding through the six senses: touch, taste, hearing, smelling, seeing, and intuition.

Figure 4.20. This 2nd grader's artist–writer's mini notebook was used during an inquiry research project to record questions and new learning on the *lamalama i'a* (torch fishing) method of catching fish.

Translation: How do you torch fish? Torch: you need a torch at night so you can see the fish. Spear: you need a spear to pierce the mullet or other fish. Canoe: you need a canoe.

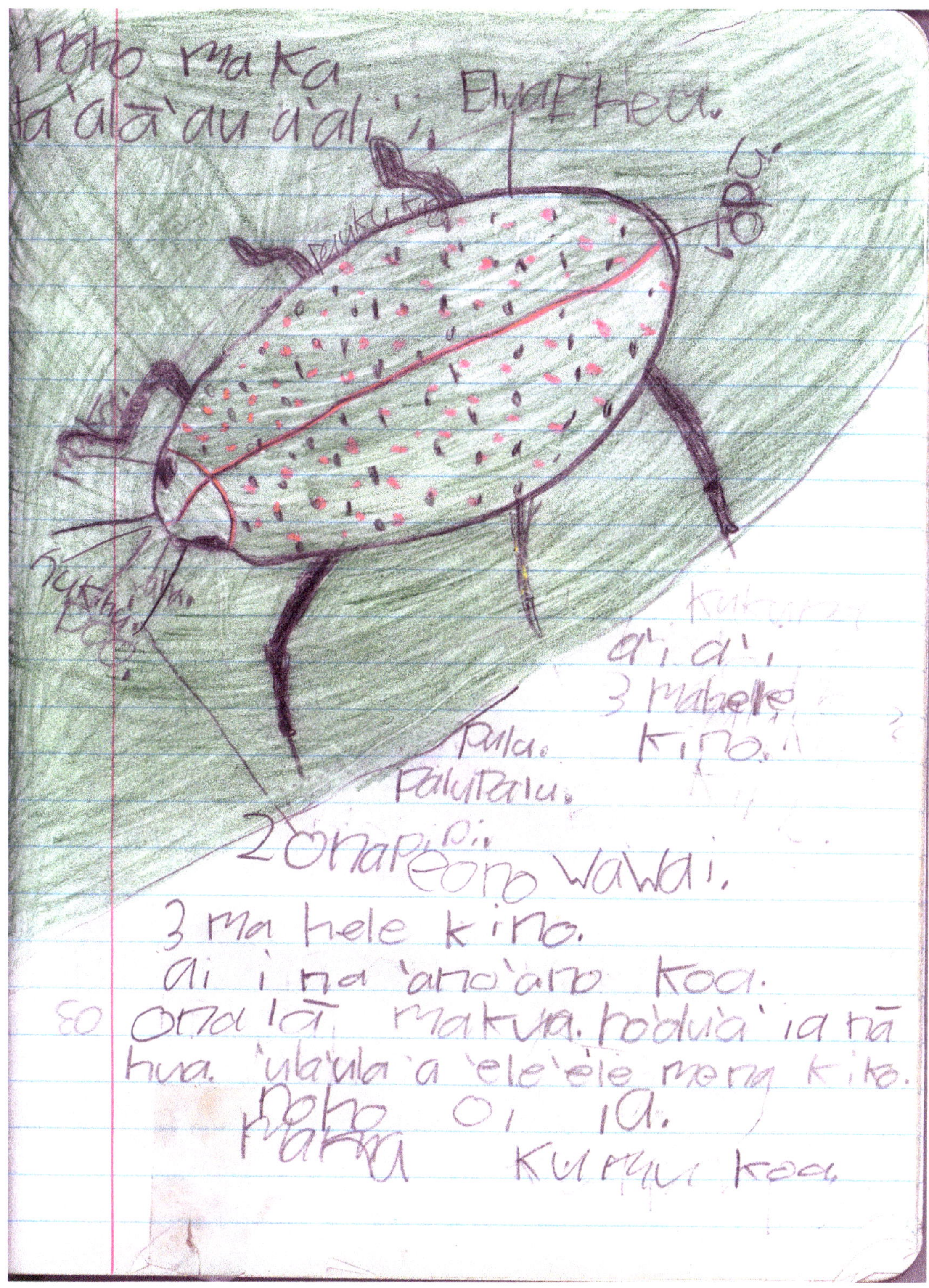

Figure 4.21. This notebook entry during prearting and prewriting records new learning during an inquiry project on native Hawaiian insects.

Translation (from top to bottom): lives on the *‘a‘ali‘i* (a native Hawaiian shrub); two wings; abdomen; thorax; eyes; antenna; transparent; 3 body parts; soft; 2 feelers; 6 legs; 3 body parts; eats *koa* (a native Hawaiian tree) seeds; flimsy eggs; red and green with spots; it lives in *koa* trees.

Notes to Chapter 4

1   Thumbnail sketching refers to a kind of shorthand drawing for artists. Thumbnail drawings are small, quick sketches used to develop an idea or series of ideas.
2   An "any-kind" drawing is a non-specific, generic rendering of an object such as a face, a flower, a fish, or a tree (see Appendix B, "Any-Kind": An Explanation).

Chapter 5

Envisioning

Stage 2: Envisioning

Envisioning is the stage in which the artist and writer begin to explore possible directions a work may take, imagining the end result. Artists experiment with form or media. Writers try out form or genre. In this stage, a safe environment is critical; when experimentation is encouraged, there is no such thing as a mistake and infinite possibilities are invited.

Envisioning in Arting

Envisioning is a kind of daydreaming, a "what if" stage in the creative process. In this stage, an artist gathers and chooses which images to work with from the many doodles, drawings, thumbnail sketches, and notes created during prearting. Envisioning allows an artist to imagine the possibilities of the work by answering questions about the form which the art might take: "What form should this piece take in order to best communicate my message to an audience and elicit a response? Should this piece be a painting, sculpture, print, or photograph? How large should the work be – two panels, four panels, or a series?

For the visual artist, translation is the entry point into envisioning. Translating is active seeing and examining through all six of the senses, digesting visual and other kinds of sensory information. It is an inner perceiving, mediating, and conceptualizing from what is seen or imagined into an artistic representation, the expression of what is perceived or imagined into line, shape, object, or form. Experimenting with tools of the visual arts, trying to articulate a form (see Figures 5.1 and 5.2), and integrating aesthetics takes one through the exploration of translating from one medium or type of representation to another, and into the messiness of envisioning.

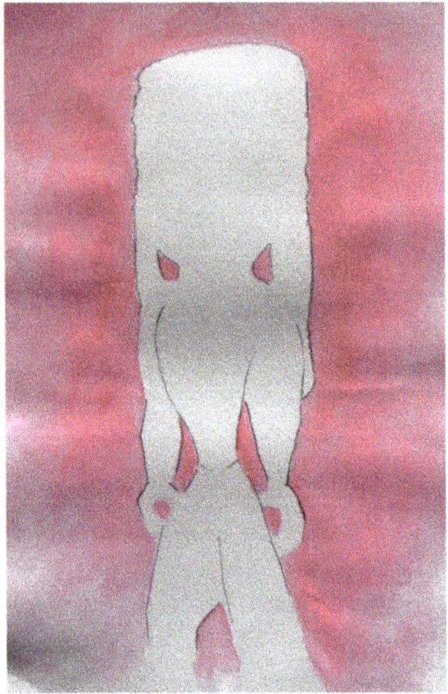

Figure 5.1. This first arting exercise, created by Kendra Medeiros, develops the ability to observe a three-dimensional object and translate it into a two-dimensional form on the page.

Figure 5.2. This second arting exercise, uses line, shadow, and highlighting to create dimensionality on the two-dimensional page.

After translation, an artist moves into a "digesting" phase of envisioning, synthesizing, and distilling what has been translated. This takes the artist to a deeper understanding of the what, the how, and the why of her creating. This stage of the arting process is always formative because concepts and plans are still malleable and experimental; still being stretched and played with; and still being redrawn, reformulated, and more deeply contemplated. The intuitive mind is fully engaged and directs this part of the process.

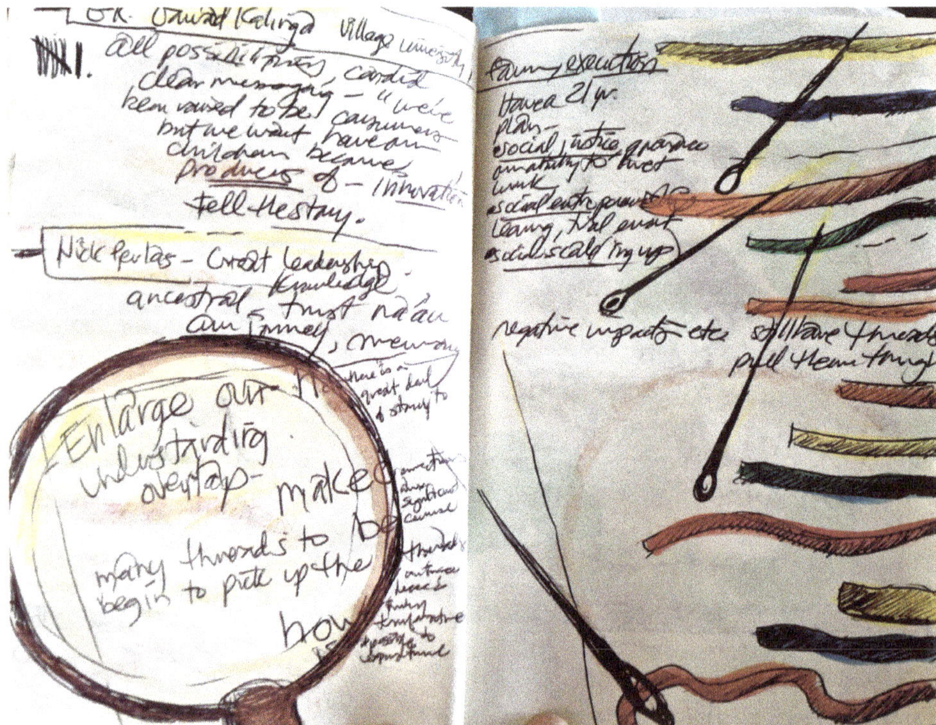

Figure 5.3. Prearting notes (on the left) in this artist's notebook lead to envisioning (on the right) a metaphor of needles and threads symbolizing the coming together of many people.

Artists envision in numerous ways. The first way of envisioning is from an intuitive place; it is an organic process. Something catches the eye, an idea resonates and incubates in the *na'au*. A piece of wood holds a bowl within, and the artist conjures and holds it in her mind's eye. At other times the voice or idea of a work persists, repeatedly appearing in the sketches and words of one's notebook. The idea of the piece begins to take shape and form, inspiring the direction the work will ultimately take. A sudden rainstorm and the puddling of water conjures a series of working sketches, or a sunrise inspires morning colors splashed onto a page.

A second source of envisioning arises from the reason a work is created, guiding the form of what is visualized as its purpose: turning a bowl to honor a marriage, beating and stamping a piece of *kapa* (barkcloth) to be used in a hula performance to honor a chief, or painting a portrait to honor a grandmother.

A third manner of envisioning that an artist might use is when she is given or chooses a medium in which to create: a photograph to commemorate a person or event, a sculpture made to honor the story of a place, or a film that communicates the lifestyle and values of a people. The choice of medium is an aspect of envisioning the outcome of the artistic work.

Envisioning takes time, the time needed to work with an idea that is still taking shape. There are no formulas for this part of the process. This is the point when the artist may feel she is entering the difficult stage of a transmediated (t^3) experience, not knowing exactly where she is going and how she will get there, and imagines the range of possibilities. It's trusting that the *na'au*, intuition, will guide and inspire the artist through this uncharted journey. Without this t^3 experience, there can never be a T^4 "aha" moment.

Envisioning in the visual arts often includes:

- Creating working sketches, visual drafts similar to written drafts of a writer. The visual artist creates multiple working sketches to develop her ideas, similar to the process of a writer refining and clarifying his ideas with each successive draft;
- Researching further about the subject matter and ideas;
- Considering the cultural context, time period, and place of work;
- Experimenting with various media or forms;
- Selecting media that best express the intended message: painting, drawing, print, photo, etc.;
- Working with masterworks as models or inspirations;
- Choosing the function, form, and purpose of the piece: to provoke, inform, respond, incite, challenge, persuade, entertain;
- Defining the intended audience: self, family, friends, community, or the world at large.

Envisioning: An Artist's Perspective

An artist is often amazed by what appears on canvas, in clay, or on film because the materials often direct the work in unexpected ways. Raw wood or stone challenge a visual artist to discover what is within. She listens to the voice of the raw materials and intuits their unseen potential. She selects the type, quality, shape, and size of these materials. For example, an Indigenous artist may contemplate using an indigenous palette (see Appendix C, An Indigenous Color Palette) of black, white, red, and yellow that comes from organic materials: charcoal, coral or chalk, blood and soil, tumeric or

Figure 5.4. *Kumu* (Teacher) Meleanna assists 3rd and 4th graders in envisioning their class mural.

ochre. Directed and inspired by her materials, she may envision the poetry of the piece through color.

Envisioning asks the artist to contemplate new thoughts and ideas as she brings together the many images created during prearting. Envisioning can be exhilarating when these new thoughts and ideas inspire and propel the artist to new mental spaces where she is able to envision the direction in which the work is taking her and/or the final product. One also encounters roadblocks or diversions that can frustrate an artist; but patience and perseverance through these challenges always leads to new vistas, resulting in work that resonates, evolves, and takes shape from the inside out. As a piece develops, care and interest in the work engages the artist, enabling her to work with more commitment and intentionality. This is how and when the artist becomes invested in and feels a responsibility for her creation.

It is essential that a visual artist view and study the work of others. Talking about and analyzing her own work, that of her peers, and that of established and traditional artists broadens her vision and deepens her appreciation for other perspectives. The importance of passing on the experience and expertise of an art form and cultural tradition can be found in the rigor, training, and lifetime study that students of the arts are exposed to and trained in (Chun, 2011).

Envisioning: Nurturing the Artist

As teachers of budding artists, we share three types of study as essential to empowering young artists to envision possibilities. First, the study and exploration of different media, along with their specific methodologies and techniques, helps students to understand the creative potential of the various types of media. Second, the study of masterworks – their craft, their quality, and the cultural/historical context in which they were created – gives students a solid foundation from which to work. Finally, the study of master artists and how they work assists students in understanding and developing their own creative processes.

It is important to give students the foundational knowledge of elements and principles of design (see Appendix D, Arting Elements and Principles of Design). This transmission (t^1) knowledge of line, shape, color, form, etc., is foundational to an artist's toolkit. It can then be used and practiced as transaction (t^2) with tools – charcoal pencils, brushes, or chisels – specific to each medium. This type of study and interaction assists young artists in gaining an understanding and appreciation for the inherent nature of each medium. For example, young artists can discover, through hands-on experience, how various drawing mediums are used and how one begins to work intuitive ideas or images into concepts toward a final vision. The confidence of young artists grows as they apply the elements and principles of design and master techniques and skills. With serious, in-depth study, teachers immerse their students in deep inquiry and research, engaging them in work which is rich in color, line, form, voice, and spirit. Learning to be specific and rigorous in one's exploration, as in not accepting "any-kind," non-original creations or non-specific generalities, is essential if students are to become adept at articulating and formulating their own understanding of ideas, envisioning of the work, and its execution.

Figure 5.5. View of Hilo Bay, 1888 – Oil painting by Joseph Nawahī: This early landscape was one of the first works done by a Native Hawaiian artist in the western painting tradition. Reprinted by permission of Kamehameha Schools.

The study of masterworks, a t^1 activity, exposes students to a wide range of exemplars to learn from and aspire to. Analyzing and talking about what works and doesn't work in a piece is a t^2 activity, assisting young artists in envisioning their own work. These activities develop an artist's vocabulary, helping her to articulate what she is understanding, feeling, and wanting to communicate.

Studying master artists, how painters, sculptors, photographers, and well-loved illustrators work and live, gives young artists insight into how others process, envision, and complete works within their art form. It helps young artists to understand the growth, perspective, and depth of that artist. Understanding how the social, historical, and cultural contexts influenced a master artist's work informs the young artist about what could inspire and compel her own work. In-depth study empowers young artists to better understand their lives and their own arting process.

Figure 5.6. *Kumu* (Teacher) Meleanna's sketch of a Herb Kane painting is used to demonstrate how an artist uses a masterwork for study.

A teacher may also use student work as a model to support and inspire young artists. Students sharing informally during arting workshop can describe how they tried out new techniques and strategies. They can become a teacher, showing their peers what they've learned and applied, revealing their thinking process, and how those techniques or strategies have moved their work forward. As a result, students will be more willing to take risks and try out new ideas.

Figure 5.7. A creative child spontaneously finds her own space to draw.

Most importantly, it is through constant practice on the part of the young artist and ongoing feedback from others that develops familiarity, expertise, and confidence to envision and create works of substance and beauty. The alchemy of form and function drive this stage of the process. Artists begin to experience the joy of discovering the work of their hands. Entering into the realm of t^3, transmediation, the realm of possibility, students must be provided a safe space so they are willing to take risks. They should be encouraged to synthesize and reshape what they are learning to formulate original ideas and work with greater assurance.

Envisioning in Writing

Envisioning for a writer is an internal seeing and imagining of possibilities. What a writer can envision, a writer can create. Envisioning happens in the early stages of the writing process, often during prewriting or the early drafts of composing. Envisioning is when a writer discovers or is able to determine the direction a written piece will take: he sees its form or direction; he hears its voice. Sometimes envisioning happens almost instantaneously, and a writer is able to move quickly from prewriting into composing. Other times, a written piece evolves slowly through the early drafts of composing, taking on form and voice as a writer explores and experiments. The clarity of a writer's vision enables him to write with greater purpose and intentionality.

We note three ways writers, like artists, envision: (1) form is inherent in the writing; (2) a writer's purpose determines form; or (3) form is predetermined for the writer. Envisioning is often organic, as the form and voice of a piece arise out of the incomplete ideas, jottings, wonderings, and rambling sentences within a writer's notebook and speak to the *na'au* of the writer. The form of the piece starts to appear; the voice of the piece shouts, "I am a poem!" or "Make me into a story!" The writing sounds like a poem, or it looks like a story. In other words, form and/or voice are inherent in the piece.

The purpose of the writing often determines its form. To honor a family member, a writer may choose to compose, using a genre of his home culture, a genealogy chant, or a song. In order to express an opinion and inform others on a local issue, a writer considers whether to compose a letter to the local legislator or a testimony to be read at a hearing. To make a point in a creative and entertaining way, a writer decides to write a satire or a story with a moral or a blog post to reach a global readership. Which form will best serve the purpose of the piece? Who is the audience?

Frequently, form is predetermined for a writer. A writer may be given or assigned the form in which to write: a chant or song is requested to commemorate a special event; a remembrance is written to share at a funeral; or an article is penned to inform the public on the status of a rare native species. A writer envisions, working within the structure and elements of a specific genre or form.

Envisioning includes:

- Deciding on the function or purpose of the piece, such as inform, entertain, respond, persuade;
- Choosing the intended audience, such as the teacher, friends, family, community, or the wider world;
- Experimenting with genre or form;
- Researching the text structure and elements of a genre or form;
- Selecting the genre or form;
- Finding "mentor texts" as models.

Envisioning: A Writer's Perspective

A writer gathers his collection of words, thoughts, photographs, sketches, and musings in his writer's notebook, journal, laptop, or smart phone for safekeeping. Here seed ideas, thoughts, and images incubate. Rereading seed ideas in his writer's notebook may inform and stimulate envisioning. A writer may be surprised by what finds its way onto the pages of his notebook or into his smart phone memory. Particular ideas capture the writer's interest, attention, or imagination, demanding to be taken beyond the writer to an audience. Having something to say moves a writer's desire to venture beyond prewriting and the self to envision possibilities, to give voice to thought, and to share with others.

When form is inherent within the voice of the incomplete snippets of text, a writer immediately envisions the direction his composition will take. A quote from *tūtū* (grandma) or an old photograph holds a special memory and a writer may envision a memoir. Words and phrases jotted down next to a sketch have a poetic rhythm and a writer hears the beginnings of a chant or poem.

When a writer has a specific purpose for his writing, envisioning also opens up possibilities. This stage allows a writer to explore various directions his piece could take before selecting the genre or form that best communicates his message to the intended audience. He explores whether writing a letter to a local legislator or a testimony to be posted on a social media site is appropriate. He tries out whether a short story written for classmates and friends about competing in a local contest or an article for the school newspaper or a class webpage is best.

Often a writer is given or assigned the form a composition will take. In this case, envisioning the range of possibilities within the given structure of the genre or form and understanding its subtle nuances enables a writer to take full advantage of the genre or form to amplify the impact of his composition on the audience.

A writer's ability to envision is enhanced and fine-tuned through the study of genres: their structure, elements, and how they are written. He may sometimes take the time to hone his vision, studying a genre or written form, to better understand its features and nuances before beginning to compose. Studying the life of particular authors, as mentors, and their writing processes enables a writer to learn more about his own process and style, expanding his repertoire of possibilities.

Figure 5.8. A 2nd grader from Ke Kula ʻo Samuel M. Kamakau begins envisioning through study, during research on native Hawaiian insects.

Figure 5.9. In her notebook, this young artist–writer envisions the form and direction her arting and writing piece may take to inform classmates and others about the native Hawaiian damselfly.

Translation: The interesting things about the Damselfly This native damselfly has a large body. It has three body parts the head, the thorax, and the long abdomen. It has six red legs. It has two short antenna. Its whole body is red, yellow, and black. Its eyes are very big.

Envisioning: Nurturing the Writer

The study of mentor texts and mentor authors (Calkins and Harwayne, 1990; Fletcher 2010; Ray, 2006), nurtures the capacity of young writers to envision. It also teaches them to seek out models for their own writing. Writers learn about the structure, particular features, and nuances of various genres and written forms. They read and listen carefully to identify the voice and tone of a work. Mentor texts, that is, texts by published and more experienced writers, including the teacher, become models to refer to throughout the writing process. Teachers who write with their students can provide an inside view into the process and experience of creating a writing piece. They provide young writers with text to study, analyze, and imitate.

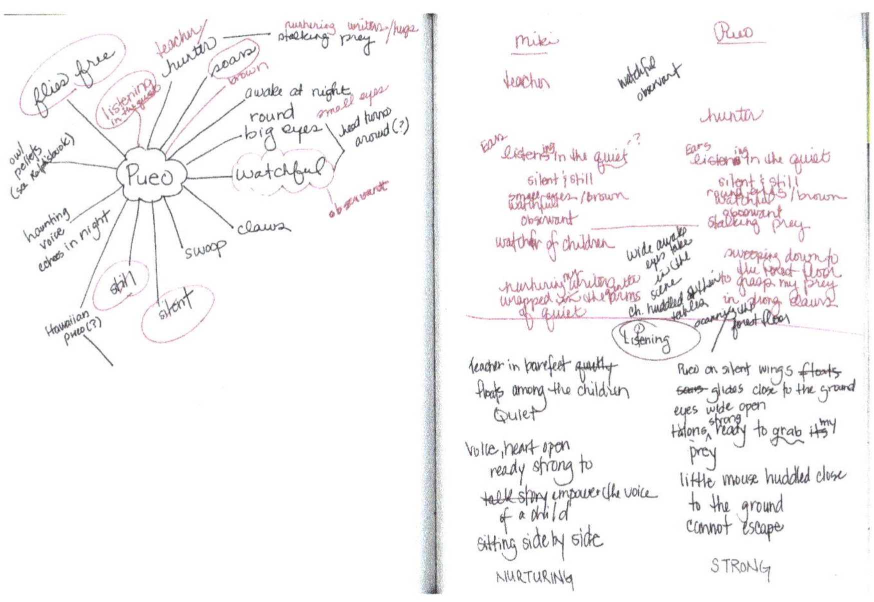

Figure 5.10. In her notebook, Miki moves from a brainstorm about the *pueo* (owl), on the left page, during prewriting, to envisioning, on the right page, a two-voice poem that compares teaching to a *pueo* (owl) hunting.

When teachers surround students with interesting texts they can emulate, their students are inspired saying, "I want to try that" or "I can write like that." For the youngest writers, an appropriate text may be simple with repetitive sentences such as *Brown Bear, Brown Bear What Do You See* by Bill Martin (Martin, 1967). For the more experienced writers it may be studying how *Out of the Dust* by Karen Hesse (Hesse, 1997) uses a collection of poems to tell a story.

The study of other authors illuminates their writing processes, how they weave their thoughts and ideas into a single cohesive composition to be shared, read, and loved (or not) by others. Inviting student writers to be mentor authors, sharing their process and techniques with peers, also creates a community of writers. Teachers can invite their students to share how they tried out a new writing technique or strategy. Teachers can also invite their students to be the teacher, modeling how they used a technique or strategy, revealing their thinking process, and sharing how the technique or strategy enhances their piece. Peer writing as mentor texts also serves as models for envisioning, elevating the work of the students so that they sit side-by-side with professional authors.

Writers need to read and study texts in the genre in which they are writing, especially when envisioning a genre for the first time, in order to capture the essence of that genre in their writing (see Figure 5.11).

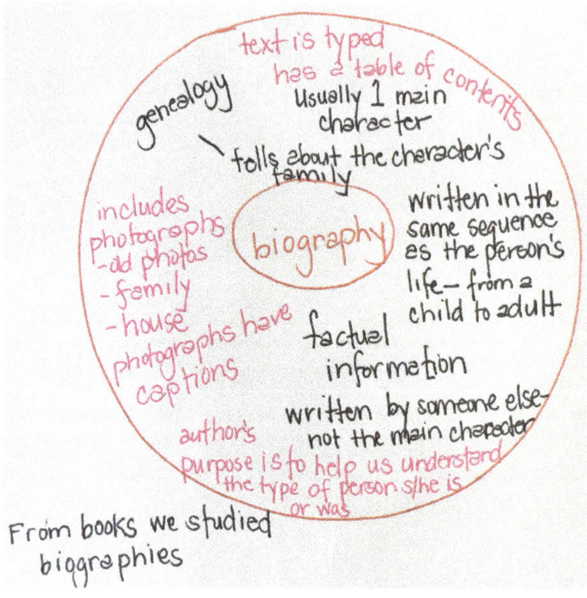

Figure 5.11. This class chart was created with 2nd graders after a genre study on biographies. It assists students in envisioning their own biographies.

Figure 5.12. Miki's self-portrait.

Figure 5.13. *Kumu* (Teacher) Miki uses her arting and writing pieces as models for her 6th grade students in a unit on identity.

The Kentucky Hills
By Miki Hayes Maeshiro

I am the granddaughter of Sabra Prater Hayes, born and raised in Hueysville, Kentucky. Sabra married Mitchell Hayes of Mousie, the town over yonder, down the windy dirt road that wandered through the dark hills.

The hills are quiet with down home folk. It is a place where family cemeteries with plastic flowers dot the steep hillsides and people move as slow as their Kentucky drawl. I remember Grandma Sabra's drawl, as s-l-o-w and thick as the molasses she used to make cookies. Hill life was a hard life; most people were coal people with large families and little money. There was women's work and men's work. Grandma Sabra gathered greens and berries in the woods; grew vegetables in the garden, lots of green tomatoes; canned fruit and vegetables to last the winter; and could kill and pluck a chicken.

My father, Roy Mitchell Hayes, the oldest of five children, was born in Maytown, down the hill, across the bridge and past the weeping willow tree. It is a place I never knew growing up. My father left the hills of Kentucky to "see the world" and never looked back. He has spent his life trying to escape his "hillbilly" past. But no matter how far away he got from his past, it was always there, staring back at him in the mirror.

Fried green tomatoes, spinach greens with vinegar, pickled corn and cornbread – not the sweet kind – were a regular part of my family meals alongside the shoyu chicken, teriyaki meat, musubi, and saimin.

The strong work ethic of hard-working country folk was instilled in me. Work hard! Sometimes it was even, do it the hard way, just like my father.

Stubborn and bull-headed, I was born a Hayes. And from what my aunties tell me, seems I always will be, even though I've added the "Maeshiro" to the end of my name. The Kentucky hills still run deep in the blood of this island girl.

Figure 5.14 Miki's writing piece

The envisioning stage of the writing process expands the repertoire of young writers and enables them to compose with greater intentionality and direction, yet is rarely included as part of writing instruction. We encourage teachers to spend time immersing students in the inquiry and study of texts and genre.

Teachers can assist young writers in envisioning possibilities through the inquiry and study of mentor texts, the study of authors, their processes, and their lives. Well-meaning teachers often shortcut the envisioning stage by providing students with a list of rules or criteria to follow. When taught in this way, students follow a formulaic "recipe" to complete a writing assignment, which rushes them into, and through, the composing stage. This type of writing instruction does not nurture students to become writers; it does not touch the heart nor develop their capacity with language and self-expression.

The study of mentor texts is an aspect of the t^1 transmission dimension, in which teachers guide their students to learn the structure of various genres, techniques of craft, and interesting ways writers use punctuation. Studying mentor texts and authors assists students to envision possibilities for their own writing. Mentor texts and mentor authors also promote a t^2 transactional learning dimension, in which young writers interact with the texts, other authors, and one another. Writers engage in a dialogue, internal and/or interpersonal, by asking and answering questions, and wondering and conjecturing about the intentions of the author. In the t³ transmediational dimension, envisioning requires the application of what one has learned from these mentors. It may be a messy endeavor as one explores and experiments with genre, form, traits (Spandel, 2011), technique, craft, grammar, and punctuation as a piece evolves and the writer discovers the form or direction the writing will take. Students become writers when they experience the joy of discovering something new within their own writing and envisioning its possibilities – the awe of hearing the voice of a poem speak from the barely legible scribbles of their notebook; envisioning the way a final poem will look and sound on the page.

Envisioning in Arting and Writing

Envisioning is about possibilities, generating an ability to comprehend the whole in all its complexity, of how two art forms come together, either side-by-side or fully integrated. Arting informs the writing, and writing informs the arting – one enhances the other in communicating the message. When arting and writing are fully integrated, the text becomes part of the visual message and vice versa (see Figures 5.15, 5.16, and 5.17).

Figure 5.15. *Hoʻohuli*: The words of an ancient Hawaiian prophetic chant inspired this piece and are included as an integral part of the mural at the Bishop Museum in Honolulu.

Figure 5.16. The words of the *Kumulipo*, a Hawaiian creation chant, inspired and contextualized this arting and writing project.

Figure 5.17. These original student drawings and poetry of 2nd and 3rd graders from Ke Kula ʻo Samuel M. Kamakau sit alongside the traditional text so that this piece embodies past, present, and future.

Note to the Reader: Our Envisioning Process

During the envisioning of this book, we studied our favorite professional educator books and art books. We analyzed the style, the voice, and the layout in which they were written and illustrated. We synthesized what appealed to us, as readers, viewers, and educators, in order to create a meaningful work to challenge and inspire you, the reader.

Chapter 6

Composing

Stage 3: Composing

Composing is the stage in which the artist begins the work: drawing, painting, sculpting. The writer writes. This stage of the writing process is also commonly known as *drafting*.

Composing in Arting

Composing is when an artist puts into action what is envisioned. The ability to compose with purpose and intentionality is the result of one's research, thinking, dreaming,

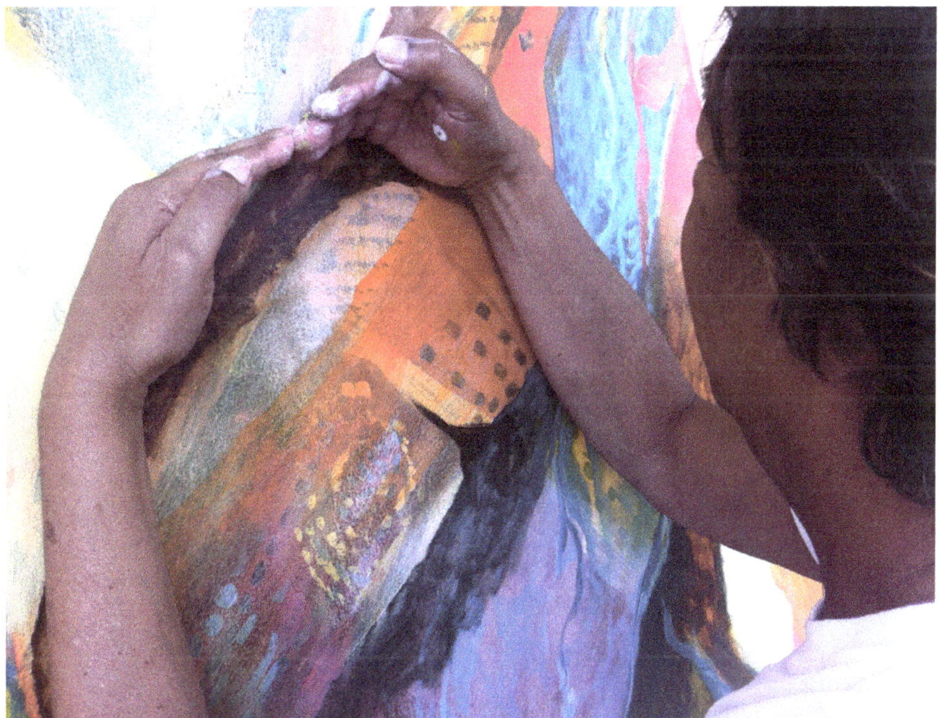

Figure 6.1. *Kumu* (Teacher) Al Lagunero plans his next move on the *Hawaiʻi Kākou* mural composition.

formulating, experimenting, and practicing in prearting and envisioning. Composing is the stage of the arting process when the brainstorming of ideas, the utilization of tools, and the mechanics of the art form are actualized. The composition is a result of all that an artist has learned over time until that moment. Composing requires time, patience, practice, practice, and more practice. Success is not guaranteed. It involves experimenting with and learning about the materials and how they interact with various media (e.g. different types of paint with different brushes and types of paper or canvas). It is continued exploration and learning from mistakes, utilizing a repertoire of skills to demonstrate aesthetic understanding and personal voice and vision. The act of composing is different for every artist.

Figure 6.2. *Hawai'i Kākou* mural at the Hawai'i Convention Center in Honolulu.

Composing allows an artist to individuate – that is, to make personal choices and stylistic adaptations – in evolving ideas and in contextualizing information within the work. Composing, to an artist, means working out how ideas, feelings, and images can be realized in physical media. It is the real work of bringing a thought or emotion beyond a general idea or vague shape, transforming it into a form that has an aesthetic – details, utility, personality, and dimensionality.

Composing: An Artist's Perspective

An artist begins composing from her home, host/indigenous, local, or global orientation by putting pencil to paper, paint to canvas and creating working sketches to further draw

Figure 6.3. A 3rd grader from Ke Kula 'o Samuel M. Kamakau composes using his working sketches.

Figure 6.4. A student gives form and color to her painting.

out ideas. What has been created from the artist's hand undergoes a kind of metamorphosis, becoming something new, unfolding like a flower bud – a creation, a living, breathing thing. The approach to a blank page or canvas is no different for the first or thousandth time. There is exhilaration and trepidation, both at the same time. The humility of an artist is in never really knowing how things will come out. Uncertainty is fundamental to the creative process. It requires courage because one must be willing to go on an adventure, to step out and step up to the task of creating in new ways, and to work without knowing the final outcome. It is a t^3, transmediational, dimension.

An artist understands composing as an evolution. Each attempt or layer informs what is to come next as the artist moves toward her vision. In composing, the visual artist begins synthesizing earlier research and ideas generated through prearting: thumbnail sketches, journaling, and all other forms of recording. Ultimately, one's best work comes from utilizing those parts of what has been gathered, incorporated, and worked at that resonate with each other. Artistic composition builds toward what one has envisioned or upon hunches of the *na'au* (intuition). Composing is about defining, redefining, and bringing clarity to an idea or emotion gradually, over time. A first pass at composition is never the last pass.

A visual artist needs patience to give thoughts time to take shape and form, to develop and grow. During the early stages of composing, this often means keeping the artist's internal self-doubter and self-critic at bay. Ideas and feelings often need to be coaxed, invoked, conjured, and persuaded onto the canvas and left there for a while.

Then, when the artist is ready to do so, it becomes a matter of stepping aside, of shutting off the critical mind, letting the intuitive mind take over and giving reign to being one with the experience of the artwork itself, moved and driven by the work as a channel or conduit of expression. Composing, at its best, can be likened to being in the flow, in a zone of focus, or in a kind of meditative state filled with intensity and emotion. This is a t^3 moment when many things begin to come together synchronously. It is the moment when the artist's creation, which has been personally vested with *hā* (breath) and *mana* (energy) has been given shape, form, and life.

Composing: Nurturing the Artist

As teachers of artists, it is essential to silence the critic during the composing of initial ideas. This is a critical juncture when great inspiration and passion can be easily squelched if teachers do not create a safe haven for ideas and work to flourish. Often, in their eagerness to teach, teachers are quick to critique and judge. Critical input at this stage can easily stifle beginning and emergent ideas. What is most needed during the artist's composing stage is a genuine interest in what students are struggling with and striving to express or discover. Listening carefully, asking thoughtful questions, providing encouraging words to coax and inspire their ideas out onto paper, canvas, clay, wood, or stone – all are teaching behaviors that can facilitate a student's composing. There is no such thing as a mistake in this stage of the process. The objective of composing is to get ideas and concepts

Figure 6.5. Kindergarten students at Ke Kula 'o Samuel M. Kamakau use their prearting drawings to envision and compose their larger mural drawings.

down on paper, canvas, or in clay. At this point, what has been an inspired thought or strong mental image comes to life through line, form, and color.

Coaching and constructive feedback delivered with encouragement supports the growth and confidence of young artists. Teachers who understand prearting and envisioning as foundational to composing assist artists to think through, create, and work up their designs and ideas with confidence. When composing, students need space and time to learn, to explore, to practice, and to create. Acknowledging the creative process, nurturing a young artist's compelling ideas, and recognizing and encouraging her desire to express herself will move the artist forward, from the conceptual to the concrete.

Composing lives in transmediation, the t^3 dimension. It synthesizes and reshapes prearting and envisioning, allowing creativity to move from the inside out. Teachers must nurture the healthy struggle of creating, helping students understand that composing requires courage: the courage to take risks, to explore, to accept uncertainty without guarantee of the work progressing as envisioned. Teachers need to provide time for students to experience and work in flow, mediating the messiness of creative activity through the conscious act of generating and giving form to inspiration. Composing is a rigorous endeavor, challenging young artists to experiment and persevere to work through their ideas. The result is often different, or better, than what was originally conceived.

Dedicated time for arting within the school day or integrated within a core subject area is ideal. The more teachers learn technique and understand process in the visual arts, the better able they will be to support the development of their students in their arting activities. Modeling is a must. Teachers are not, however, expected to be art experts, but to be learners themselves, arting and learning along with their students.

Composing in Writing

Composing is the act of writing down and bringing to life what has been envisioned. It is playing with words and sentences: selecting, arranging, and weaving them together to create meaning for a reader. Sometimes a writer's vision is very clear, enabling him to compose with intentionality. At other times, composing overlaps with envisioning. A vision is fuzzy, a bit out of focus, and composing allows form and direction to evolve and shift through experimentation and exploration until a vision is fine-tuned. A writer's capacity to compose with intentionality and direction increases with clarity of vision.

In order for a writer to move forward through composing, it is essential to silence the critic within, to give oneself permission to first write poorly in order to capture the essence of what one wants to say. The first draft is not the only draft. This first draft of a composition is the foundation on which a writer builds subsequent drafts, improving and becoming more focused toward the vision.

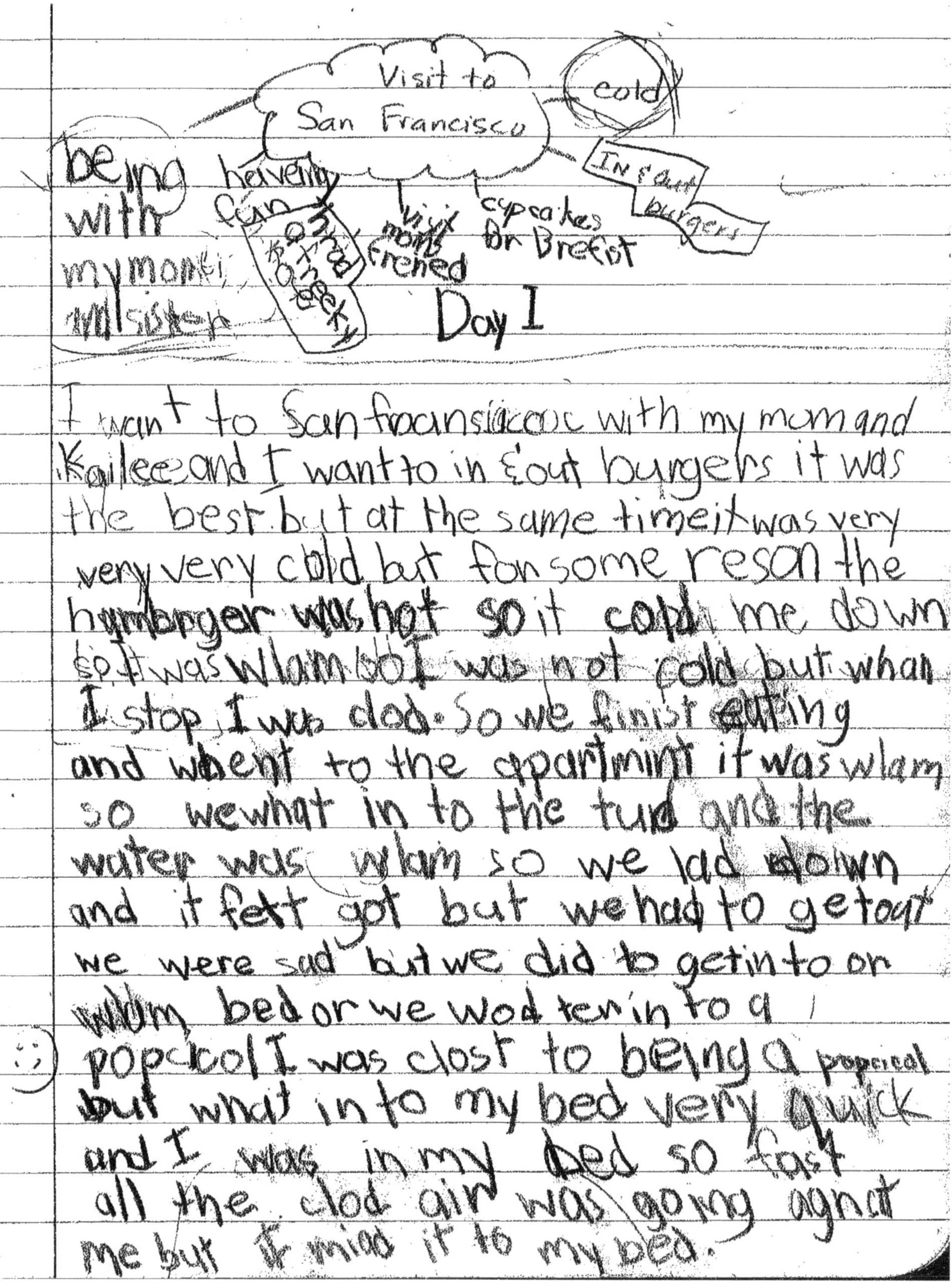

Figure 6.6. In this writing example, a 2nd grader used his prewriting web to compose a first draft about his trip to San Francisco.

Composing: A Writer's Perspective

The first sentence is committed to the page, only to disappear into eraser stubble or to be thrown into the trash. A sentence is pecked out on the keys of a laptop, simply to disappear with one tap of the Delete key. The utter whiteness of the blank page! The monumental task of conjuring something from nothing! Although composing can be the most exciting part of the writing process, getting something down on paper or screen can be a challenge and, indeed, the most frustrating part of writing. The condition of the writer's composition prior to composing can be likened to the unshaped mound of clay for the potter, the block of wood for the woodcarver, the piece of stone for the sculptor, or the blank canvas for the painter.

An experienced writer understands composing as an evolution or process, a progression of development, of drafting and redrafting, in an attempt to approximate what has been envisioned. In the writing world, the first draft is never the last draft! In fact, a first draft is often quite rough, even for an experienced writer. A writer needs to give himself permission to write poorly in order to write well (Murray, 1996; Lamott, 1994). The aim of the first draft in composing is to get thoughts down, even if unorganized and incomplete. That means silencing the writer's inner critic. Thoughts and ideas of the first draft need to be coaxed, persuaded, and enticed out onto the page and left there, exposed, to breathe. So our advice to writers at the composing stage is: get rid of the eraser, and don't use the Delete key. Instead, just write, write, and write some more. The point of composing is to get all of the writer's thoughts, ideas, information, images, examples, and stories – home, host/indigenous, local, global – down onto the page. Then leave them there, at least for a while. This first draft will probably be one of many, and it provides essential raw material for further development of the writer's vision in written form.

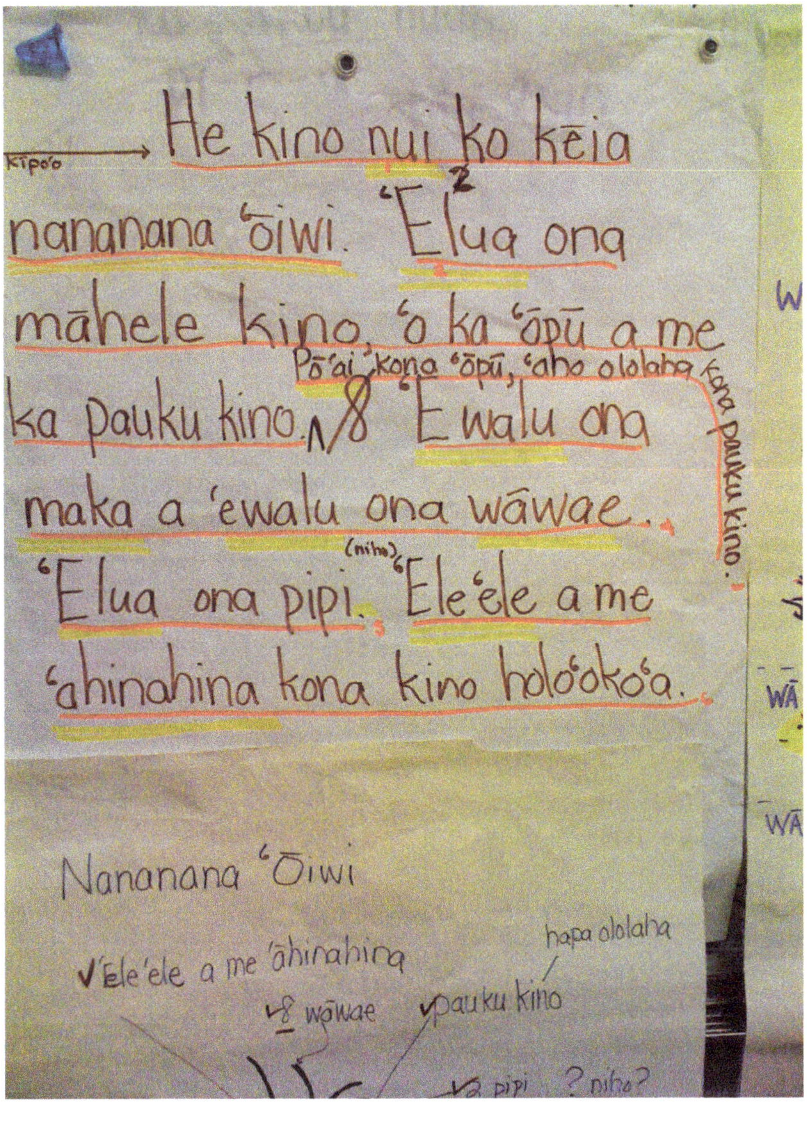

Figure 6.7. *Kumu* (Teacher) Miki demonstrates composing an informational piece on the native spider to 1st and 2nd graders.

Translation: The native spider has a large body. It has two body parts, an abdomen and a thorax. His abdomen is round and his thorax is ovalish. It has eight eyes and eight legs. It has two feelers. His body is black and grey.

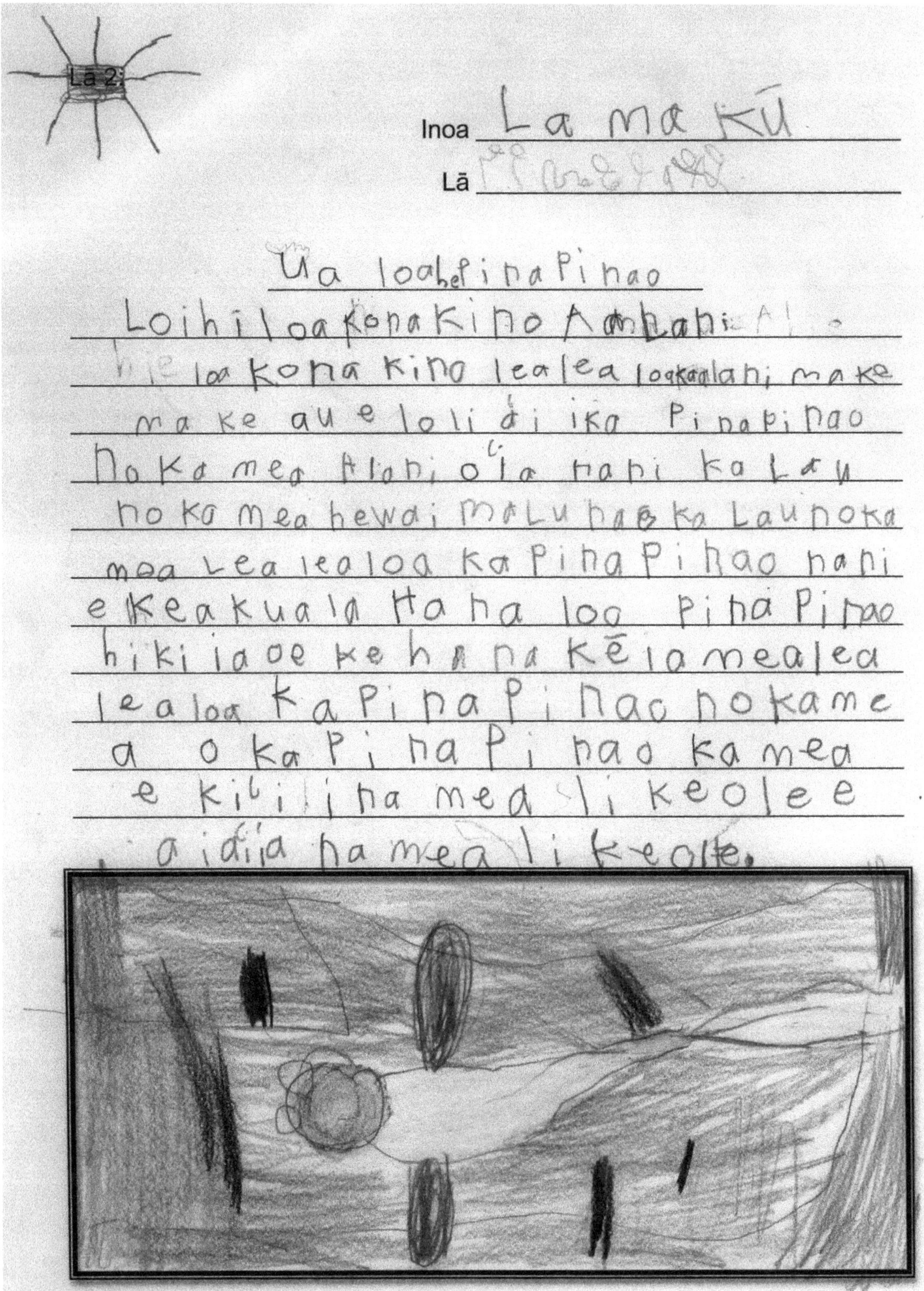

Figure 6.8. A 2ⁿᵈ grader has composed his first draft of an informational piece on the native Hawaiian dragonfly.

Translation: Dragonfly Its body is very long(.) Its body is light orange(.) The orange is very fun(.) I want to become a dragonfly because he is orange(.) The leaf is beautiful because there is a waterdrop on top of it(.) …

Composing: Nurturing the Writer

Writers need a nurturing environment where they feel supported to write about what is on their mind and in their heart and soul. They need to feel that they can take risks, without fear of criticism. It is important for teachers to know their students: their interests, dreams, hopes, strengths, challenges, and capabilities in order to provide feedback that propels the writer to keep going. When working with students during composing, active listening and a strategically placed question or two can coax, persuade, and entice young writers' ideas and words onto the page. It is vital to give writers specific, positive feedback about what they are doing well so those behaviors, strategies, and techniques continue. It is also important to teach students new strategies and techniques through lessons and individual or group conferences to further support application of writing techniques and skills.

During composing, student writers need permission from their teachers to write poorly in order to write well. In their eagerness to teach the writing rather than the writer, teachers are sometimes quick to correct and judge, wounding the pride and deflating the soul of the writer. Once trust is broken between teacher and novice writer, risk-taking atrophies. The writer is no longer invested in his work. He learns to write only what is safe. The result is the all-too-common unoriginal, voiceless, formulaic compositions that teachers, unfortunately, know all too well.

Teachers must silence their own critic and also help students learn to silence their inner critics. Encourage students to write on paper with a pen or to freewrite on the computer

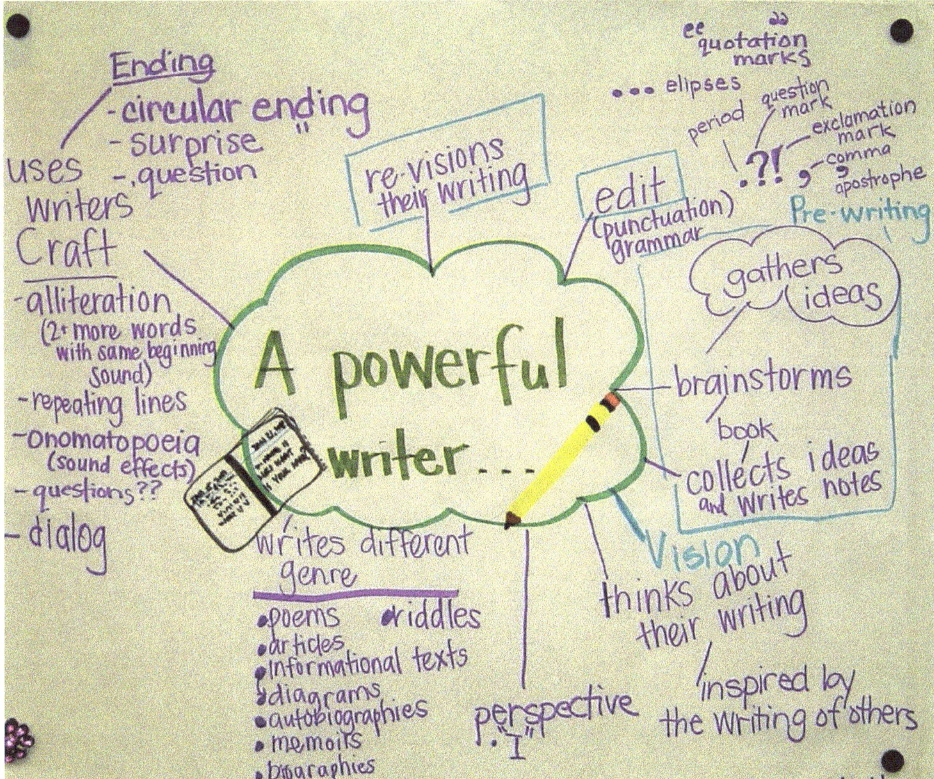

Figure 6.9. As students learn writing techniques and skills, they are added to a Powerful Writer chart of this 3rd grade class at Hau'ula Elementary School on the north shore of O'ahu.

without deleting or moving any text on early drafts. If they are writing by hand, you can allow them to cross out words as long as they are not lost and can be retrieved for later use. Keep students from using the Delete key to encourage the accumulation of words and ideas, rather than prematurely editing or second-guessing themselves.

Once students have become more fluent writers, usually by 3rd grade, teachers can also begin each writing session with a quickwrite. You can set a timer and have students write fast, getting as many words down as they can on their topic. This removes the mental block of the blank page and banishes the expectation of producing perfection on the initial draft. Donald Murray says, "Write fast, uncontrollably fast. What will happen? You'll produce a draft, a draft that needs work, of course, but you'll have a piece of writing" (Murray, 1990: 142).

It is valuable to teach students to write around hard parts. You can permit students to draw a line for an unknown word, circle a word to mark it as temporary, use ellipses for unfinished sentences, or leave a paragraph unwritten. These writing habits help students understand that writers can return to their drafts to work meticulously through the hard parts. In so doing, obstacles are navigated, diminished, or eliminated, helping student writers get their ideas down onto the page.

Young writers need the time and space to write – lots of time! Writing daily or as often as possible is best to build rhythm and writing momentum. They need dedicated writing time during the school day to enter into flow, the zone where a writer is fully immersed in the creative process. Like arting, composing in writing lives in t³, transmediation, where writers reinterpret, reformulate, and reconstruct what they have learned to generate

Figure 6.10. Arting is used as a springboard with emergent writers to inform and generate their written compositions. This Hawaiian language immersion artist–writer uses his *kalo* drawing to compose a descriptive piece.

original work. Writing can get messy in this mediating stage, when writers experiment with ideas and techniques. Sometimes those ideas and techniques work; sometimes they don't, sending a writer back to the drawing board, prewriting and envisioning.

Teachers must nurture the healthy struggle of young writers and encourage them to persevere as they work through the hard parts to develop a piece of writing. Composing isn't easy; but it can be exhilarating as a story or poem comes together, new insights are revealed, or words come together to say something in a new way.

Composing in Arting and Writing

Composing in arting and writing begins the work of actualizing what one has envisioned. It is an exploration into how image and word relate to each other, or not. It's the stage of creation and expression that determines how text and image come together, overlap, or diverge within a composition. When composing, arting informs the writing, and writing informs the arting: one enhances and builds upon the other. The combination of the two is more than the sum of their parts because each has an important and complementary role in informing and enhancing the whole.

Figure 6.11. 2nd graders use arting and writing to research local sea creatures, learn about multiple perspectives as an arting concept, and use descriptive language to create an informational piece about their creature.

Translation: The Stingray This is a stingray; It has dark eyes; Its body is flat; Its mouth is on the underside of its body; It has a black tail[.]

In a place-based science inquiry on local Hawaiian sea creatures, 2nd graders and a multi-age class of 3rd and 4th graders at Ke Kula ʻo Samuel M. Kamakau used the arting and writing processes to research, create, and exhibit/publish a descriptive informational piece (see Figure 6.11) and a Hawaiian riddle class book (see Figures 6.12, 6.13, and 6.14). During prearting and prewriting, students observed real sea life: sea urchins, sea cucumbers, and reef fish. They also examined representational models and studied photographs of these sea creatures. Their working sketches and written notes were the foundation of their compositions, allowing them to compose their arting and writing pieces as experts. Their detailed drawings enabled students to use specific language while composing their descriptive informational piece or riddle and accompanying informational text as the answer. The details of their written descriptions equally informed and supported further embellishment of their drawings.

These two art forms when woven together have a greater capacity to engage students in new and creative ways. It is important to remember that arting, like writing, is an expressive language, a vehicle for communication. Arting offers teachers an opportunity to capitalize on their students' visual language and understanding to further expand and develop text and story. Rather than ask students to stop drawing or painting and start writing, the teacher can ask them how drawing will inform their writing and vice versa, so that the two interrelated processes will co-evolve, with students going back and forth between arting and writing in a natural flow in which the different media support each other. This convergence of image and text is the dimension of transmediation (t^3) where one arrives at metacognitive awareness, as knowing catches up with intuition – an "aha" moment of synthesis. This allows students to cross over the threshold and enter a transformational experience of the T^4 dimension.

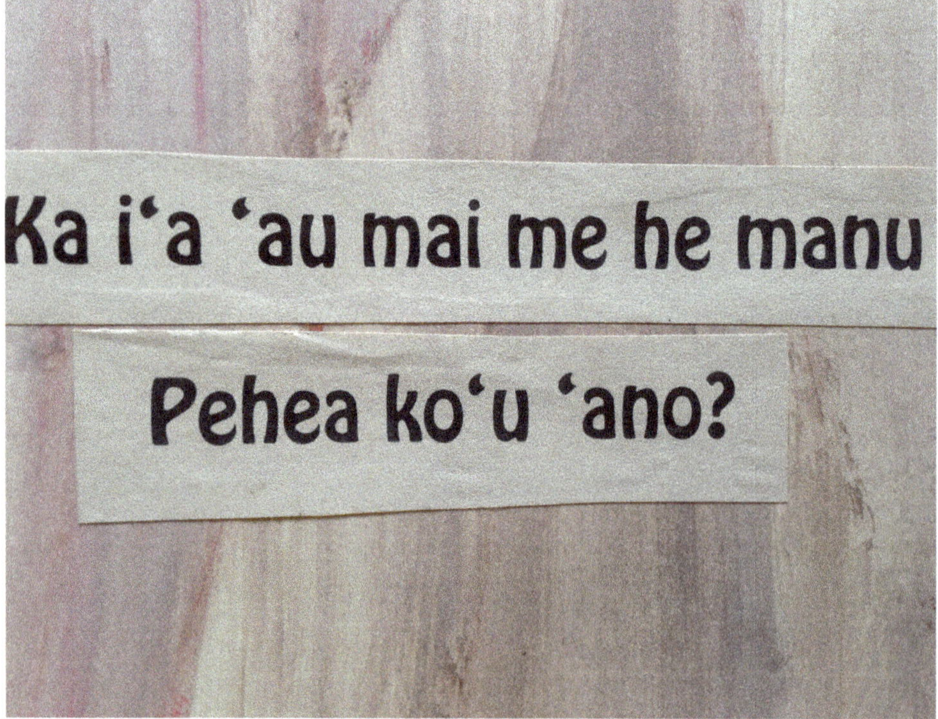

Figure 6.12. The child's visual and written riddle was paired with a traditional Hawaiian riddle. Translation: The fish that swims like a bird. Who am I?

Figure 6.13. In this arting and writing project, the child composed a visual and written riddle.

Translation (clockwise from top): I have thousands of babies. I have a green beautiful back. I live in the ocean on the reef. I live on the sand on the land sometimes.

Figure 6.14. The Hawaiian riddle solution also includes informational writing about the sea turtle. Translation of riddle solution (the larger bold caption): I am a Sea Turtle.

Translation of informational writing:

Sea Turtle

By ʻAikuʻe Napolean-Ahn

I am a sea turtle. I live in the ocean and on the sand. *Honu* is my species.

I have a beautiful green back and bumpy skin. There are 13 large plates on my back. I have two large eyes. My entire body is greenish-brown.

I don't move very fast on the sand. I swim like a bird flies. I eat seaweed. I am a herbivore.

I give birth to my young in the sand. I lay eggs in a hole that I dig in the sand. Then I leave. The eggs hatch and the babies must dig their way out of the hole and race to the ocean.

Chapter 7

Conferring and Revisioning

'A'ohe 'ulu e loa'a i ka pōkole o ka lou.
"No breadfruit can be reached when the picking stick is too short."
There is no success without preparation.
– 'Ōlelo No'eau no. 213

Stage 4: Conferring and Revisioning

Conferring and revisioning together comprise the stage in which attention is focused on the logic and message of the work – reseeing, reconsidering, and reworking the piece until it comes together as a whole, logically and aesthetically. Conferring with others guides the artist and writer towards realizing the potential of a work and its impact on an audience. It is in this stage that refinement of the work begins.

Conferring and Revisioning in Arting

Revisioning is a stage of honing and refining the work at hand: cleaning up a line to more precisely articulate a shape, correcting a shade of color to tie two contrasting areas together, and/or putting a wash in to unify a composition. Time and conferring with others provides new insights and added perspectives, giving an artist the opportunity to see her work with new eyes, to refocus and clarify ideas, intention, and meaning in the piece.

At the conferring and revisioning stage of the process, the artist reexamines the interior logic and ordering along with the aesthetic unity of the whole. She reviews her own work and actively seeks out the feedback of others. First, there is an introspective, personal revisioning that involves no one but the artist. Second, there is an interactive conversation when the artist has an opportunity to confer with others and invite their input. Third, there is a teacher-to-student review in which feedback is instructive. Through review and analysis, conceptual and mechanical aspects of the work are revisioned as the work is being developed.

Personal review or analysis is a kind of talking to oneself, as an artist is always reflecting on her process, intention, and the evolution of her piece throughout the entire creative journey.

In addition to personal analysis, an artist confers with others, seeking outside feedback regarding her work. Because the artist often projects her intention, seeing more than what is actually present in the piece, seeking out other opinions about the work gives her an opportunity to talk with others, thus affirming or providing additional information, needed direction, alternative options, and fresh insights. Feedback can be an ongoing conversation that informs the artist about the quality and progress of her work. It should not be relegated to the end of the creative process, but should be happening throughout the evolving work.

An artist often confers with her teacher and/or mentors; mentor-to-student feedback is instructive and is ongoing throughout the process. A teacher or mentor can offer knowledgeable insights into the work along with helpful suggestions on techniques to enhance the piece. Do lines need to be moved or softened, revealed or emphasized? Do the colors compel an emotion in the viewer and convey the meaning intended? Are other elements and principles needed to clarify and enhance the work? Does the overall composition move the viewer? Having years of experience to offer, teachers and mentors can share their expertise in many ways that are useful to a novice artist as she works to refine her piece.

When a composition isn't working, the spatial relationships may be misaligned or the colors incompatible. There may be a lack of movement or harmony: it just doesn't feel right. When this happens at the conferring and revisioning stage, an artist may need to take great risks to wrestle with and rework the piece. Conferring and revisioning demand persistent effort to resolve those parts that aren't working.

Figure 7.1. Artists revision their work on the Hawai'i Kākou Mural Project at the Hawai'i Convention Center.

Figure 7.2. *Kumu* (Teacher) confers with this young artist on his composition and technique at Ke Kula 'o Samuel M. Kamakau.

Conferring and Revisioning: An Artist's Perspective

Conferring and revisioning can be likened to a sculptor chiseling away at her artwork, continuing until the piece reveals itself from within. It is in this stage that an artist has to be courageous, daring, and compelled by the work and the vision within it to make needed changes that will complete the piece.

It is often at this stage when extraneous lines or unwanted shapes get covered up and swallowed into the composition, and when things that do not belong are deleted. Conferring and revisioning aim to create coherence throughout the entire work. Culling and/or adding details are ways to strengthen form and meaning towards an even better rendering and execution of the artist's vision.

Conferring and revisioning consider the whole range of an artist's toolkit – tones, tints, shades, point of view, multiple perspectives, scale, proportion – to create compositions that are compelling for both the artist and the viewer. There are no guarantees that a work will be successful just because one's intentions are earnest and a lot of hard work went into creating the piece. However, when an artist is courageous and diligent, trusting in her *na'au* and the creative process, novel pathways open toward clarity, resolution, and completion of the work.

Conferring and Revisioning: Nurturing the Artist

Teachers need to nurture, support, and assist young artists in seeing the value of this stage to affect the quality of their work. It is important for young artists to understand that conferring and revisioning involve analyzing, taking things apart to understand the relationship between the parts. These conjoined processes also consider the whole and its relationship to its parts. It is in this stage that the artist is ready for and open to conferring, actively seeking out feedback from others.

It is important for the teacher to withhold judgment in order to assist young artists in building their own capacity to analyze and make corrections to their own work. Specific, non-judgmental feedback is the best way to nurture and support students, particularly the young and inexperienced. Probing to understand the intention of young artists fosters an ability to better articulate ideas, story, and voice. Conferring with the young artist often provides a teachable moment in which specific techniques can be offered for consideration.

Conferring with peers and mentors provides an opportunity for additional feedback and assistance. The timing of this feedback is important, because artists need to be ready to hear and act on feedback being offered. They then need the time to further develop and hone their craft, skill, and message in order to further refine the piece so that it conveys the intended vision, voice, and energy.

The visual impact of the art piece at this point of the process gives young artists the encouragement to persevere as they work through this stage. Great work is not easy to create. Trusting in the process ultimately shapes the quality of the final composition. At this juncture, artists take pride in seeing the evolution of their work and the many steps it took to create a work of beauty and excellence.

Working through the t^2 and t^3 dimensions, the artist continues to finesse and fine-tune her work. As the piece is reworked, the artist's vision develops clarity and resolve. She is ready to bring all aspects of the work together. Conferring and revisioning are dynamic aspects of the arting process encompassing the dimensions of t^1, t^2, and t^3 simultaneously.

Both the analytical and intuitive mind interface to work towards mediating a potentially transformative experience.

Conferring and Revisioning in Writing

Conferring and revisioning begin when the writer pauses and desires constructive feedback to gain an understanding about what does and doesn't work; he is ready to test out his draft on others having gone as far as he can with his piece. The revisioning of a composition is informed by conferring with others, particularly mentors and fellow writers, whose expertise, opinions, and impressions matter. Conferring is integral to revisioning. For example, a writer may feel that he wants to try out different story endings to see which one provides the best resolution; he may want to investigate whether a main character's words and actions are believable and compelling; or he may wish to invite the suggestions of others to find a way through or around a mental block or other writing challenge. Do the words convey the meaning I intend, or do I need to rework and clarify parts of the piece? Do words and sentences need to be deleted? Is it organized so that others can follow, or do sentences and paragraphs need to be rearranged? Moreover, through conferring, a writer's ideas gain substance and detail by having to clarify them for others.

Figure 7.3. A 2nd grader revisions his piece using the * symbol to indicate the addition of information.

Translation: I am a dragonfly. I am a native insect. I have three body parts. *I have a little oval head. I have a short stocky thorax. I have a long and skinny abdomen. I have two tiny pincers (on my front legs). I have six legs. My body is roundish. I have six green legs. I have a tiny head. I have large wings. I have feelers and eyes. I have a green and blue and yellow body.

Armed with new insight and information from conferring, a writer is ready for revisioning, to resee his composition, to sharpen its focus and clarify ideas, meaning, and intent. Revisioning is the part of the writing process when the fine detail work happens. At times, it is inserting new content (e.g. in the way of examples, clarifications, or elaborations) that strengthens the overall message. At other times, it is deleting content that detracts from the meaning and flow of the composition. This stage involves organizing sentence and paragraph order to enhance coherence. It entails adjusting word order and grammatical structures to emphasize meaning. It includes selecting just the right word to communicate subtle details. Revisioning means, literally, reseeing, as if with new eyes, in order to refine the images or mental schemas that the composition creates in the mind of the reader. It also requires rehearing the tone, rhythm, and cadence of the words with new ears to refine the way sentences and individual words work together in fluency and rhythm when read aloud, so they roll off the tongue with ease. Lastly, but perhaps most importantly, it involves sensing what the aesthetic response in the *na'au* of readers might be – their deep, instinctive or "gut" reaction to the work.

Conferring and Revisioning: A Writer's Perspective

In this stage of the writing process, the writer has completed an initial composition and is attempting to resee his piece from fresh perspectives such as might be gained by letting a piece "sit" for a while and then revisiting it, or by conferring with others.

During revisioning a writer is ready for, is open to, and seeks out constructive feedback. Conferring with mentors and peers is an opportunity to request assistance through a difficult part of a composition, to ask for specific feedback, or just to try out a piece on others. True conferring requires a safe space where a writer can take risks, open himself up to others without worrying about failure or that his ideas will be made fun of. Conferring with others can give a writer new ideas and perspectives to consider when going back to rework and revise a composition. Doing so expands one's vision when considering others' home, host/indigenous, local, and global perspectives in reworking a piece. In addition, it is critical to check one's facts: the writer can, for example, consult experts such as host/indigenous practitioners to verify the structural integrity of a cultural piece or verify information about a local or global issue.

Revisioning is honing and fine-tuning the ideas of a composition. It is not recopying; nor is it editing. The work of revisioning is like that of a camera lens refocusing a fuzzy image to bring clarity and detail to what is seen. Revisioning is a writer's opportunity to focus a composition by adjusting unclear ideas, adding specific and important details, and deleting words and images that do not belong or that otherwise detract from the message, the rhythm, and the coherence of the composition.

Revisioning may also encompass a major directional shift of a composition that isn't effective, such as rethinking and reworking a piece in another genre, from another point of view, or in a different tone or voice. If a writer revisions a very different composition than the one at hand, it necessitates returning to the prior stages of envisioning and composing to rework the piece in this new direction. Students will be much more likely to do this meticulous work if they are encouraged to always keep their vision and purpose as the ultimate goal and reason for writing.

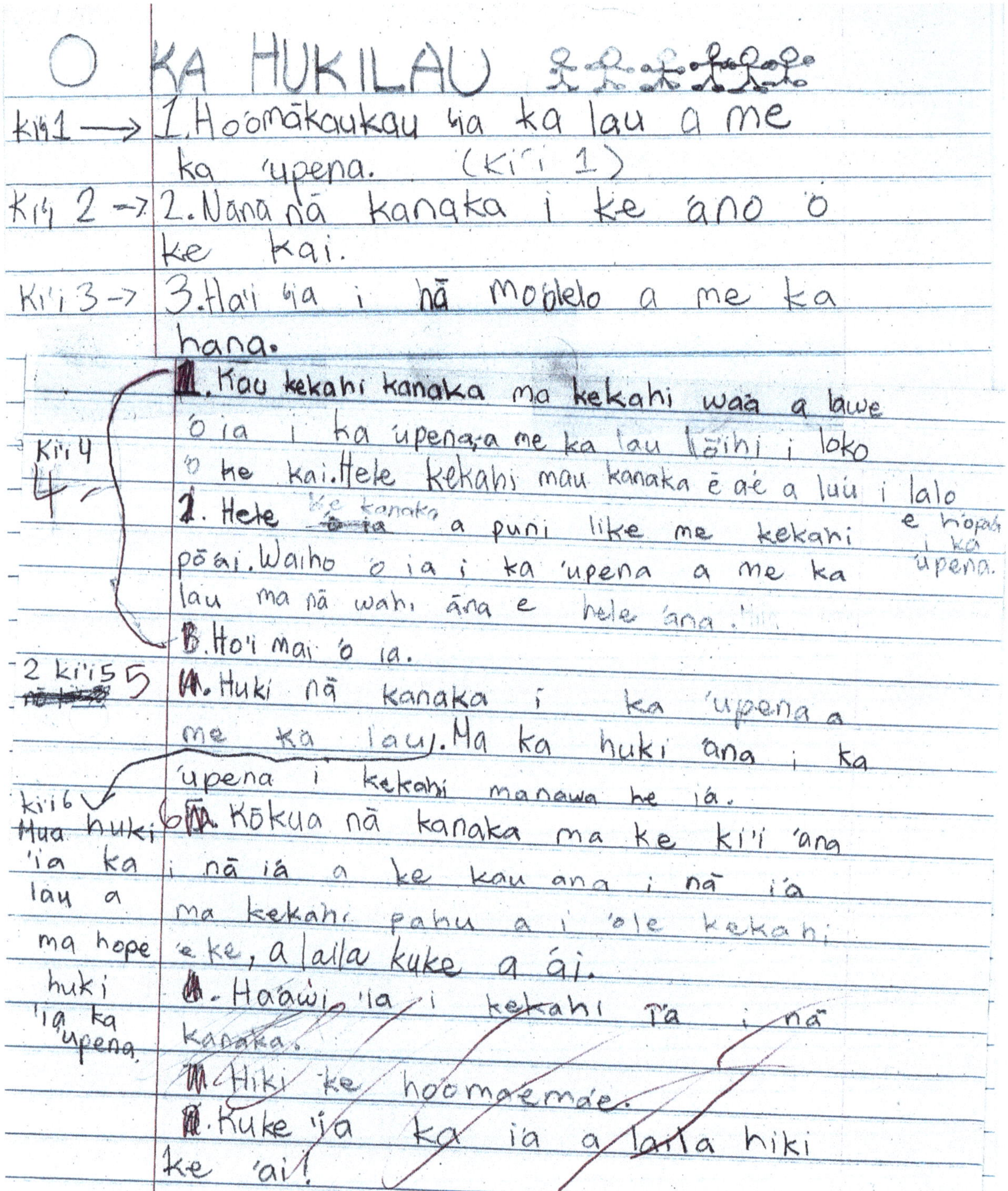
O KA HUKILAU

Kiʻi 1 → 1. Hoʻomākaukau ʻia ka lau a me ka ʻupena. (Kiʻi 1)

Kiʻi 2 → 2. Nānā nā kanaka i ke ʻano o ke kai.

Kiʻi 3 → 3. Haʻi ʻia i nā moʻolelo a me ka hana.

Kiʻi 4 4. Kau kekahi kanaka ma kekahi waʻa a lawe ʻo ia i ka ʻupena a me ka lau lōʻihi i loko o ke kai. Hele kekahi mau kanaka ē aʻe a luʻu i lalo e hopu i ka ʻupena.

Hele ke kanaka a puni like me kekahi pōʻai. Waiho ʻo ia i ka ʻupena a me ka lau ma nā wahi āna e hele ʻana.

Hoʻi mai ʻo ia.

2 kiʻi 5 5. Huki nā kanaka i ka ʻupena a me ka lau. Ma ka huki ʻana i ka ʻupena i kekahi manawa he iʻa.

Kiʻi 6 Hua huki ʻia ka lau a ma hope huki ʻia ka ʻupena. 6. Kōkua nā kanaka ma ke kiʻi ʻana i nā iʻa a ke kau ana i nā iʻa ma kekahi pahu a i ʻole kekahi ʻeke, a laila kuke a ʻai.

Hāʻawi ʻia i kekahi iʻa i nā kanaka.

Hiki ke hoʻomaʻemaʻe.

Kuke ʻia ka iʻa a laila hiki ke ʻai!

Figure 7.4. A 3rd grader revisions her procedural piece on the Hawaiian *hukilau* method of fishing. She uses arrows to indicate the addition of information and crosses out information that will be deleted in the next draft. On the left margin, she also envisions the addition of photos to be included in her final draft.

Conferring and Revisioning: Nurturing the Writer

When conferring and revisioning, teachers need to understand the intentions of their student writers to know how to confer and help them articulate their messages more clearly and powerfully. It often helps to paraphrase what writers have said to ensure that one has understood correctly. It is important to ask students questions to draw out their ideas, probing for their intentions and thoughts. Often it is when talking about their own writing that their intention crystallizes, becoming more succinct, and also more concrete for others to understand. When conferring, it is important to consider questions such as: What is the message this writer hopes to communicate to the reader? What does he want the reader to feel? What will the reader understand as a result of reading this piece? How will the reader be changed or different after reading this piece?

Conferring is also about noticing what students have done in their composition, paying attention to the selection and rhythm of words, the character or voice used to tell a story, and the way information is organized. Is there unity and coherence of ideas? Should paragraphs be moved, deleted, or added? Do the sentences and paragraphs bridge and transition clearly from one to the next? Is the message clear, orderly, and cumulative from beginning to end? What works or detracts in communicating the message? What details may enhance the telling?

During conferring and revisioning, writers are analyzing the specific parts of their piece and how they come together (or not) to create the whole piece. Teachers can support their young writers in analyzing the effectiveness of the structure and organization of their pieces, as well as the use of the various elements of craft and how they contribute to the overall rhythm, tone, and message.

Conferring and revisioning are appropriate for all writers, even our youngest, when carried out at their developmental level. When conferring, the challenge for teachers is deciding upon the appropriate feedback that will assist the writer in moving forward. What is this writer ready for? In our youngest writers, revisioning usually consists of adding on additional information, whether in a picture or text. Once they are able to revision by adding on, revisioning expands to include substitution – for example, changing overused, mundane words, such as *sad* or *happy* to a more specific word choice, as in *disappointed, worried, thrilled,* or *ecstatic*. The deletion of superfluous or tangential text is often the most difficult challenge in revisioning for all writers.

When students first begin conferring and revisioning, rereading their piece aloud to themselves helps them to hear how the piece sounds to others. Starring sentences or parts of the piece they are pleased with and circling words, sentences, or parts they would like to rework and develop gives them and the teacher visual cues to focus the revisioning work. It is also useful to teach appropriate proofreading symbols: a caret to indicate the insertion of words, arrows to indicate where a sentence or paragraph will be moved, a single line or squiggle through text to indicate a deletion. We often modify revisioning symbols for our youngest writers.

During revisioning, although there can be many changes made, there should be no erasing, so that changes remain visible. This allows the writer to return to previous threads of thought where the writing is viewed as a work in progress. Using a colored pen (other than red) to make adjustments to their pieces helps students and teachers track revisions and record the evolution of their thinking.

Conferring is the context where teachers, as mentors, can offer a new technique or skill via a lesson or mini-lesson, or can remind students of a craft technique that will enhance the work at hand. Transmission (t^1) of information, offered at this teachable moment assists young writers in applying new techniques and skills more readily. It is important to use tentative rather than directive language and to offer more than one possibility for writers to consider. For example, a teacher may suggest, "Some writers might use dialogue to help their readers understand that a character is feeling angry. Other writers may use specific verbs to show anger: a character *slammed the door* or *stomped his feet*. You might want to experiment with these techniques to see how they work in your piece." It is important to remember that the composition belongs to the writer. It is essential that teachers manage their language and feedback so that students always have the sense that they are in control and own the direction of the composition by making their own decisions.

While conferring, it is important to focus students on the ideas and organization of the piece. In the t^2 and t^3 dimensions, the writer continues to tinker with and polish his ideas, playing with different possibilities and experimenting with new techniques. As the piece continues to be reshaped, the writer's voice gains substance and clarity. As in arting, the whole mind, both the analytical and the intuitive, interface in this stage to work through mediating toward a transformative experience. Conferring and revisioning are dynamic aspects of the process encompassing the dimensions of t^1, t^2, and t^3 simultaneously.

In conferring and revisioning, writers focus on bringing out the details and clarity of what is unclear, vague, or confusing. It is important for teachers to help young writers experience and understand the value of this stage of the process. Once young writers experience this stage and its ability to evolve and develop the quality of their piece, they are empowered and more willing to undertake conferring and revisioning. They often take great pride in having numerous revisions and seeing the development of their composition as it changes and evolves over time. It is important to postpone the emphasis on the writing conventions of spelling, grammar, and punctuation for editing until the time when the composition is more complete and closer to its final form.

Revisioning is not recopying! All too often we have seen the writing fire extinguished in writers by having them copy and recopy their compositions. We are not against recopying for the purpose of rewriting a composition neatly and clearly for publishing so that others may read a student writer's words. However, that is for publishing, a different stage of the writing process. The revisioning stage is not the time to insist on neatness or to teach handwriting. Revisioning is messy work. It involves marking up one's piece with carets to include additional information, crossing out unnecessary information, and using arrows to indicate where sentences and paragraphs will be moved.

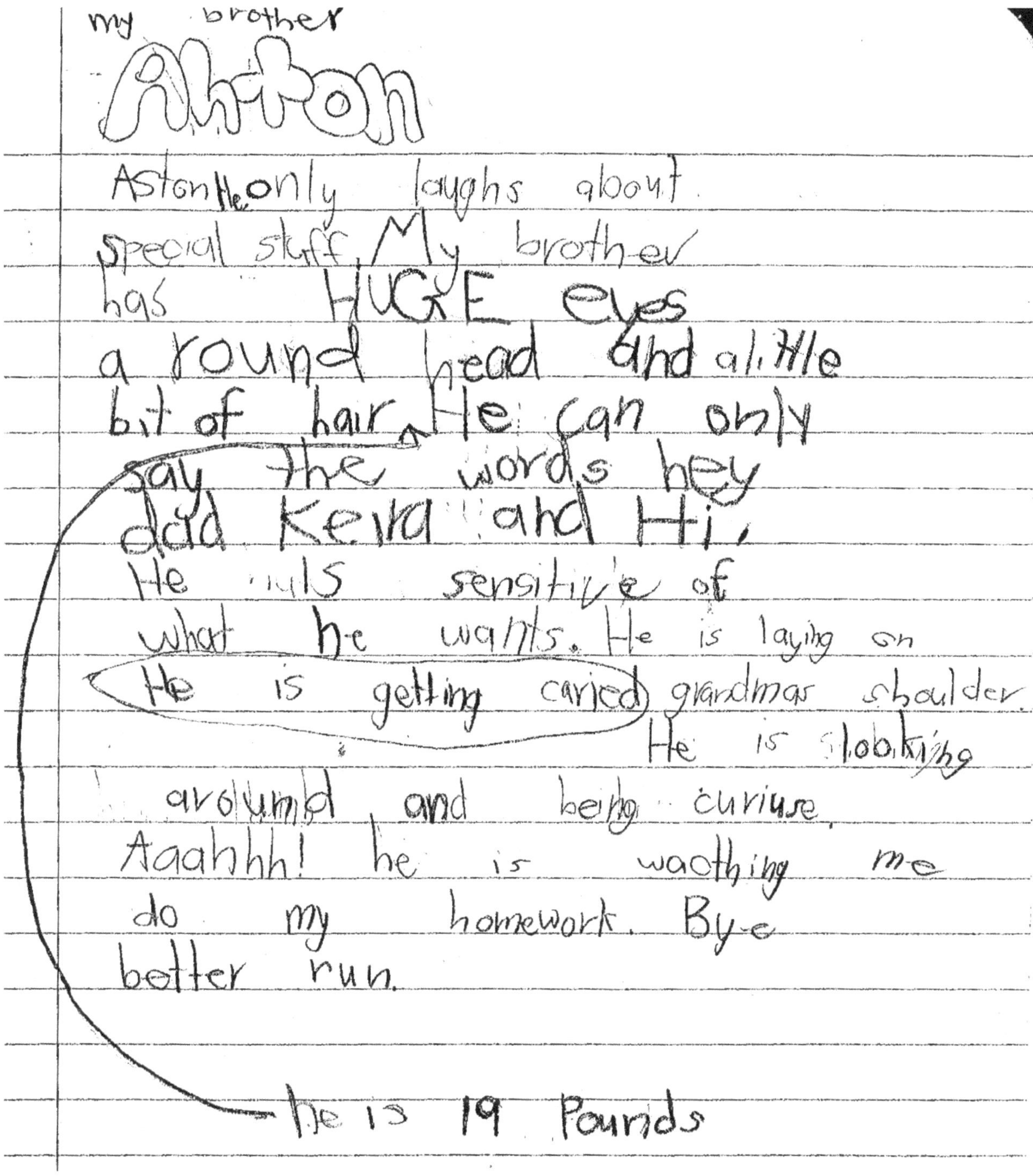

Figure 7.5. In this composition, a 2nd grader from Kamehameha Elementary School, Kapālama, Oʻahu, revisions his writing piece by inserting an additional detail about his baby brother in the middle and adding descriptive information to the end.

Conferring and Revisioning in Arting and Writing

Conferring and revisioning are about clarifying one's message and making one's work the best it can be. At this stage, arting and writing are worked on independently of one another because each form has its own interior structure, integrity, and craft. However, when working on one form, the artist–writer must always keep the other form in mind because adjustments to one inevitably affect the other. Conferring and revisioning are ultimately about the rigorous visual and literal honing of the work to bring clarity and the successful integration of art and text, to give the work its full voice.

In a culturally based science project (see Figures 7.6, 7.7, and 7.8), 2nd and 3rd graders researched classifications of sea creatures and their anatomy. Through arting and writing, students researched the Hawaiian cosmological evolution of sea creatures. The students observed actual animals, representational models, and photographs (see Figure 7.6) to create realistic drawings and poetic descriptions of their sea creatures. Through practice over time, conferring with their teachers and peers, their drawings were refined and writing included more detail. Through t^3, the transmediation dimension, both image and text informed each other as what the artist–writer envisioned was *revisioned*, becoming more detailed and complex.

Figure 7.6. Students study photographs and illustrations of a Hawaiian sea creature to capture its details in their drawings and inform their writing.

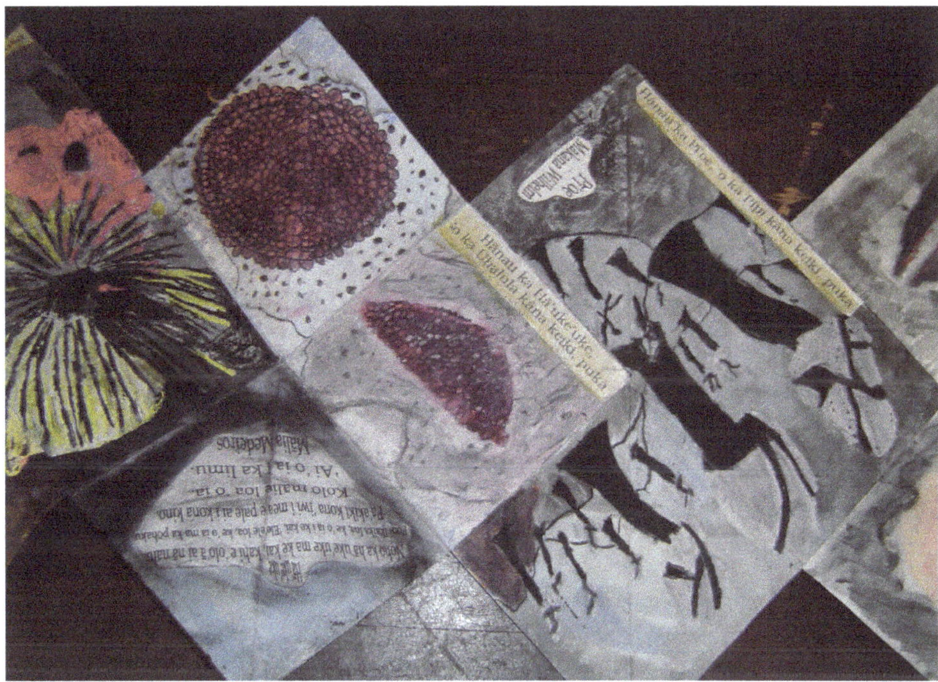

Figure 7.7. The final drawing of Figure 7.6 is included in this *origami* style book where arting and writing come together creating a complete composition, visual and written.

Figure 7.8. Past and present meet on the pages of this child-created book. The words from a traditional Hawaiian chant sit side by side with the poetry and images of the young artist–writers.

Chapter 8

Critiquing and Editing

E kuhikuhi pono i nā au iki a me nā au nui o ka ʻike.
"Instruct well in the little and the large currents of knowledge."
In teaching, do it well; the small details are as important as the large ones.
– ʻŌlelo Noʻeau no. 325

Stage 5: Critiquing and Editing

When in the *critiquing* and *editing* stage, the overall structure and proper mechanics of the work are reviewed, refined, and corrected, first by the artist–writer and then by peers and more experienced others. The meticulous work required during critiquing and editing cleans up and sharpens a piece so that it presents and reads in its most compelling and powerful state. When arting, an artist typically first goes through a critique before doing any edits or refinements to a work. That is, critiquing precedes editing. When writing, a writer may first self-edit and self-critique, polishing his own piece before presenting it to others for critique. In such a case, editing precedes critiquing.

Critiquing and Editing in Arting

Critique, informal and formal, internal and external, is the stage of arting when all ideas and aspects of an artist's work are considered in their totality. It is a thorough and final assessment of all aspects of the work, considering quality as well as impact on the viewer. It is in critique and the subsequent editing that the artwork becomes ready for an audience: to inform, enthrall, challenge, inspire, or persuade them, or simply to express beauty. It is the last opportunity an artist has to scrutinize the fine details of her work and whether she has succeeded in bringing the painting, print, or sculpture to life. She checks over the surface of the image to assure that all visual considerations are accounted for – balance, proportion, and internal harmony; a logic or unifying concept to the composition; a rhythm of color, line, form, texture and pattern – before it goes out on display for public viewing.

Figure 8.1. This Kamehameha Schools, Kapālama, Oʻahu, 2nd grader shares his arting process with peers and teachers.

Critiquing and Editing: An Artist's Perspective

Internal or personal critique is important because it is the necessary activity of seeing one's work through a critical lens. It is through the combining of line and color, light and form, and the alchemy of creativity that the artist communicates to the viewer how she wants her work to be seen and read. Does it say something? Does the piece affirm its purpose or reason for being? Have all technical aspects of the medium been successfully integrated? Have all personal visions and intentions of the artist been realized? Personal critique is rigorous and difficult because the work itself has often become too familiar or too precious to its creator.

External or formal critique allows peers and mentors to respond to the artist and provide critique. In critiquing, only the most subtle adjustments, edits, are made at this final stage since the work is typically resolved and very nearly finished as so much time and effort has been vested in prearting, envisioning, composing, and revisioning. Critique for an artist, therefore, is that moment of honest and thorough examination to experience one's work in its totality before it is made public.

Critiquing and Editing: Nurturing the Artist

Critique, before the work goes public, is the stage when peers and mentors are invited to give constructive feedback. Critique requires the artist to speak informally to others about her work, about its genesis and the resolution it underwent to arrive at its current form. Editing is an artist's opportunity to make final corrections informed by the critique.

The work of an artist embodies who she is, her personality, and ways of seeing and being in the world, making her vulnerable during critique. It is important for teachers to remember that critique for a young artist should not be critical, but instructive. An artist identifies with her work as it is imbued with her spirit.

Student artwork compiled into a portfolio for review is also a vehicle for critique and presentation of work that nurtures and informs the young artist. It offers both student and teacher the opportunity to review the best examples of the student's work, demonstrating growth and ability. The technical or more formal art conventions – elements and principles of design, technique, application, and execution – are judged. The aesthetic quality of the work and the artist's inherent sense of her own voice within the pieces are also evaluated. Typically, in this form of critique for younger students, specific visual genres – still life, portraiture, and perspective drawing or painting – are included and reviewed. The intention of portfolio review is to give constructive critique to the young artist to help her develop her vision and expression in a unique "visual voice." It also allows a student artist the opportunity to do editing before presenting her work to a wider, more public, audience.

Critiquing and Editing in Writing

After revisioning, ideas have greater detail, words have specificity, and the composition has a coherent structure. Attention then shifts to critiquing and editing. Often at this stage, the writing process is the reverse of the arting process – that is, editing precedes critiquing.

Editing requires precision. It is rigorous work primarily within the dimensions of t^1 and t^2 when a writer applies his technical knowledge of spelling, word meaning, and the conventions of genre, grammar, and punctuation to ensure precise meaning, clean up imperfections, and smooth passages' rough edges. It is careful editing on the writer's part that enables a reader to more easily read, comprehend, and interpret a piece.

Editing involves correcting spelling so that it is accurate and correcting grammar so that it follows conventions such as noun-pronoun agreement, subject-verb agreement, and consistency of verb tenses. It is also correcting and adjusting punctuation, because these conventions which, together with the grammatical structure, communicate how to read a composition. Punctuation marks signal the grammatical organization, tone, cadence, tempo, and flow of the words, thereby enhancing and emphasizing the meaning of the written word. The piece is now ready for critique by others.

Critiquing is a metacognitive activity in which the writer takes a step back, distancing himself from the piece to assess the work as a whole. A writer wants to know, "Does the piece communicate my intended meaning and purpose? Is this the most effective point of view and form the work should take to express these ideas and views? Do the internal parts and structure coalesce toward a compelling and integrated whole?" Therefore, to gain a broader perspective, the writer invites others into the process to react and provide feedback.

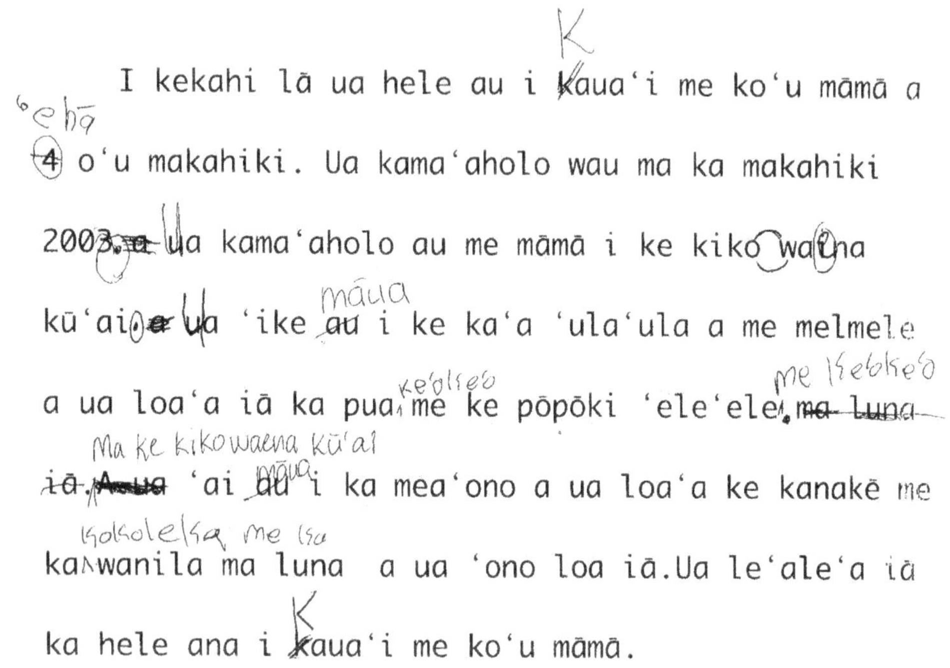

I kekahi lā ua hele au i Kaua'i me ko'u māmā a
o'u makahiki. Ua kama'aholo wau ma ka makahiki
2003. Ua kama'aholo au me māmā i ke kiko waena
kū'ai. Ua 'ike au i ke ka'a 'ula'ula a me melmele
a ua loa'a iā ka pua me ke pōpōki 'ele'ele ma luna
iā. Ua 'ai au i ka mea'ono a ua loa'a ke kanakē me
ka wanila ma luna a ua 'ono loa iā. Ua le'ale'a iā
ka hele ana i Kaua'i me ko'u māmā.

Figure 8.2 A Hau'ula Elementary School 2nd grader has edited (as much as she can) her piece before conferring with her teacher.

Translation: One day I went to Kaua'i with my mom and I was 4 years old. I jogged in the year 2003. I jogged with my mom to the shopping center. We saw a red and yellow toy car and we got a white flower and a black and white stuffed cat at the shopping center. We ate dessert and I had candy with white chocolate on top and it was so delicious. It was fun going to Kaua'i with my mom.

Editing and Critiquing: A Writer's Perspective

Writing conventions enable readers to make sense of the written word. Editing is the opportunity for the writer to scrutinize the conventions of his composition: correct spelling mistakes and typographical errors; add and/or delete words and improve weak word choice; alter punctuation; and rectify grammatical inconsistencies before publishing a piece for others to read. There are numerous ways in which a writer may choose to grammatically construct and to punctuate a sentence. Therefore, it is essential to know and understand the possibilities and subtle differences of these options to skillfully capture the nuances of meaning.

When using the host/indigenous language of a place, it is important to verify that words have been used appropriately in the context of the piece and spelled correctly. In order to capture a region's distinct dialect and local language, a writer will need to carefully examine sentence structure and word choice, while also being careful to use the expected register (e.g. in terms of style and level of formality) for the type of writing he is doing.

After editing, the writer seeks out the opinion and critique of others: a respected mentor, content and/or cultural experts, other writers, or close friends. A writer often gathers together with others to share his work and receive constructive feedback with the hope of actualizing the potential and intentions of the writing. He asks, "What are your impressions? What parts are weak or strong? Are there words that need to be changed?" Critique allows the writer to test out his piece. When the writing is reviewed, a writer gains insight into the way in which others understand his work, thereby deepening and broadening his perspective of the writing.

For a proficient writer, the stages of conferring and revisioning and of editing and critiquing often happen simultaneously. A writer constantly rereads his piece attending to meaning: adding thoughts; fine-tuning word choice, grammar, and punctuation; and deleting ideas that detract from the overall meaning and direction of the piece. The writer is always asking himself, "Will this make sense to my audience? Is it clear enough? How can I make it better? Is this how I want it to sound? Does this sentence or paragraph capture the essence of what I am trying to say?"

Editing and Critiquing: Nurturing the Writer

This stage is an opportunity for teachers to assess and instruct students in the mechanics of writing within a real and meaningful context. Repetitive spelling, editing, and grammar exercises in isolation without context are often meaningless to students and are rarely applied in their writing. It is essential for teachers to assist young writers in understanding the importance of this stage of the writing process. If a piece is going to be published for a wider audience beyond the classroom, polishing a piece to remove errors and checking for proper conventions are important so that others can more easily comprehend what is written.

Viewing grammar and punctuation as the intentional communication of writer to reader emphasizes the purpose of editing – rather than seeing this as the stage when the teacher marks up and corrects the paper. This new perception changes the behavior of young writers from a mechanical process of searching for errors needing to be corrected to an intentional, thoughtful process of rereading (preferably, aloud) in order to make choices as to word selection, grammar, and punctuation according to the meaning and intention which the writer wants to convey.

When students have spent a great deal of time and thought on a piece of writing, laboring through the entire process, it can be discouraging and overwhelming to receive a piece marked-up with corrections made by the teacher. Teachers can nurture young writers by requesting that they edit their writing themselves or with a peer, as much as they are capable of doing. Analyzing the remaining errors is a formative assessment indicating skills for further development informing instruction. Thereafter, teachers can meet with students individually or in small groups to reteach skills, review their application, and select one or two new skills that writers are developmentally ready to learn as demonstrated in their writing. For example, a child using dialogue in his piece can be taught the use and application of quotation marks.

Teachers can act as editors in the same way that professional writers have editors who review, make corrections, and give suggestions for improvement. At this point, when the student has edited the piece as far as he is developmentally able to, the teacher may then complete necessary edits for the student, remembering to note the skills for future instruction. This prevents overwhelming or discouraging the student writer with too much information that he may not be ready for.

Once a piece has been edited, the writer is ready for critique by others. Most children through the 3rd grade are not developmentally ready to metacognitively distance themselves from their work. Therefore, for our youngest writers, the critique aspect of this stage is when teachers promote the child's understanding of themselves as writers by using encouraging words and reinforcing what the child is able to express and do. Teachers as the most experienced writers in the room take on the metacognitive role for these youngest writers. They provide specific feedback which contributes to improving the piece and the development of the student as a writer. The teacher needs to know her/his students and be strategic in when to nudge, how much to nudge, and what this writer is ready to receive as constructive feedback. It is important to use tentative rather than directive language and to offer more than one possibility for writers to consider, leaving the choice to them.

For older students, participating in peer critique is one of the most powerful ways to grow as a writer. Therefore, it is essential to teach older students the value of critique and the process: listen for understanding, begin feedback with strengths, ask clarifying questions, and offer specific feedback that will improve the work, not judge it. A writer may request specific feedback on content, organization, or flow of a piece. He seeks out feedback in order to see his piece through the eyes of others and broaden his own perspective. Critique requires writers to have a nondefensive, learning mindset. Critique, when done well, can inspire writers to revision their writing and continuously transform themselves as writers. It is therefore a way for writers to actualize the fullest potential of a writing piece and their own fullest potential as writers.

Critiquing happens primarily within the t^2 and t^3 dimensions and enables T^4, Transformation. The transactional nature of critique often requires the writer to move into a mediated space of healthy struggle, where the writer persists to resolve problems and strengthen the writing. Teachers must support the healthy struggle of this stage to encourage persistence, to hold on to the vision of the piece.

Critiquing and Editing in Arting and Writing

Critiquing and editing make up the final stage in which a piece is made ready for an audience. Based on critique or feedback from others, the artist–writer revises or edits, reconsidering how the artwork will be touched up and the writing cleaned up – first, independently of one another and finally in tandem with each other. This stage tightens the relationship between arting and writing. Critiquing and editing is the stage in which all ideas and aspects of an arting and writing piece are considered together, in their totality.

When considering the interrelationship within the t^3, transmediation, dimension of how arting and writing work effectively together, the artist–writer asks questions such as the following:

- Do the visual image and text tell a parallel story with the pictures and words sitting side-by-side? (Examples of this can be seen in the sea creature arting and writing in Figures 6.11, 8.3, 8.4, and 8.5.)
- Is the image and text complimentary, with each form adding information to the overall understanding of the piece? Does the art augment the text or vice versa? (Examples of this can be seen in the riddle book arting and writing in Figures 6.12 and 6.14, in the *Kumulipo* arting and writing in Figures 7.7 and 7.8, and in the *kalo* arting and writing in Figure 9.4.)

The interplay of the arting and writing during this final mediation coalesces to become more than the sum of its parts. When brought together to sit side-by-side, the result is greater than what would have evolved independently of the other, making the work ready to go public.

Figure 8.3. A kindergarten student from Ke Kula 'o Samuel M. Kamakau draws an illustration to sit side-by-side with the text from a class story, *He Ka'ao no Hauwahine lāua 'o Meheanu: A Bilingual Tale of Hauwahine and Meheanu* (Ke Kula 'O Samuel M. Kamakau, 2008).

Figure 8.4. A 3rd grader from Ke Kula ʻo Samuel M. Kamakau uses images and words to explain "How to Paddle a Canoe."

Translation (from top to bottom, left to right): Canoe Paddling by Mahie Wilhelm; Necessary materials: paddle, outrigger canoe, people, ocean, bailer. The steps: Begin by putting the canoe into the ocean; Start to paddle (on one side), then switch sides; Switch sides; Continue. Directions: Take the canoe into the ocean and get inside and put the paddle forward and bring the paddle back toward you. Be alert because your hands and feet need to be on the right side of the canoe and switch sides after 12 paddles.

Figure 8.5. This 2nd grade informational arting and writing piece provides the audience with interesting facts and multiple perspectives of the jellyfish in its habitat. The visual image and written text are complimentary with each adding information.

Translation:
Jellyfish
This is a jellyfish
He has a slimy body
The top of his body is round
His tentacles are underneath
It has small tentacles
It has lots of tentacles

Chapter 9

Going Public: Exhibiting and Publishing

Aia no i ka mea e mele ana.
"Let the singer select the song."
Let him think for himself
– ʻŌlelo Noʻeau no. 67

Stage 6: Exhibiting and Publishing

Exhibiting and publishing is the culminating stage of the arting and writing processes that celebrates completion of the work. It is "going public," sharing work with a larger audience.

Figure 9.1. A 3rd grader from Koko Head Elementary School shows off her self-portrait. The image on the right was a prearting drawing done prior to instruction. The image on the left was completed after instruction and self-study using a mirror.

Exhibiting and Publishing in Arting

Exhibiting and publishing for a visual artist is the final stage of the arting process, having one's work seen by a viewing audience. It is a purposeful vehicle for sharing one's art. Exhibiting typically involves the showing of new or recent works. Publishing involves displaying artwork in books or websites and has become a newer and more common kind of venue that can be considered a form of publication.

This stage is complicated by myriad considerations of what exhibiting artwork entails: (1) framing and mounting, including the color, size, and shape of mats and frames; and (2) the placement and sequencing of work, including the presentation of pieces, how they are hung, the flow and order of the works, the lighting, and the traffic of the room. All of these considerations are part of the final deliberations involved in exhibiting works of art. Exhibition design and the considerations that go into this aspect of final presentation of work are complex, variable, and time-consuming.

Exhibiting and Publishing: An Artist's Perspective

The exhibiting and publishing of completed works enables an artist to experience her inspired visions in concrete ways, giving her a sense of accomplishment and belief in having created work that has a voice and that contributes to a larger world story. Exhibiting and publishing gives an artist the opportunity to appreciate her newly created body of work in one place at one time, having reached the pinnacle, a Transformative ($t^1 \times t^2 \times t^3 = T^4$) experience. It also makes it possible for others to experience the work – possibly at multiple other sites, such as through electronic transmission of images – and be transformed by it. It provides an artist with a way to intimately understand and appreciate her own process and a way of having her perspective of the world seen and experienced by others. It is her commentary on and unique contribution to the home, host/indigenous, local, or wider global cultural conversation. It puts creating paintings and photographs into a context that is both real and personally meaningful. Having the opportunity to exhibit and publish work validates the creative process, as it provides the context and purpose for doing the work in the first place.

Exhibiting and Publishing: Nurturing the Artist

Exhibiting and publishing for artists is a celebration. It is a rite of passage, essential to support the development of young artists. Exhibiting and publishing involves creating opportunities for students to arrive at a T^4 experience, creating something meaningful that has an impact on others. Through exhibition and publication, artists receive feedback, genuine reactions, and reinforcement from others.

Once they have experienced transformation, they want to recreate the experience again. Standing away from their work, seeing through the eyes of others, taking a step back to appreciate the results of the process and final product are what gives artists a deep sense of accomplishment. Reflection and introspection build an appreciation for the arting process and its results. When children have been immersed in arting, doing the important work that real artists do, and experiencing transformation, they grow to see themselves as having voice and agency, as their views and personal visions contribute to society.

Figure 9.2. These boxes are the result of an interdisciplinary study connecting the Hawaiian culture (1st box on the bottom) and science concepts (2nd and 3rd boxes) to understand the present (4th box) to form a vision of the future (5th or top box).

Exhibiting and Publishing in Writing

Exhibiting and publishing is the culmination of the writing process and all of the writer's hard work. It unleashes a writer's voice to be read by others. Today exhibiting and publishing writing can take many forms. It might be reading a story in front of the class or for family members; it might be posting a story on a class bulletin board or posting a review of a movie, restaurant, or product on a website; it might be writing and reading aloud a testimony at a public hearing or a eulogy at a funeral; it might be printing an electronic or hard copy memory book of a recent trip, with photos, captions, and reflections; it might be writing a letter to the editor that appears in a newspaper; or it might be publishing a personal blog for friends and interested followers. It could also be compiling a family cookbook which includes short biographies and stories for a family reunion. It could be getting an article published in a local or literary magazine or a book printed by a major publishing house.

Exhibiting and publishing one's writing is also the occasion to take pride in and to celebrate the fruit of one's hard work and effort. Authors celebrate completion of their work, exhibition and publication, via author signings and readings, book launches, and publishing parties. These public venues provide an opportunity for authors to read aloud and share their work with an audience. In addition, student works might be printed or exhibited and published in-house to be shared with each other and family members or with others in the community, such as seniors in a retirement home.

Figure 9.3. Kindergarteners at Ke Kula ʻo Samuel M. Kamakau present their class song about the various reef creatures to parents at a Family Night Learning Celebration.

Exhibiting and Publishing: A Writer's Perspective

Sharing a finished work with others, the final stage of the writing process, is the culmination of a writer's creativity and effort in prewriting, envisioning, and composing along with painstaking attention to detail in conferring and revisioning and editing and critiquing. Because every written form has its own unique features and stylistic characteristics, at this stage a writer considers layout and design of his completed composition. What will this poem look like? Does the layout of this cookbook, website, travelogue, or brochure fully integrate text and visual image? Is the format accessible and clear to the reader? When exhibiting and publishing, a writer must make these kinds of aesthetic decisions regarding the presentation of his completed work. At this point, a writer brings to fruition what he envisioned in the early stages of the writing process.

While completing a work can be transformative, exhibiting and publishing a work is arriving at the pinnacle of a T^4, Transformative, experience. Having produced a finished composition to be read, heard, thought about, commented on, and enjoyed by others gives a writer a sense of fulfillment and accomplishment that he has done and said something important and made a difference. This type of transformative experience is what keeps many writers writing. The act of exhibiting and publishing acknowledges hard work, the joy and gratification which come from contributing to a larger body of knowledge and participating in a broader conversation with others.

Figure 9.4. A kindergarten student from Hauʻula Elementary School learned about her genealogical connections to the *kalo* (taro) plant, sharing her knowledge with others through this arting and writing project. (Translation can be found on page 174.)

Exhibiting and Publishing: Nurturing the Writer

Exhibiting and publishing, the sharing of work with others, provides a real-life context and motivation for writers to write. Reading their writing aloud for an audience, having exhibits and publications viewed and read by others, and receiving positive responses encourages young writers to work through the writing process to achieve their vision and to complete literary works of art. Student-written books fill the classroom and school library, sitting alongside those of professional authors, transforming young writers into real authors. Pieces can be exhibited and published on the class webpage, cafeteria bulletin boards, and in the school hallways. Student writing published beyond the school in community newspapers, newsletters, and brochures launches young writers' visions and voices into the world.

It is important for teachers to incorporate a wide variety of ways and opportunities for celebration to acknowledge the hard work of their young writers. The opportunity to be the center of attention by reading at the front of the class in the Author's Chair strengthens young writers' voices and confidence by providing them the opportunity to read their own words aloud and hear the positive comments of friends and peers. An Authors' Tea is a celebration of student writers when families come to school to listen with undivided attention and proud smiles, and afterwards to ask for autographs. Exhibiting and publishing is the important final step in the writing process, fueling writers' passions and giving a sense of accomplishment and transformation.

Exhibiting and Publishing in Arting and Writing

This final stage of the arting and writing process is as critical as any other. The artist–writer considers placement, layout, and presentation of a completed work. The ability to

Figure 9.5. This banner announces the upcoming student-authored book sale.

sequence and juxtapose image and text, while considering the impression and message the work presents to an audience and reader is what this stage of the process is all about. This is when aesthetic considerations of image, text, and space are fully integrated. The work, its voice and aesthetic impact, must be felt and responded to, maximizing the potential for a T^4, Transformative, learning experience. Exhibition and publication are essential for an artist and writer, generating opportunities to be change agents by sharing meaningful work with others.

An example of arting and writing coming together is Golden Pencils, Inc., a children's publishing project created at Kamehameha Elementary School, Kapālama, Oʻahu (see Figures 9.5 and 9.6). Students created this project as a way to engage in authentic arting and writing. Students publish books individually or collaboratively with peers, or they contribute to themed classroom anthologies that are published for peers and families.

Figure 9.6. Student-authored books for sale.

Figure 9.7. This book, *'Aumakua*, is an example of a student-authored book sold at the Golden Pencils book sale.

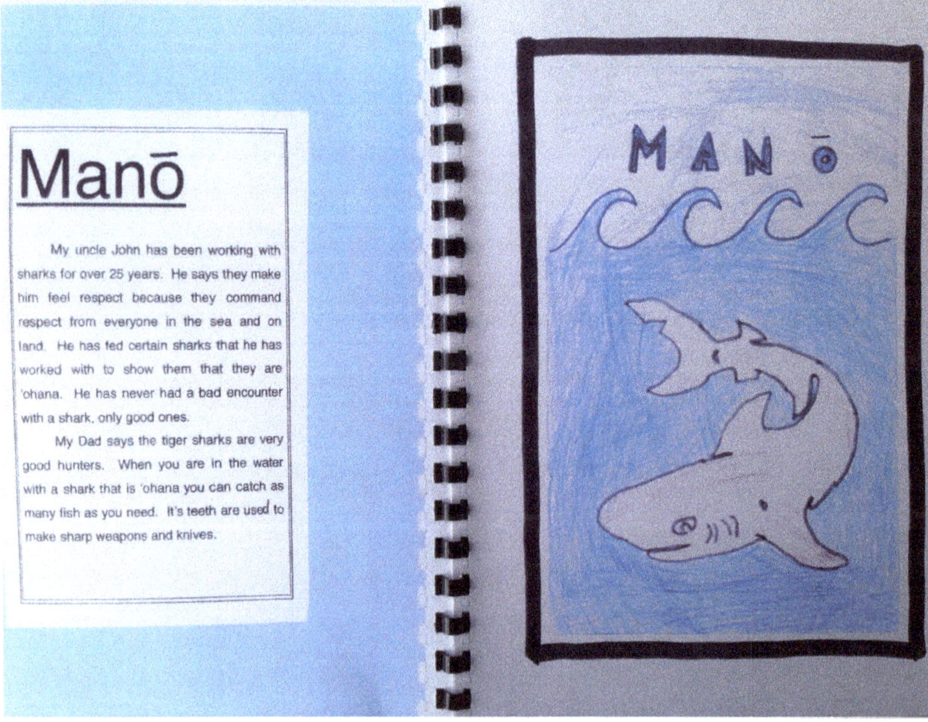

Figure 9.8. These pages on the *manō* (shark) are from the *'Aumakua* book about this Hawaiian child's family guardians.

Figure 9.9. Anna with student author, Kekauleleanaeʻole Kawaiʻaeʻa, and his book, *Kohala Kuamoʻo: Naeʻoleʻs Race to Save a King* (Kawaiʻaeʻa, 2010).

To support home–school connections, family members are encouraged to work with their child to share and write family stories. One example is an informational book a 2ⁿᵈ grader published on the various Hawaiian *ʻaumakua*, or family guardians, manifested as animals, birds, sea life, plants, rocks, or clouds (see Figures 9.7 and 9.8). He interviewed family elders for information on the various *ʻaumakua* in his family. Another example is a *kupuna* (grandparent), who passed on a story of an ancestor that played a pivotal role in protecting the infant chief Kamehameha from a rival chief seeking to kill him. Kekaulele, a 2ⁿᵈ grade student, heard his grandfather retell this story many times as a child and began writing it during a writers' workshop session at his school.

When the writing was completed, Kekaulele's father illustrated the text as a family project. A local publisher specializing in Native Hawaiian cultural materials contracted the stunning project, and the book is now sold on Amazon.com, at Barnes and Noble and other bookshops. The final work, *Kohala Kuamoʻo: Naeʻoleʻs Race to Save a King*, won a Moonbeam award and was selected to represent the State of Hawaiʻi at the 2011 National Book Festival in Washington, D.C. This was indeed a T^4, Transformative, moment for the child and his family.

Arting and Writing in Education (AWE)

The arting and writing workshop is an exciting, often messy or chaotic, place to teach because students are often working at different stages of the creative process. This ensemble workshop blurs the lines between content areas and traditional curricular time allocation by fostering a more seamless, integrated and holistic learning environment.

How valuable it is to teach the budding artist and aspiring writer about inspiration, process, content, and context rather than focusing exclusively on the skills and mechanics of arting and/or writing! To engage students in these collaborative processes is how the alchemy of real learning can begin for an artist or writer.

The intention of the arting and writing workshop is to engage and liberate the creative spirit within each child, allowing for the possibility of T^4, Transformation. When teachers nurture artists and writers with patience, the creative spirit within will flourish as they grow into a greater understanding of their own voices and talents. Young artists and writers become empowered when they understand what it means to be creative, to care about what it is they are learning, and to give expression to their thoughts by sending their images and words out into the world. When the two modalities are combined in lessons, units, and projects, as in the examples in Part III, the expressive power of the work, and so the power to transform, is exponential, $t^1 \times t^2 \times t^3 = T^4$.

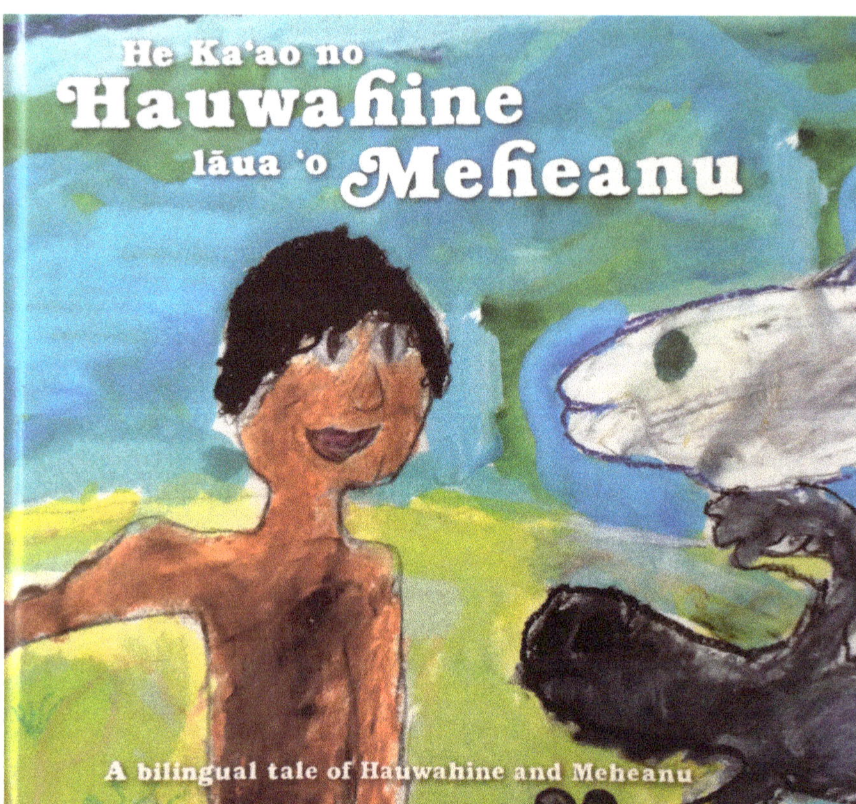

Figure 9.10. Student-illustrated and -authored book, *He Kaʻao No Hauwahine Lāua ʻo Meheanu.*

Figure 9.11. Student artist–writers from Ke Kula ʻo Samuel M. Kamakau autograph their published book during an author signing at Native Books shop, *Nā Mea Hawaiʻi.*

Figure 9.12. This 3rd grader from Hauʻula Elementary School completed a life-size self-portrait of his future self in a paper mosaic format. The final writing piece is his recipe for becoming a firefighter (written on the background of his mosaic).

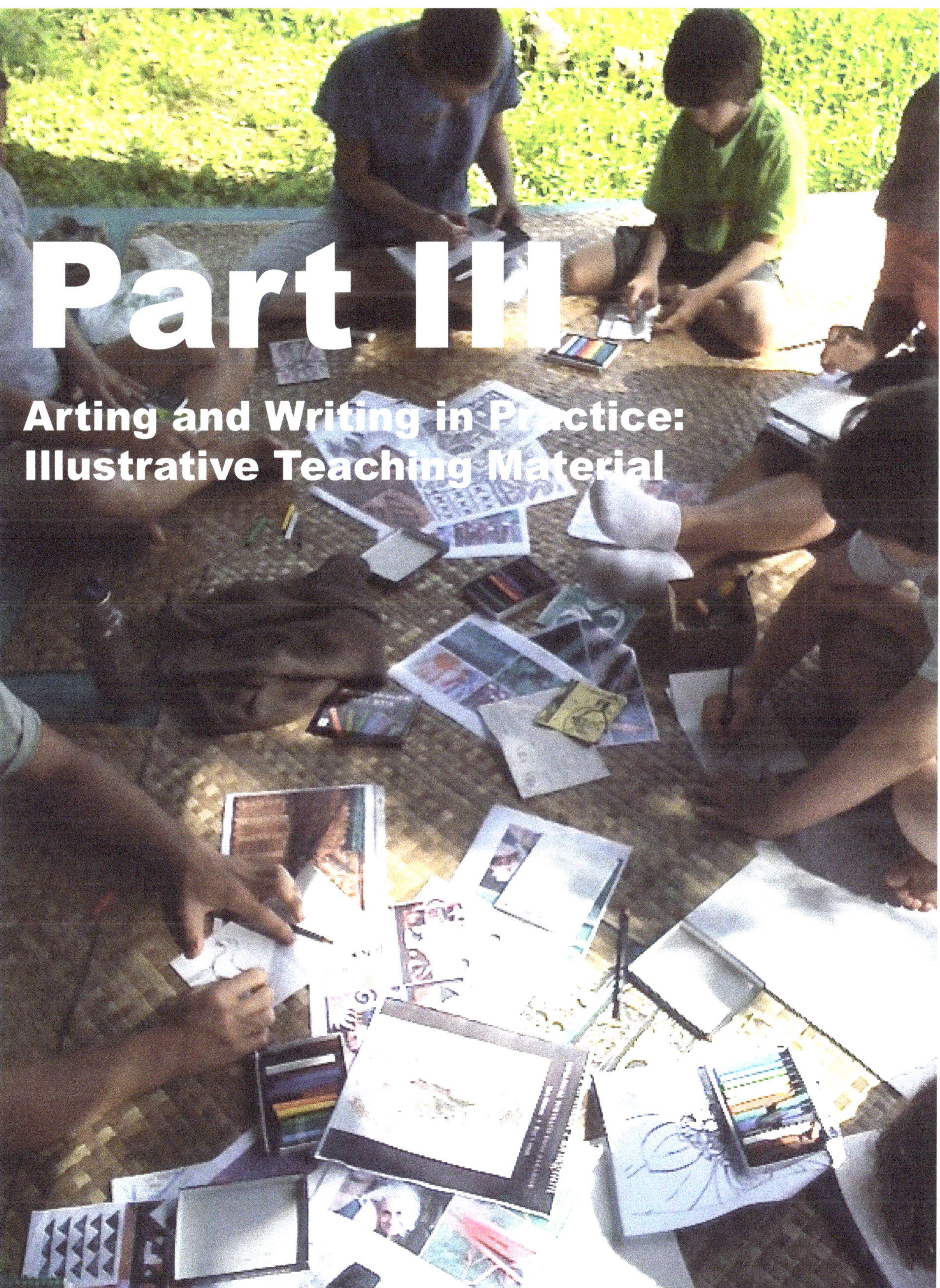

Part III
Arting and Writing in Practice:
Illustrative Teaching Material

Chapter 10

Active Seeing: Relationships to all Living Things

Nā aliʻi o ke kuamoʻo o Hāloa.
"Chiefs of the lineage of Hāloa."
Said of high chiefs whose lineage goes back to ancient times – to Hāloa, son of Wākea.
Wākea mated with Hoʻohōkūkalani and had two sons, both named Hāloa. The older
Hāloa was born a taro, the younger one a man. It was this younger brother that the high chiefs
name with pride as their ancestor.
– ʻŌlelo Noʻeau no. 2204

Figure 10.1. A student studies a *kalo* plant he has harvested from the *loʻi kalo* (taro patch).

UNIT OVERVIEW – TARGET GRADE LEVELS: K-2

The unit is a study, through observation, of a culturally significant plant of the host/indigenous culture of your specific locale to learn about the relationship the people had with the plant, the land, and other living things of your place. The children will establish their own relationship with the plant as a way to nurture a relationship with nature and with place. The children will learn descriptive words and plant-part vocabulary related to the specific plant studied. We urge you to explore the possibility of bilingual work by including languages other than English, the primary one of the school system, such as the host/indigenous language of your community or the mother tongues of children in your class.

Allow the flora, fauna, and stories of the host culture of your place, as well as any other cultures represented in your students or community, to be a window with which to view and understand the relationships between us, as people, and plants, animals, the land, and all living things. We encourage you to bring nature indoors, into your teaching spaces, or to venture outside beyond the walls of your building to explore the natural environment of your place – your home.

Objectives

- Establish a relationship with a plant and nature.
- Understand the role of *kalo* (taro) or other plant in the host/indigenous culture.
- Explain the host culture's relationship with a specific plant, the land, and all living things. In our Hawaiian example, the relationship between the people and *kalo* is familial; therefore, a reciprocal responsibility (*kuleana)* exists. People care for the *kalo* and the environment as the *kalo* plant feeds and the environment provides for the needs of the people.
- Explore and appreciate the host/indigenous culture's valuing and honoring of the relationships between humankind and the natural environment.
- Learn vocabulary related to local plants and culture (with the possibility of bilingual work on words in English and an indigenous language or children's mother tongue).

Arting and Writing Activities

- Observational drawing (prearting and prewriting as research).
- Listening/reading and retelling stories of the host culture.
- Identifying and labeling the parts of the plant.
- Examining the environment of the plant and what it needs to grow: sun, rain, soil, cultivation by humankind.

Assessment

- Formative assessment, observation of children and examining work products, is ongoing throughout the unit.
- Summative assessment is the final arting and writing product; self-assessment and personal reflection on the learning process and outcomes.

Hawaiian Cultural Context

The Six Senses

In a Hawaiian worldview, people know and observe the world through, not five, but six senses: sight, hearing, smell, taste, touch, and intuition. Hawaiians recognize and acknowledge intuition as a way of knowing and consider it an essential medium for being in the world. Hawaiians access intuition from their *na'au*, or gut. Knowing through intuition brings an understanding to things, both seen and unseen, and to vision beyond sight.

Figure 10.2. *Kalo* continues to be cultivated in the traditional Hawaiian method in *lo'i*, irrigated terraced gardens similar to rice paddies.

The Kalo (Taro) Plant

Kalo has sustained the Hawaiian people for generations. It continues to be cultivated in the traditional Hawaiian method in *lo'i*, irrigated terraced gardens similar to rice paddies (see Figure 10.2). Large valleys on all of the Hawaiian Islands were filled with these terraced gardens; a few of them remain in cultivation today. All parts of the *kalo* are eaten. The Hawaiian staple, *poi*, is made by cooking and pounding the corm into a thick paste, which is then mixed with water.

Kalo is a metaphor for family. When a *kalo* stalk is planted, it is referred to as the *makua*, or parent. Smaller plants then grow off of and surround the parent plant. These smaller offshoots are called *keiki*, or children. These offshoots are also referred to as *'ohā*, which is the root word of *'ohana* (family). The stalk of the plant is called the *hā*, stalk or breath.

Kalo is found throughout Polynesia. Other taro varieties are found around the world.

Figure 10.3. Harvested *kalo* lies on the bank of a *lo'i kalo*, taro patch.

The following story explains the familial relationship between the Hawaiian people and the *kalo* plant.

Figure 10.4. Elder Brother of the Hawaiian people, Hā-loa-na-ka-lau-ka-pa-li-li.

Hāloa, The First Hawaiian

There was a time, long, long ago when only the *akua*, the Hawaiian gods, lived upon the land in Hawai'i. Wākea (Sky father) took Ho'o-hō-kū-ka-la-ni (creator of the stars in the sky) to be his companion. She soon became pregnant with their first *keiki* (child). They were overjoyed and looked forward to the day their first child would be born.

The day finally arrived and Ho'ohōkūkalani gave birth to a still-born son. It was heartbreaking. But Wākea and Ho'ohōkūkalani loved their little son so much they named him Hā-loa-na-ka-lau-ka-pa-li-li (trembling leaf of the long stalk/breath) and buried him near the eastern corner of their house. That way he would always be close to them. They visited him and cared for that tiny plot of land every day.

Soon after, they noticed an unusual plant growing, one they had never seen before, sprouting from the very spot where Hāloanakalaukapalili was buried. This plant had green, heart-shaped leaves connected to a long stem. Below the stem, in the ground grew the corm. This amazing plant was the very first *kalo*! Wākea and Ho'ohōkūkalani were so happy and cared for this plant. The *kalo* continued to grow bigger and was soon surrounded by many little plant shoots called *'ohā*. These shoots were planted and grew into kalo plants which would ultimately feed the people.

Wākea and Ho'ohōkūkalani soon had a second child, a healthy boy. They named this little baby Hāloa, after his older brother. He grew up to be a strong man. He was the first Hawaiian *kanaka* (person). In this way the *kalo* plant was first born and is the *kua'ana* (older sibling) of the Hawaiian people. Hawaiians are the *kaikaina* (younger siblings) of Hāloa. It is the *kuleana* (responsibility) of the elder *kalo* plant, Hāloanakalaukapalili, to care for his younger siblings by feeding them so they never go hungry. In return, it is the *kuleana* (responsibility) of Hawaiians to care for their elder brother, the *kalo* plant. This relationship continues to be honored today. *Kalo* feeds the Hawaiian people and the Hawaiian people continue to care for the *'āina* (land) and for the *kalo*.

As descendants of Hāloa, the Hawaiian people, continue to honor these important ancestral relationships, as they are seen as part of their origin mythology.

LESSON 1: ACTIVE SEEING IN NATURE

(1–2 class periods)

OVERVIEW

In this lesson, children learn active seeing through observing leaves. They describe leaves, sort and classify them based on characteristics (shape, color, texture), then draw and write about what they see using one particular leaf. Through these activities, the children learn to observe for specific details, use accurate vocabulary to describe the details, and include the details in their drawing and writing. Encourage the students to avoid "any-kind" drawings (see Appendix B, "Any-Kind": An Explanation).

OBJECTIVES

- Describe, sort, and classify leaves into groups based on their characteristics.
- Cite similarities and differences between leaf groups.
- Create an observational drawing and writing (prearting/prewriting) piece.

MATERIALS

- Objects or pictures of shapes: circle, oval, triangle, square, rectangle, diamond.
- Leaves of different shapes (it's helpful to also know the names of the plants).
- Drawing pencils, crayons, or colored pencils.
- Erasers (recommend Magic rub brand).
- Drawing paper (12" × 18" or larger size).

BACKGROUND KNOWLEDGE

Children should be familiar with the basic shapes, visually and by name: circle, oval, triangle, square, rectangle, diamond. As shapes are the ABCs for children learning to draw, it is important to establish this foundation, particularly for the youngest students. Basic shapes are the foundation for more complex drawings.

Hawaiian Leaf Images

Figure 10.5. *Kalo* (taro).   **Figure 10.6.** *Kī* (ti).

Figure 10.7. *'Uala* (sweet potato).

Leaf Shapes

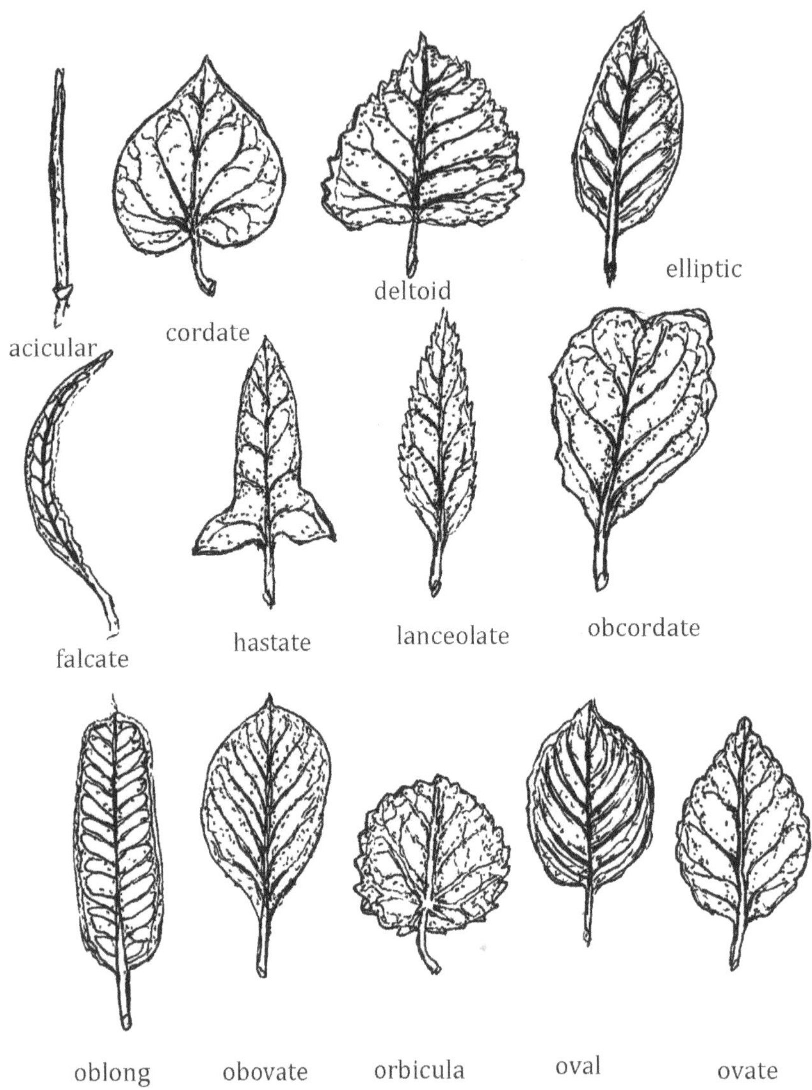

Adapted from: Swink, Floyd and Wilhelm, Gerould (1994).

As students begin active observation of plants and their leaves, a beginning primer, such as the one above, assists them in identifying leaf shapes.

Figure 10.8. Leaf shapes.

LESSON PROCEDURES

1. **Creating Connections**
    Bring in a select variety of leaves. In small groups, children observe, describe, and group the leaves based on common characteristics. Each small group reports to the whole class about their groupings of leaves (shape, color, size, parts, texture) and explains their reasoning, citing similarities and differences.

2. **Naming**
    Introduce children to the names of the plants of the various leaves. After the children describe and learn the characteristics of the leaves, names are more easily learned. Naming is important as it assists learners to become more familiar and specific with the content – in this example, plants.

3. **Arting and Writing Teacher Demonstration**
    Use one of the leaves for the demonstration. Think aloud what you notice about the leaf prior to drawing, incorporating vocabulary the children mentioned during their sharing. Demonstrate, beginning with shape, to draw what you observe. Add the descriptive vocabulary as you draw. For example, in Figure 10.9, "ti leaf" and "oval" were written immediately after the shape of the *ti* leaf was drawn. Then the specific details – veins, color differentiation, spots, midrib, and stem – were drawn in and the words were added to the piece.

Figure 10.9. Teacher arting and writing example of a *ti* leaf.

Translation: ti leaf, oval, long, spotted, midrib stem, yellow, green

4. **Independent Student Drawing and Writing**
    Children select a leaf to art and write about. Encourage writing as part of the process along with the arting. Assist the children in noticing and then arting and writing the details. During their independent drawing and writing, it is helpful to show examples of the children's work-in-progress, pointing out specifically what the students have done. Encourage creativity and variation.

5. **Sharing**
    Children share and read aloud their prearting and prewriting pieces.

Figure 10.10. A kindergartener from Hau'ula Elementary School engages in serious study to inform her work.

6. **Assessment**

   (These assessments are formative and performance-based.)

   (a) Observe children for application of the skill of active seeing (color, line, shape, texture) in their work products and during sharing.

   (b) Observe children for application of knowledge and accurate language when describing leaf characteristics (shape, color, size, parts, texture) in their work products and during sharing.

7. **Reflection**

   Ask children to share what they learned and give feedback on the arting and writing process. What did they learn about the plant? How did they feel about arting and writing about the plant? What did they like? Why? What was challenging? Why?

Figure 10.11. This Hau'ula Elementary School 2nd grader finds a leaf to draw.

LESSON 2: "HELLO, PLANT"

Introduction to Plant

(1–2 class periods)

Figure 10.12. This Hauʻula Elementary School kindergartner meets his *kalo* plant.

OVERVIEW

In this lesson, children are introduced to a specific plant of cultural significance.

All indigenous cultures have unique relationships with specific plants and animals. In this Hawaiian example, the *kalo* plant is selected because it has sustained the Hawaiian people for generations. They are related to it and it feeds them; it has fed them from the beginning. Examples of other culturally significant plants include: corn (Iroquois/Navajo of North America), rice (Chinese/Japanese of Asia), and quinoa (Aymara/Quechua of South America).

Bring in an actual plant or go outside to where the plant is growing. If a live plant is unavailable, bring in pictures for children to view.

OBJECTIVES

- Understand the role of *kalo* (taro) or other plant in the host/indigenous culture.
- Explain the host culture's relationship with a specific plant, the land, and all living things. In our Hawaiian example, the relationship between the people and *kalo* is familial; therefore, a reciprocal *kuleana* (responsibility) exists. People care for the *kalo* and the environment as the *kalo* plant feeds and the environment provides for the needs of the people.
- Explore and appreciate the host/indigenous culture's valuing and honoring of the relationships between humankind and the natural environment.
- Learn vocabulary related to local plants (with the possibility of learning words in English and a host/indigenous language or the children's mother tongue).
- Establish a relationship with the plant.

MATERIALS

- Plant or photographs of plant (in our example we will use the *kalo* plant).
- Story that explains the cultural significance of the plant (in our example, we will use "Hāloa, the First Hawaiian" – located in the unit overview).

LESSON PROCEDURES

1. **Creating Connections**
   Introduce the plant to the class. ("Hāloanakalaukapalili, this is the kindergarten class. Class, this is Hāloanakalaukapalili, a *kalo* plant.") Children introduce themselves, one by one, to the plant. For example, "Hello, Plant! I am Moani from Hauʻula." At this age, the delight in engaging in conversation with a plant is remarkable, as children instinctively know there is something wonderful about talking to another living thing.

2. **Teacher Storytelling/Read Aloud**
   Tell or read aloud a cultural story about the plant. For our Hawaiian example, we use the story, "Hāloa, The First Hawaiian."

3. **Follow-up to Storytelling/Read Aloud**
   Create a follow-up activity to the story, reinforcing the main idea of the story and human relationship with the plant, including both drawing and writing. A follow-up activity to the Hāloa story could be to have the children draw and write about their favorite part or the most important part of the story.

4. **Sharing**
   Children share their follow-up drawings and writing about the story and the plant.

5. **Assessment**
   (These assessments are formative and performance-based.)
   (a) Observe for children's knowledge and conceptual understanding of the importance and relationship of the plant to the host culture during sharing and in their work products.
   (b) Observe and listen for children's demonstration of appreciation and respect for the plant.

6. **Reflection**
   Children share thoughts and feelings about their relationships with plants and nature.

LESSON 3: OBSERVATIONAL DRAWING

Getting to Know the Plant, Part 1

(1 class period)

Figure 10.13. A kindergarten student works on his observational drawing of a *kalo* plant in the class garden.

OVERVIEW

In this lesson, the children learn that observation is *active seeing*. They continue to practice *active seeing* by looking closely and noticing details of the plant: shape, color, texture, pattern, and outline. They use descriptive vocabulary to describe what they see and then draw what they see. Observation, or active seeing, is an essential skill to develop as artists and writers. Artists and writers slow down and take the time to notice small details that others miss in today's fast-paced world. For Indigenous people, observation is a way of learning about and knowing the world.

OBJECTIVES

- Observe and draw the plant with its details.
- Deepen relationship with and knowledge about the plant.

MATERIALS

- Plant(s) or photographs of plant (in our example, we will use the *kalo* plant)

- Drawing paper (9" × 12")
- Drawing pencils and erasers
- Crayons

LESSON PROCEDURES

1. **Creating Connections**
   Review what the children learned and remember about the plant from the previous lessons.

2. **Arting and Writing Teacher Demonstration**
   (a) Before the drawing demonstration, tell the children that you are observing and practicing "active seeing" and think aloud about what you are noticing as you look closely at the plant.
   (b) Begin your drawing with the outline or shape of the plant. As you continue the drawing, demonstrate a range of lines – heavy and dark, soft and light, wide and thin – so the children see how they can use the pencil as a basic arting tool to create a variety of lines. Incorporate the basic vocabulary of arting elements and principles of design: line, color, space, shape, perspective, texture, and pattern (see Appendix D, Arting Elements and Principles of Design).

3. **Focus on Observation**
   Point out that you are drawing what you see, not what you know in your head. Show them how you are observing the details of this specific plant and drawing what you see. You are not doing "any-kind" drawings (see Appendix B, "Any-Kind": An Explanation).

4. **Independent Student Drawing**
   Children begin their first observational drawing of the plant, paying attention to as many details as they can. All efforts should be supported and encouraged as the children practice or "draft" their drawings. Remember that today's drawing/arting activity is practice, one of several practice drawings the children will be doing to learn about this special plant. They can't really make mistakes because it's practice! The more we practice, practice, practice, the more we improve.

5. **Share and Reflect**
   Children share their drawings and one thing they learned about the plant through their observation and drawing.

6. **Assessment**
   (These assessments are formative and performance-based.)
   These initial drawings will inform you about how well students observe and see. Are they drawing what they see? Or are they attempting to draw what they think they know? (See Appendix B, "Any-Kind": An Explanation.)
   (a) Observe children for application of the skill of active seeing (color, line, shape, texture) in their work products and during sharing.
   (b) Observe and listen for children's demonstration of appreciation and respect for the plant.

LESSON 4: OBSERVATIONAL WRITING

Getting to Know the Plant, Part 2

(1–2 class periods)

OVERVIEW

In this lesson, the children will be learning the scientific and cultural vocabulary naming the parts of the plant and labeling their drawings with these new words. They will be making the connections between their observations, their drawing, and their expression through spoken and written language. In this way, they will be coming to know the world and themselves through the arting and writing process.

OBJECTIVES

- Deepen knowledge about and relationship with the plant.
- Learn vocabulary related to local plants (with the possibility of learning words in English and a host/indigenous language or the children's mother tongue).
- Express in writing the knowledge, understanding, and feelings about the plant.

MATERIALS

- Plant(s) or photographs of plant.
- Chart with plant picture (either drawn or a photo).
- Plant diagram with plant parts labeled (see Figures 10.14 and 10.15 as examples).
- Teacher created observational drawing (from previous lesson).
- Drawing pencils and erasers or crayons (for writing).

Figure 10.14. This diagram of the *kalo* plant displays specific vocabulary for the three major parts of the plant: leaf, stem, and corm. The students use this as a reference while working on their own arting and writing projects.

LESSON PROCEDURES

1. **Creating Connections**
   Display chart with plant picture. Have children recall what they learned about the plant through the story, the follow-up activity, and their observational drawings. Record children's responses on the learning chart for them to reference later during writing. "We have sure learned a lot of information about this plant."

2. **Naming**
   Introduce the plant vocabulary diagram to the children. First, introduce the plant vocabulary which the children used during the creating connections activity. In our Hawaiian example, during the creating connections activity the children might have said, "I learned these lines on the leaf are yellow." At this time, we would introduce the specific word "veins," or *a'a lau*, and point it out or ask students to find it on the diagram (see Figures 10.14 and 10.15). The other plant vocabulary can then be introduced.

Possible *Kalo* Vocabulary

- *a'a* (rootlets)
- *a'a lau* (veins)
- *hā* (stalk)
- *lau* (leaf)
- *lū'au* (new leaf shoot)
- *kalo* (corm: the underground swollen stem base of some plants)
- *piko* (leaf node: where a leaf is connected to the stem)
- *'ohā* (offshoot of corm)

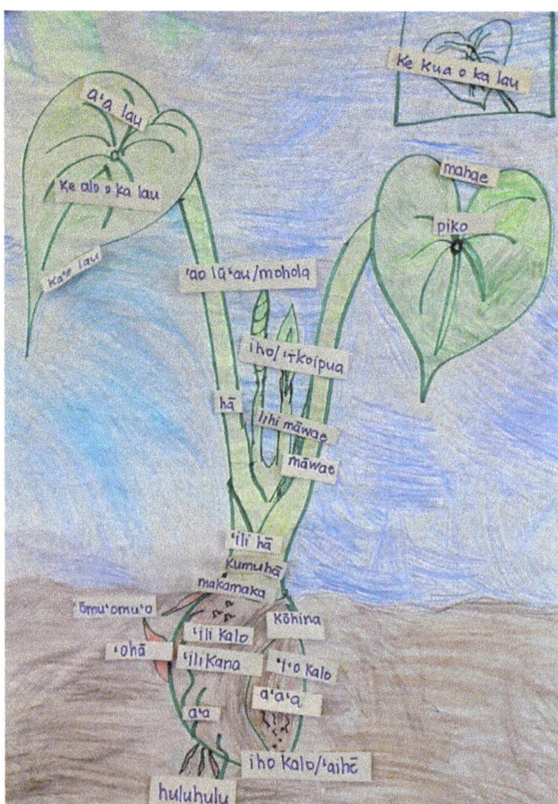

Figure 10.15. This teacher-created plant diagram supports students in learning the cultural and academic vocabulary for the names of the *kalo* plant parts.

3. Writing Teacher Demonstration

"We will be recording the important information we've learned about the plant on our drawings." First, demonstrate labeling the parts of the plant on your own observational drawing from the previous lesson and second, show students how they add observations and important ideas around the drawing (see Figure 10.16). Model adding your own thoughts and how to use the *kalo* diagram and chart for ideas. Encourage them to be creative and experiment with the way they write and use words.

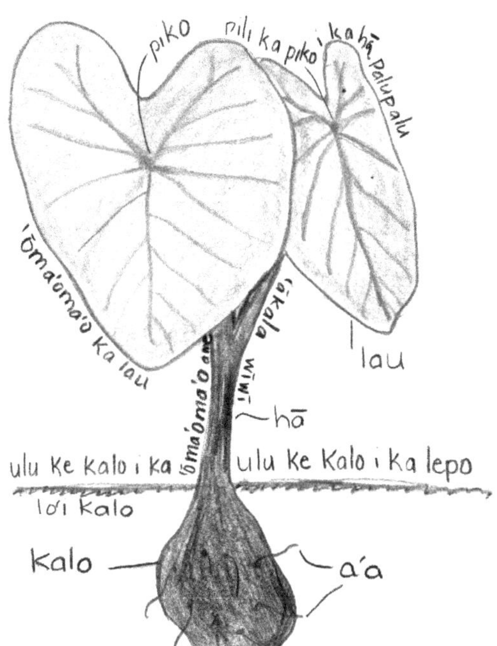

Figure 10.16. This teacher drawing demonstrates using new vocabulary for plant parts to label the drawing and adding observations made while arting.

Translation: The leaf is green. The *piko* is connected to the stem. Taro grows in a taro patch. Taro grows in the dirt.

4. Independent Student Work

Children work independently to write or copy plant part words from the diagram to label their drawings. Children also compose their own sentences or select and copy words and sentences from the class-generated chart onto their drawing.

5. Sharing

Children read aloud words and sentences and share their drawings.

6. Assessment

(These assessments are formative and performance-based.)

These initial written observations will inform you about how well students observe and see. Notice what details the children are paying attention to in their arting and writing as the children share. Point out something positive in each piece that the children can learn from and strive toward as they continue to practice observing, arting, and writing. Involve students in this process of noticing and reflecting on their work.

7. Display Gallery

Create a gallery wall or space to display the children's arting and writing pieces.

8. Reflection

Ask children to give feedback on the arting and writing processes. How did they feel about the arting and writing? What did they like? Why? What was challenging?

LESSON 5: ARTING AND WRITING USING THE SIX SENSES

Scientific and Sensory Vocabulary

(2–3 class periods)

Figure 10.17. Kumu Miki and a kindergartener from Ke Kula ʻo Samuel M. Kamakau make observations to record in their arting–writing mini notebooks.

OVERVIEW

In this lesson, the children will expand the plant observations to include all of the senses. In a Hawaiian worldview, people know and observe the world through not five but six senses: sight, hearing, smell, taste, touch, and intuition. Each student will use a mini notebook to practice multiple drawings of the details of various parts of the plant along with recording scientific and descriptive vocabulary.

OBJECTIVES

- Deepen knowledge about and relationship with the plant.
- Represent the plant and its details, in arting, using the six senses.
- Use scientific and sensory vocabulary, orally and in writing, to describe the plant.

- Learn vocabulary related to local plants (with the possibility of learning words in English and a host/indigenous language or the children's mother tongue).

MATERIALS

- Plant.
- Class word bank chart.
- Plant-part diagram.
- Cut-and-fold mini notebook for each child (see Appendix E, How to Make a Cut-and-Fold Mini Notebook); pre-fold for the youngest children (kindergarten).
- Drawing pencils and erasers.
- Colored pencils or crayons.
- Clipboards (optional).

LESSON PROCEDURES

(Prearting and Prewriting – thumbnail sketching and brainstorming)

1. **Creating Connections**
   Introduce the students to the mini notebook. Then give these instructions: "We are going to continue learning about our special plant. The last two classes we made observations mostly with our eyes to learn about the plant. The next few classes we are going to use all of our senses to learn more about the plant. We observe and learn about things and the world by using all six senses. This mini notebook is to practice drawing and writing your observations using all six senses: seeing, hearing, smelling, touching, tasting, and feeling or intuiting."

2. **Arting and Writing Teacher Demonstration**
   Show children how to redraw the plant, focusing on a different sense on each page in the mini notebook. They will write observations based on the specific sense in words and sentences. Children should draw and write so that their pictures and words sit side by side or overlap, similar to a collage. Let them be creative. Encourage experimentation in writing with various sizes and styles of print. (see Figures 10.18 and 10.19.)

3. **Independent Student Work**
   In the cut-and-fold mini notebook, children focus on using their senses to observe the plant and to: learn, know, draw and redraw, write and add more writing about the plant, focusing on each sense, over several class periods. Encourage the children to have a conversation with the plant. What is it saying? (see Figure 10.20 for a kindergarten example.)

Figure 10.18. This spread from a teacher's mini notebook focuses on the sense of taste (on the left page) and intuition (on the right page).

Figure 10.19. The opened mini notebook documents a study of the *kalo* plant through all six senses.

4. **Sharing**

    After each class session, choose several children to share their drawings, words, and thoughts. In this way, you can capitalize on the creative ways the children are approaching their work. The selected children's work can be models for the others. Add additional sense words and observations to the class word bank chart.

5. **Final Sharing**

    Children review their mini notebooks to find their favorite drawing and word or sentence. Children share their favorite drawing and read aloud the word or sentence(s) to the class. For example, our students shared some of the following sentences from their *kalo* mini notebook: "The *kalo* is green." "The leaf has a *piko*." "The *kalo* is happy in the rain and the sun."

6. **Gallery and Reflection**

    Unfold the mini notebooks to reveal the larger arting and writing piece (the many smaller drawings and observations put together as a whole), as in Figures 10.19 and 10.20. Display as an Arting and Writing Gallery. Encourage the children to reflect by asking them questions such as: What do you notice about these drawings? What do you notice about what your peers have written? What is interesting to you?

7. **Assessment**

    (These assessments are formative and performance-based.)

    (a) Observe and listen for children's demonstration of appreciation and respect for the plant.

    (b) Observe children for application of the skill of active seeing with the six senses (color, line, shape, texture) in their work products and during sharing.

    (c) Observe children for application of sensory and accurate language when describing the plant (shape, color, size, parts, texture) in their work products and during sharing.

Figure 10.20. This example of a kindergartener's opened mini notebook documents his study of the *ti* plant.

LESSON 6: WHERE I LIVE

Connecting to Home

(4+ class periods)

OVERVIEW

In this lesson, the children will continue to deepen their connection to plants as living things through a comparison of human needs to the needs of plants. Home, where people are from, shapes who they are. People come from a specific place. Plants grow in a specific environment. The children will make observations and learn more about the environment of the plant, where it grows, and what it needs to survive. Then they will demonstrate this knowledge to create a final arting piece of the plant in its environment.

OBJECTIVES

- Orally and/or in writing, explain the similarities and differences of human needs compared to that of the plant.
- Use the words "foreground" and "background" appropriately.
- Complete the final arting piece.

MATERIALS

- Plant.
- Chart paper folded in half, title on one half, "Children's Needs;" title on the other half, "Plant's Needs" (as in Table 10.1).
- Drawing paper 24" × 36" (white or manila), folded in half to 12" × 18"; use one-half of the drawing paper for the plant arting. The other half will be used in Lesson 7 to create the writing and frame.
- Drawing pencils.
- Oil pastels or crayons.
- Watercolor paints.

Table 10.1. Chart Paper Template for Comparing the Needs of the Children to Plants.

Children's Needs	Plant's Needs

BACKGROUND KNOWLEDGE

- An understanding of needs and wants.
  Needs: what I need to survive. If I didn't have this I would die.
  Wants: what I may desire to make things more pleasant or easier, but not a need. If I don't have this, life may be more difficult, but I won't die.
- Additional reading and science lessons on plants as living things could be integrated prior to or during this lesson.

LESSON PROCEDURES

1. **Creating Connections**
   Create a student-generated class chart of things they (children) need in order to survive.

Table 10. 2. Example of the Student-Generated Needs of Our Students.

Children's Needs
Air (oxygen)
Water
Food
Sun
Shelter
*Parents/Love

*NOTE from the authors: Our children always add the last idea of children needing parents or love. We acknowledge that without love we would not be very healthy human beings or live a fulfilled life.

2. **Teacher Introduces the Environment**
   Plants are living things, just like people are, and they also have needs in order to grow and survive. What does the plant (*kalo*, in our example) need to survive and thrive?

Table 10.3. Example of Our Completed Children's and Plant's Needs Class Chart.

Children's Needs	Plant's Needs
Air (oxygen)	Air (carbon dioxide)
Water	Water (rain)
Food	Food/Nutrients
Sun	Sun
Shelter	Dirt
Parents/Love	Love (someone to take care of it)

How are people like plants? Together, as a class, create a main idea statement about the human relationship with plants. (For our example, the children said, "Plants are just like us. We need air, water, food, sun, and love to grow.")

3. **Arting and Writing Teacher Demonstration** (Layering of the art media and writing for the final arting and writing piece)

   (a) Demonstrate drawing and coloring the plant in its environment for the final arting and writing piece. Emphasize drawing the plant large and including all of the details students have observed. Add important plant vocabulary, showing how the writing sits side-by-side with the drawing. Write with oil pastel or crayon. Lastly, remind them to draw in the environment, where the plant grows (soil or water line to show above and below the ground), and what it needs to survive (sun, clouds, rain).

   (b) Demonstrate watercoloring the background environment using the earth tone colors of the natural environment. Introduce the words "foreground" and "background." Foreground is typically at the bottom of the page. Objects, the *kalo* plant, appear larger with more detail. The background is the top half of the page. Objects, clouds and sun, appear smaller with less detail. (see Figures 10.21 and 10.22.)

4. **Independent Student Work** (final arting and writing piece)

   (a) Children draw the plant large, putting it in its environment (i.e. adding soil, sun, rain).

   (b) Children color the plant, using oil pastels. (They do not color the background at this stage.)

   (c) Children watercolor the background environment. (Let watercolor dry before continuing.)

5. **Arting and Writing Teacher Demonstration** (next class period)

   After the watercolor has dried, demonstrate revisioning, going back over the piece, after the paint is dry, with oil pastels or crayons to make improvements, accentuate details, and add words.

6. **Independent Student Work**

   Children revision the piece with oil pastels: improving it, accentuating details, and adding words.

7. **Sharing**

   Children share their pieces with partners. Guide them to notice and articulate similarities and differences between their pieces. Have them share one thing they notice or like in their partner's piece.

8. **Assessment**

   (These assessments are summative and performance-based.)

   (a) Listen to student explanations regarding how human needs are similar to the plant's needs.

   (b) Listen for appropriate use of arting terminology, foreground and background.

   (c) Examine whether the final product includes, visually and in writing, the important plant parts, plant details, vocabulary, and the appropriate environment.

Figure 10.21. A kindergartner from Hauʻula Elementary School is immersed in her *kalo* arting and writing, showing what the plant needs to grow: sunshine, dirt, and clouds for rain.

LESSON 7: *HŌʻIKE*: EXHIBITING AND PUBLISHING

Arting and Writing Together

(3+ class periods)

OVERVIEW

In this lesson, the children write an informational piece or story about the plant. The writing and drawing are then displayed side-by-side as a single arting and writing piece to demonstrate and showcase learning.

OBJECTIVES

- Write an informational piece or story about the plant.
- Design a pattern, using important plant parts and environmental elements to create a border for the writing piece (see Figures 10.23 and 10.26).
- Share knowledge with others about the importance of the plant.

MATERIALS

- Plant part diagram.
- Class learning chart.
- Student plant arting piece from Lesson 6. Use the other half, the side opposite the plant-arting, to prepare the frame. Draw in the lines of the frame on each sheet with a black marker for the youngest students.
- Scratch paper.
- Drawing pencils.
- Crayons or colored pencils.
- Watercolor paints.
- Teacher-created arting border example; select parts of the plant and/or elements of the plant's environment to design a pattern to frame the writing piece.

BACKGROUND KNOWLEDGE

Children should have an understanding of pattern and the skill to create a simple visual pattern.

LESSON PROCEDURES

1. **Creating Connections**
   Children orally compose a sentence or sentences about their plant arting and share with the class.

Figure 10.22. This kindergarten arting example includes labeling plant parts.

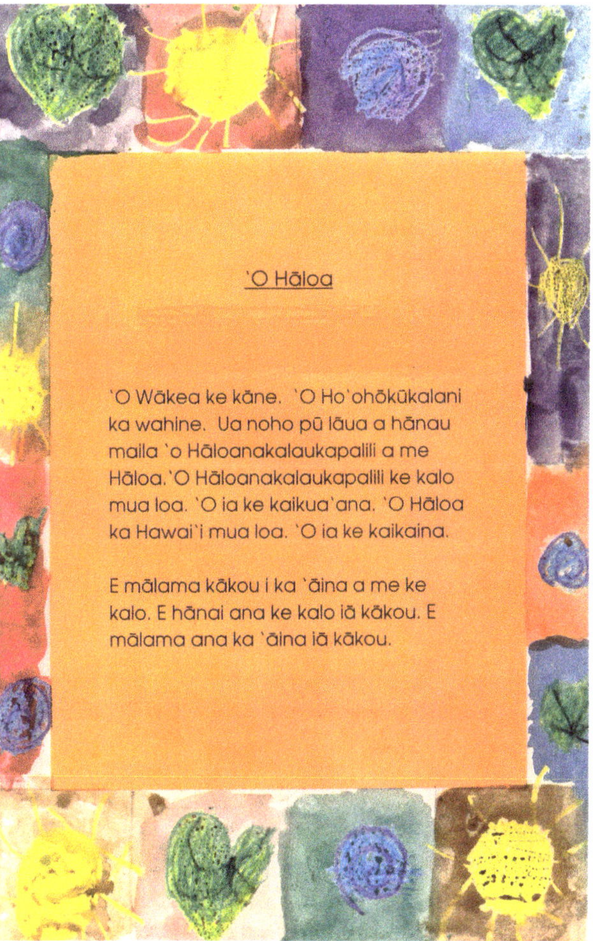

Figure 10.23. The student's drawings of important plant parts, leaf and *piko* (leaf node), and environmental elements, including the sun, frame the class-shared writing piece.

> Translation:
> Wakea was the husband. Ho'ohōkūkalani was his wife.
> They gave birth to Hāloanakalaukapalili and Hāloa.
> Hāloanakalaukapalili was the very first *kalo* plant. He was
> the older brother. Hāloa was the very first Hawaiian person.
> He was the younger brother.
> We take care of the land and the *kalo* plants. The *kalo* feeds
> us. The land will take care of us.

2. **Final Writing Piece**

A variety of writing project possibilities are presented below.

(a) Shared writing for younger students

- Generate a class-shared writing, an informational piece or a story, in which all students have an opportunity to participate, share, and add on to each other's ideas, as in Figure 10.23.

- Alternatively, each student can generate an original sentence about the plant. The sentence(s) can then accompany each individual student's arting piece, or the student sentences can be put together to create a class informational piece or story, as in Figure 10.25.

    (b) Independent writing for older students
- Each student generates an informational piece or story about the plant. Students proceed through the writing process with the final piece typed up or handwritten neatly in the arting frame opposite the arting piece about the plant in its environment. Figures 10.26 and 10.27 show a variation on this theme, with the students' informational piece typed onto transparent vellum integrated into the arting piece and their genealogy piece in the arting frame opposite the arting piece.

3. **Teacher Demonstration**

   Share the sample border that you created with the class. Explain your thinking as you discuss the pattern design. Generate some possible patterns as a group. What parts of the plant or environment might you include? Why? Have children look at their own work and select plant parts (in our *kalo* example, it might be the corm, leaf, or leaf node) or environmental elements (soil, sun, rain, wind) to include in the frame pattern. (We asked our kindergarten students to choose three things, from the plant parts and environmental elements, to include in their pattern.)

4. **Independent Student Work**

   Children design a variety of patterns on scratch paper before choosing one to use in the border framing the writing piece. Have them use oil pastels or crayon to color the border pattern. One watercolor paint color from the plant drawing is selected to carry over onto the frame. They then paint over the drawings in the frame.

5. **Putting It All Together**

   When dry, glue the writing piece inside the frame. The final framing of the writing with the patterning exercise will allow the children to see their arting and writing come together in a visually pleasing way that will give them great pride in creating a beautiful finished piece and work well done.

6. **Sharing**

   Using an Artist's and Author's Chair in the center or at the front of the room, children read and present their pieces to the rest of the class.

7. **Reflection**

   Have students reflect on the unit. What is the most important thing you learned about the plant? What was the best part of learning about this plant? What was most challenging while learning about this plant?

8. **Assessment**

   (This assessment is summative and performance-based.)

   (a) Listen for the ability of students to orally compose a sentence (for shared writing) expressing what each has learned about the plant. Or examine student informational writing, based on both completion and quality criteria, sharing what they have learned about the importance of the plant.

   (b) Review students' drawings and patterns to determine whether they successfully created a repetitive pattern.

   (c) Observe the students' ability and willingness to share information they have learned about this plant with others.

   (d) Observe and listen for students' demonstration of appreciation, connection to, and respect for the plant.

HŌʻIKE: EXHIBITING AND PUBLISHING

The culminating activity of this unit would be a *hōʻike*, or exhibition, where the children have the opportunity to share their learning with others – including their peers and possibly other teachers, parents, and the general public. It is an opportunity for them to teach their peers, younger children in the school, family members, and even the community, all they have learned about this wonderful plant along with their growing understanding of their relationship to and place in the natural world.

Figures 10.24. In this example, a kindergartener from Ke Kula ʻo Samuel M. Kamakau completed his own arting piece.

Figure 10.25. Once the *kalo* research and arting pieces were completed, the kindergarteners worked with partners to compose a sentence about what they learned. The sentences were then sequenced into a class-shared writing piece.

Translation:

Gratitude to Hāloa
Taro grows in an irrigated terrace.
Here is the parent and the child.
The roots are good because they help the taro to eat.
The stem is connected to the node of the leaf.
The leaves are happy because of the rich dirt.
The sun is an important thing every day.
There is lots of rain and wind.
The rain falls from the clouds.
The taro can grow.
Gratitude to the taro for my life here.
Gratitude to Hāloa.

Figure 10.26. 1st graders at Hau'ula Elementary School composed an original informational writing piece to sit beside the *kalo* drawing. These arting and writing pieces share their learning about the *kalo* (with the drawing) and their genealogy (opposite the drawing).

Translation:
I Have a Beautiful Taro
By Kailani del Rey

I have a purplish red taro.
It has lots of roots.
They are blackish.
The leaves are green.
The corm part is
brown and white.

Figure 10.27. Another 1st grader's final piece demonstrates the originality and personality of the artist. These 1st graders took their pieces through the entire arting and writing processes and were displayed at the end of the year celebration.

Translation:
Hāloanakalaukapalili
By No'eau Graycochea

This is a taro plant.
His name is
Hāloanakalaukapalili.
He lives in the
district of Kahuku in the
Ko'olauloa region of O'ahu.
His colors are green, purple,
and brown.

Chapter 11

Cultures: Identity through Portraiture

Kuʻu ewe, kuʻu piko, kuʻu iwi, kuʻu koko
"My umbilical cord, my navel, my bones, my blood"
Said of a very close relative.
– ʻŌlelo Noʻeau no. 1932

Figure 11.1. Robin Fifita, artist apprentice, shares her completed self-portrait. As a result of her genealogy and family origin research, the portrait details the wavy texture of her hair, the deep black of her eyes, the brown color of her skin, and the thickness of her lips to reflect her Polynesian ancestry.

UNIT OVERVIEW – TARGET GRADE LEVELS: 3–8+

Through arting and writing, students explore their own cultural identity as connected to family and place. Students explore and analyze mentor texts in order to envision, compose, and publish their own writing pieces on the significance of their name and/ or where they are from.

This unit offers several options in completing the writing component of the project. Students create a name poem or narrative in Lesson 3 and a "Where I'm From" poem in Lesson 4. You may have students complete both pieces to be included as part of the final arting and writing project. Another option would be to have students develop a draft of both the name and "Where I'm From" writing piece, then select one to revise, edit, and publish alongside the self-portrait. A different option would be to take students through either Lesson 3 or 4, depending on the time allotted, focus, and content.

The culminating project is a self-portrait juxtaposed with the writing pieces. Family participation is an integral component throughout this unit as students record their family genealogy and explore the origins of their names.

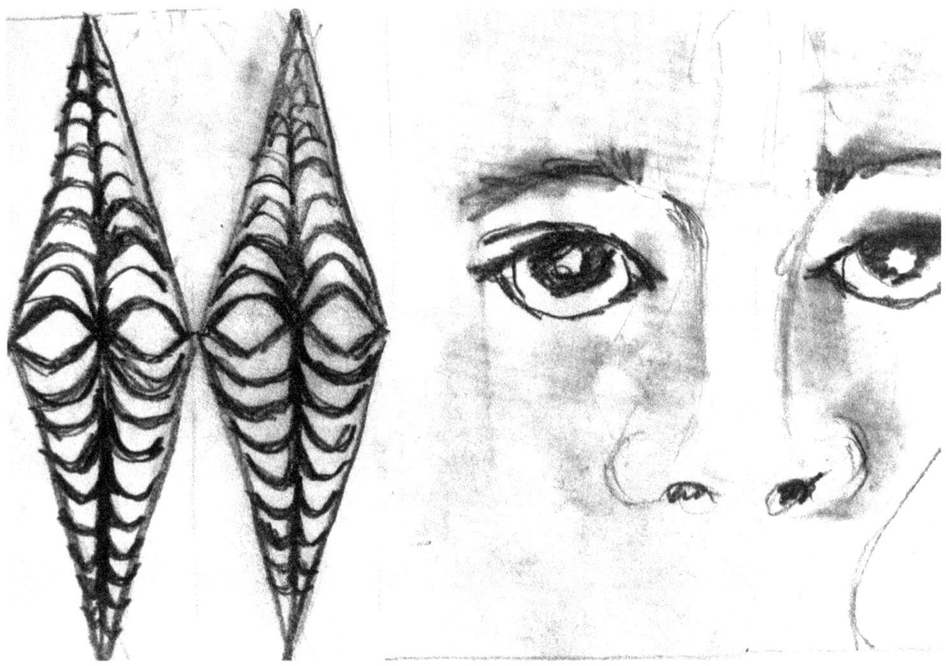

Figure 11.2. This working sketch of a Tongan geometric pattern and partial self-portrait reflect a young woman's understanding of culture as part of her identity.

Objectives

- Record at least 3 generations of family.
- Explore one's personal and/or cultural identity through personal/family names and relationships to family and place.
- Express personal and/or cultural identity by crafting writing piece(s).
- Use arting techniques to create a self-portrait with a complementary background.

Arting and Writing Activities

- Create a family tree/plant drawing.
- Research and record family genealogy for at least 3 generations.
- Find photographs of family members of each generation. Draw pictures if photographs are not available.
- Create a mini notebook exploring personal connections and relationships to family that contribute to personal identity.
- Create a mini notebook exploring personal connections and relationships to a place that contributes to personal identity.
- Complete a writing piece explaining the significance of one's personal name(s).
- Write a "Where I'm From" poem.
- Create a self-portrait with a complementary background.

Assessment

- Formative assessment, observation of students and examining work products, is ongoing throughout the unit.
- Summative assessment is the final arting and writing product, self-assessment, and personal reflection on the process and what has been learned. To assess the final arting and writing project, generate a rubric with specific grade level writing expectations/standards and project criteria. Include both completion and quality criteria.

Hawaiian Cultural Context

Moʻokūʻauhau (Genealogy)

Identity is connected to genealogy, a person's ancestors, those who came before. From a Hawaiian worldview, the naming of a person, place, event, or treasure is a significant act of defining identity within a cultural context. *ʻO wai kou inoa?* asks your name. The response tells the questioner a lot about you: who your parents are, who you may have been named after, what your name means, and where your family is from. All of these aspects of identity, relationship, and who a person is connected to are foundational to shaping and understanding the person's identity.

Place and Identity

From a Hawaiian perspective, identity is also connected to geographical place, where a person is born or raised. Traditionally, in Hawaiʻi and many other parts of the world, a person's family was associated with a specific geographic place, town or region, which aided in defining and shaping that person's identity.

LESSON 1: MY GENEALOGY – WHERE I'M FROM

My Place within My Family

(Home project and approximately 13–18 class periods)

OVERVIEW

Part 1 of this lesson is a home project engaging the students and their families in researching their genealogy through interviews with family members on family history and places of origin. Each family will also select a type of tree/plant to symbolize the family based on its significance to their family, culture, and/or place. Students should be able to explain its significance and what it represents.

Allow sufficient time for families to do research and work with their child to complete a genealogy template. We recommend that there be flexibility in the completion criteria because some families may not have all of the requested information by the suggested deadline and may need time to research information as the unit progresses. (Adopted and foster children might be able to choose their adopted/foster family or birth family, if that is an option. Since this can be a sensitive issue, we recommend having a conversation independently with these students, and with their parents or guardians, prior to the start of the project so they have time to make a decision.)

In Part 2 of this lesson, students complete the family tree and genealogy arting and writing project. They select and draw a significant tree/plant to symbolize the family and place their genealogy, completed in Part 1, onto the tree.

Note to the Reader: Involving Yourself in the Lesson Activity

We encourage you to complete your own family tree and genealogy before teaching this unit. Photograph your work at each step, documenting your process to share with students as an example, or do the project alongside your students, using your work to demonstrate each step.

Figure 11.3. This is a completed example of the family tree and genealogy project.

OBJECTIVES

- Create a family genealogy with at least three generations, identifying names of family members, year born, and place of birth. (Figure 11.4 is an example of a completed family genealogy template; see Appendix G for a reproducible genealogy template).
- Draw a tree/plant as a symbol of family.

MATERIALS

- Books, stories, and memoirs about grandparents and family/cultural origins; some recommended books (details in References) are: *I Love Saturdays y domingos* and *Where the Flame Trees Bloom* by Alma Flor Ada, *Grandpa's Magic Banyan Tree* by Jeff Langcaon, *My Tūtū Kāne and Grandpa* and *I Visit My Tūtū and Grandma* by Nancy Alpert Mower, *When I Was Young In The Mountains* and *The Relatives Came* by Cynthia Rylant, *Grandpa's Journey* by Allen Say, *The Trip Back Home* by Janet Wong.
- Sample letter to families explaining the genealogy project (Appendix F).
- Reproducible Genealogy Template (Appendix G).
- Family History Interview sheet (Appendix H).
- Optional for older students: Sample genealogy questions such as *Fifty Questions for Family* or *History Interviews: What to Ask the Relatives* (http://genealogy.about.com/cs/oralhistory/a/interview.htm).
- Photo of significant tree/plant to symbolize your family.
- Photocopy of each student's completed genealogy.
- Teacher-created completed family research template (as example for students).
- Chart/handout with genealogy symbols to be used for this project.
- Drawing pencils and erasers.
- Color pencils.
- Watercolor paints.
- Magic or painter's tape.
- Dark permanent marker.
- 2 sheets of drawing paper (at least 12" × 18") per student.
- Smaller pieces of drawing paper for practice.

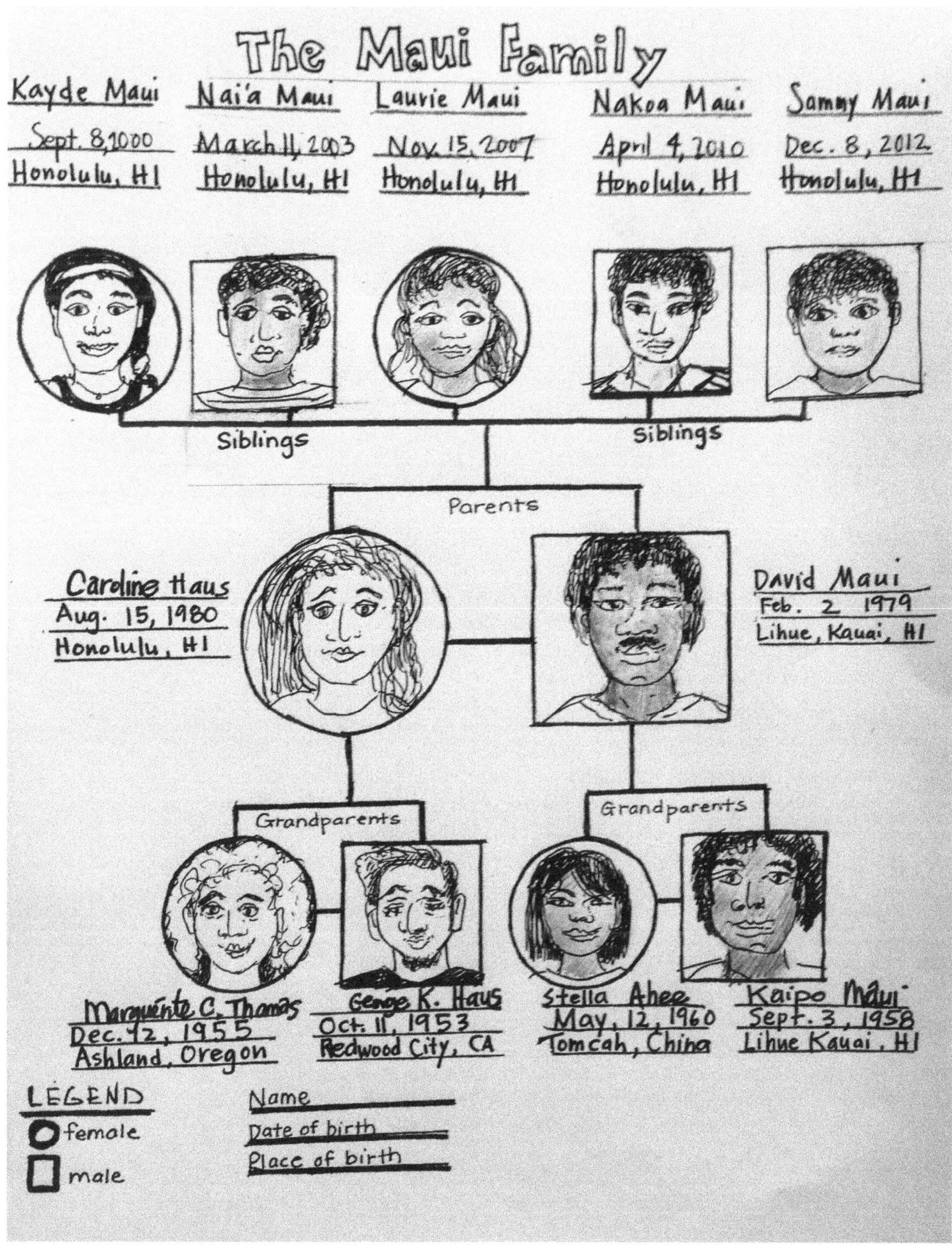

Figure 11.4. This is a completed genealogy template used to record family information for the project (pseudonyms have been used).

LESSON PROCEDURES

Part 1: Home Project on Genealogy Research

1. **Creating Connections through Story**
   Over several class periods, read aloud books, stories, and memoirs about grand-parents and family/cultural origins to initiate conversations about the ways in which family shapes the story characters. Students also respond by prewriting in their artist–writer notebooks about ways in which family has shaped their own identities.

2. **Genealogy Research**
   Send home the genealogy research packet (letter to families, genealogy tem-plate, and several copies of the Family History Interview sheet) for families to complete with their child. Use the Family History Interview sheet in Appendix H with younger students. Older students may wish to add their own questions. *Fifty Questions for Family History Interviews: What to Ask the Relatives* (Powell, 2014) has a useful list of questions for students to choose from. It is also important for the students to understand that some information, including pho-tographs, may be difficult to acquire, needing further time and research beyond the recommended due date. Let the students know that it is acceptable for some information to remain incomplete on the template when it is returned to school. If photographs are not available, students may draw their family member. The objective of this lesson is to engage students in the genealogy process and to find out as much information as they can.

3. **Maintain Project Momentum**
   While families are working on the home project, conduct a "status-of-the-class" review daily, or as often as possible, to track student progress, to allow time for students to learn from what other families have done, to raise questions, and to discuss and overcome challenges along the way. Invite a few students to share their progress and the work which the family has done on the project. This is a good way to keep the project at the forefront and maintain interest and momen-tum. Some discussion questions could be:
   - What have you discovered about your family history?
   - What family members have you to written or talked with?
   - What trees/plants are you considering as a symbol of your family?
   - What is a challenge you are facing?
   - What might your next steps be?

   All students should be able to share something about how the project is going. This also can provide you information about which students may need greater support, encouragement, or alternative options.

Part 2: Creating a Family Tree

(upon completion of Part 1: Home Project)

Do a search for "Queen Victoria's family tree 1901" for an interesting family tree image (see "Genealogical Tree of The Queen and Her Descendants" available at http://www.americanancestors.info/wp-content/uploads/2010/11/victoria_family_tree_1901.jpg).

4. **Arting Teacher Demonstration – Envisioning through Working Sketches**
    On 12" × 18" drawing paper (landscape orientation) folded in half so that there are two halves of 12" × 9" each:

    (a) Explain to the students that they will be envisioning by creating working sketches, drafts, or practice drawings in pencil of their family tree/plant. Demonstrate folding the drawing paper in half, so that there are two halves of 12" × 9" each.

    (b) Show a photograph or picture of the tree/plant you have chosen to symbolize your own family and explain your reasons for selecting this specific tree/plant and its significance to your family, clan, tribe, ethnic background, or place (see Figure 11.5).

    (c) Using a drawing pencil, demonstrate drawing a working sketch on the left half of the drawing paper. Use the actual plant or photograph to envision its placement on the page – orientation, shape, scale (e.g. how tall the tree is and where the branches will go) – and explore details (e.g. trunk texture and leaf shape). Include notes to self – things discovered or noted during drawing that you want to remember when doing the next working sketch. Include questions you have while drawing that may require further research. This is a practice drawing, so demonstrate trying out and experimenting with ideas and making mistakes. Let the students know that this is just practice, so mistakes are encouraged and welcomed (see Figure 11.6).

Figure 11.5. This photo of a *pua kenikeni* tree was used to create working sketches of Figures 11.6 and 11.7.

5. **Independent Student Arting – Envisioning through Working Sketches**
   On 12" × 18" drawing paper (landscape orientation) folded in half so that there are two halves of 12" × 9" each:
   (a) Students envision their family tree/plant by observing the actual tree/plant and/or photo to create an initial working sketch (trunk or stalk, branches and leaves, and roots) on the left side of the drawing paper.
   (b) Students should include notes to self – things discovered while drawing that they want to remember for the next drawing and questions they have while drawing that may require further research.

6. **Arting Teacher Demonstration – Composing a Final Working Sketch**
   (a) Using a drawing pencil, demonstrate composing a final working sketch on the right half of the drawing paper. Explain your thinking about incorporating the many ideas in the notes recorded during the envisioning stage to compose this final working sketch. Keep elements that work for your drawing and adjust or eliminate elements that don't work. Incorporate any new information gathered from the additional research.
   (b) Add important details to the drawing, using the Arting Elements and Principles of Design in Appendix D (see Figure 11.7).

7. **Independent Student Arting – Composing a Final Working Sketch**
   (a) Students compose a final working sketch on the right half of the drawing paper, keeping elements from the envisioning working sketches, changing elements that don't work, and incorporating new details or information gathered from additional research.
   (b) Students complete the drawing by adding important details, using the Arting Elements and Principles of Design in Appendix D (see Figure 11.7).
   (c) Optional: Students' final sketches are displayed around the room. Students do a "gallery walk," analyzing the work and contributing thoughts, suggestions, or questions via sticky notes.

8. **Arting Teacher Demonstration – Composing the Final Drawing**
   On 12" × 18" drawing paper, portrait orientation:
   (a) Demonstrate marking in, by drawing in lightly, the shape of the tree/plant onto the larger paper.
   (b) Share your ideas for completing the drawing and lightly draw in some of the details (see Figure 11.8). Demonstrate and emphasize that all parts of the tree/plant are important and should be included: roots, tree trunk or plant stem, branches and leaves,
   (c) Explain the background (where the plant grows) and its importance to the completed composition.
   (d) Show an example of a completed project explaining that the family genealogy will be placed onto the drawing.

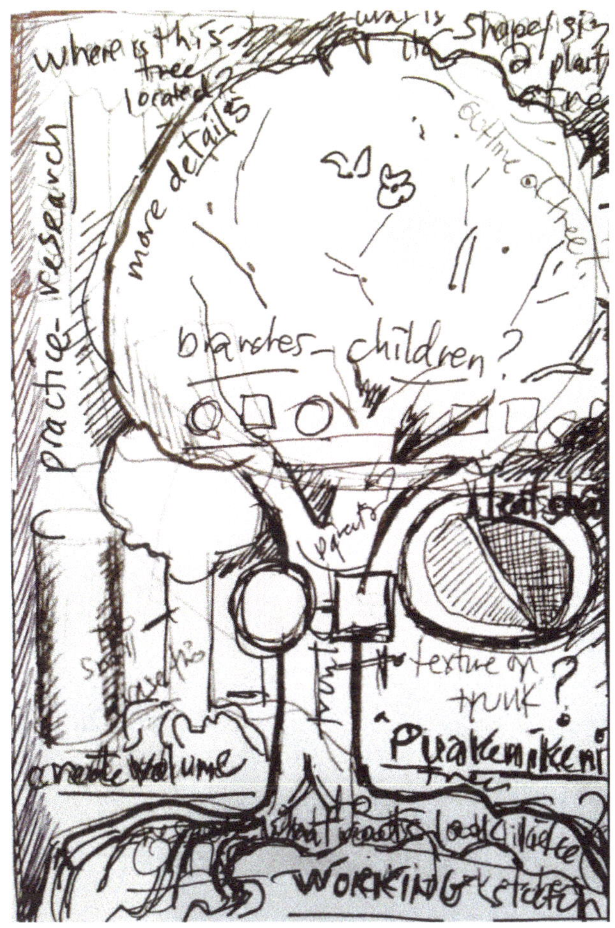

Figure 11.6. In this initial working sketch, the artist envisioned placement – orientation, shape, and scale – while also exploring important details. The artist also included notes to self – things to remember for the next sketch. Questions that arose while drawing were also included and required further research.

Figure 11.7. This final working sketch provides the artist with an additional practice in composing before proceeding to the final drawing.

9. **Independent Student Arting – Composing the Final Drawing**
    (a) Students lightly draw in the shape of their family tree/plant onto the larger 12" × 18" paper.
    (b) Students complete a detailed drawing of their tree/plant, including the background (see Figure 11.9).

10. **Arting Teacher Demonstration – Completing the Final Drawing**
    (a) Demonstrate coloring in your family tree/plant, using drawing techniques: blending, shading, and highlighting with color pencils (see Appendix D, Elements and Principles of Design).
    (b) Continue demonstration by adding a second layer of color with watercolor paint. Demonstrate holding the brush, the direction and movement of the brush stroke, and various water-to-paint ratios to create degrees of opacity and transparency (see Figure 11.10).

Figure 11.8. This example demonstrates initial steps in composing a final drawing, lightly sketching in the shapes and objects.

Figure 11.9. The completed final drawing includes the tree/plant and background.

Figure 11.10. This example demonstrates how color pencil and watercolor paint layers are added to complete the drawing.

Figure 11.11. The final arting composition is ready for the writing, the family genealogy, to be added.

11. **Independent Student Arting – Completing the Final Drawing**

    Before coloring in their final drawing, students should be given time to experiment with and practice using color pencils and watercolor paint techniques. Students then:

    (a) Color in their final tree/plant composition with color pencils.

    (b) Add watercolor paint.

    (c) Set the composition out to dry.

12. **Arting Teacher Demonstration – Critiquing**

    Demonstrate how artists critique their own work by noticing unfinished areas, then follow up by filling in white spaces, finishing lines, and doing any other clean-up work needed before exhibiting their work for an audience.

13. **Independent Student Arting – Critiquing**

    Students critique their work and go back in to fill in white spaces, finish lines, and do other clean-up work. During this independent work time, you may want to have students critique each other's work.

14. **Writing Teacher Demonstration – Editing**

    The genealogy template will be used as the writing component of the project. It will be the final published piece, exhibited for others to see.

    (a) Share the importance of editing the written piece for accuracy before it will be published for others to read. Share examples of what to look for when editing the genealogy: accuracy of dates, spelling of names and places, capitalization, and accurate genealogy protocols.

    (b) Demonstrate tracing text and symbols with a dark permanent marker.

15. **Independent Student Writing – Editing**

    (a) Students reread the genealogy information, editing for accuracy. Peer editing can be included.

    (b) Students trace over text and symbols with a dark permanent marker.

16. **Writing Teacher Demonstration – Assembling the Finished Arting and Writing Piece**

    (a) Use a photocopy of the completed genealogy template. Cut out each family member and corresponding information.

    (b) Explain to the students how the different parts of your tree/plant represent the generations of your family (e.g. the trunk or stalk of the tree/plant represents your parents' generation, the branches represent you and your siblings, the roots represent your grandparents, great grandparents, and all of the generations that have come before).

    (c) Position the circles and squares, along with the corresponding information, onto the drawing – parents on the trunk, self and siblings in the branches, grandparents in the roots.

    (d) Glue the family members and information onto the drawing.

    (e) Draw in the genealogy lines (e.g. generational and marriage lines) with pencil onto the final drawing.

    (f) Trace over the penciled lines with dark permanent marker.

17. **Independent Student Writing – Assembling the Finished Arting and Writing Piece**
    (a) Students position family member photographs/drawings and corresponding information onto the family tree.
    (b) Students then glue the family member photographs/drawings and information onto the tree.
    (c) Students draw in the genealogy lines with pencil.
    (d) Students trace over the penciled lines with dark permanent marker.

18. **Exhibiting**
    Students share their family tree genealogy projects in small groups and/or with whole class, highlighting three things they learned about their family or themselves. Exhibit student projects (see Figure 11.3 for an example of a completed family tree and genealogy project).

19. **Reflection**
    Students complete a reflection on the project by answering the following questions:
    • What are the three most important things you learned about yourself or your family?
    • What are two things you enjoyed about this project?
    • What challenge did you encounter or is there a question that you still have?
    This reflection can be written or conducted as an interview.

20. **Assessment**
    (Both formative and summative assessments are included.)
    (a) During the home project, check in on students and allow class time for students to share information, stories, progress, challenges, and plans; and to informally assess student progress, troubleshoot any challenges that arise, and determine which students may need additional supports or alternative options.
    (b) Examine each student's family genealogy template for sufficient information. If students do not have access to family information, modifications to the project may be necessary.
    (c) Design criteria or a rubric with the class to determine completion and quality criteria for the project. Students self-assess their own family trees/plants to determine whether they have met the project completion and quality criteria.

Figure 11.12. The family member drawings or photographs and corresponding information on the genealogy template, Appendix G, is cut out and positioned on the completed family tree drawing.

LESSON 2: DEFINING ME: CONNECTIONS AND RELATIONSHIPS

Explorations in Identity

(3 class periods)

OVERVIEW

Through researching their family genealogies, students have learned more about their family history, members of their family, and place(s) their family is from. In this lesson students begin to explore their personal identities or what makes them who they are. Students will create mini notebooks with drawings and words describing themselves.

OBJECTIVES

Students identify physical characteristics and personal attributes, through arting and writing, which contribute to one's personal identity.

MATERIALS

- Drawing paper (12" × 18") to be folded and cut into a mini notebooks (see Appendix E, How to Make a Mini Notebook).
- Completed "Defining Me" mini notebook to be used as an example for students.
- Drawing pencils and erasers.
- Crayons, color pencils.

1. **Creating Connections**
   Have students share interesting facts, information, and personal discoveries they learned about their families and themselves during Lesson 1 while doing the genealogy research and creating their family tree.

2. **Arting and Writing Teacher Demonstration**
   Explain to students that they will be exploring their personal identities, what it is that makes them who they are. Share your own personal "Defining Me" mini notebook (instructions in Step 3), explaining the reasons for your choices and reading aloud some of your prewriting thoughts. Provide a variety of examples and multiple levels of thought (literal, metaphoric, and symbolic) to encourage the students to think more deeply about themselves.

3. **Teacher Guided Prearting and Prewriting**
   Have students fold and cut their mini notebooks as you demonstrate (see Appendix E, How to Make a Mini Notebook). Take your students through their mini notebooks. Follow the directions in steps a–e below, allowing about 5–7 minutes per page spread (2 pages side by side) to get initial ideas in thumbnail sketches and words onto the page. Let students know that they are not expected

to complete the arting or writing during this short guided exercise. They will have additional independent arting and writing time to go back into and complete their mini notebooks.

Directions:

(a) Front cover: Write your name and draw your favorite facial feature (nose, eyes, smile, long hair). Describe this feature or tell about why it is your favorite (see Figure 11.13).

Figure 11.13. Prearting and prewriting about a favorite facial feature activates personal reflection in this mini notebook.

(b) First spread (pages 1 and 2): Draw and write about at least 3 things that you love about yourself: physical features – such as long hair, fast feet for running – or talents, interests, and passions – such as catching a football, playing piano, reading, drawing (see Figure 11.14).

Figure 11.14. This first spread of the mini notebook shows the things this artist–writer loves about herself: being a creative person who works with her hands; her writing, drawing and painting; and being a photographer.

(c) Second spread (pages 3 and 4): Draw and write about at least 3 geographical features and landmarks of home, where you are from, such as a mountain, the ocean, a river or lake, a tree, the skyline (see Figure 11.15).

Figure 11.15. On this spread, the artist–writer draws and writes about the important landmarks and geographical features of her home: the mountain peaks and their names, the marshland area, and the beach.

(d) Third spread (pages 5 and 6): Draw and write about at least 3 things that are culturally important and that represent you, your family, and/or your culture: a basket woven by aunty; my fishing spear or hunting bow; reindeer for the Sámi; corn, beans, and squash for the Iroquois; *kalo* for Hawaiians (see Figure 11.16).

Figure 11.16. The artist–writer reflects on the importance of her culture and draws and reflects on three culturally significant objects: a feather *lei* (garland), a *pū* (conch shell), and an *'umeke* (calabash bowl).

(e) Back cover: Draw and write about something that represents a significant or favorite member of your family: auntie's *'ukulele*, dad's football, mom's favorite flower (see Figure 11.17).

Figure 11.17. On this last page of her mini notebook, the artist–writer draws an *'ukulele* to represent a favorite aunty and writes about her feelings and memories of this special person.

Note to the Reader: Reflecting and Expanding on Options

Following the work on the front cover and the first spread, it is helpful to pause and highlight, do a brief share – or have students share – some of the different ways the students are experimenting and playing with arting and writing. This provides an opportunity for students to expand their own arting and writing possibilities and to experiment with different ways of arting and writing. For example, some students may brainstorm a word list and others may choose to write sentences. Some students may choose to write first, others may choose to thumbnail first. Some students may choose to do several smaller drawings on a spread, while others may do one large drawing that incorporates different elements. Encourage students to try out a different way of brainstorming on second and third spreads and back page.

4. **Independent Student Arting and Writing**
    Students continue to draw and write in their "Defining Me" mini notebooks. Some students may need further conversation, scaffolding, and/or direction in completing the third spread on culture.

5. **Sharing**

   Throughout the lesson, have students share their drawings, reread their words, and explain their thoughts and feelings about their work. In this way, you capitalize on the creative ways students are approaching the work as examples for the others.

6. **Final Sharing**

   Have students review their "Defining Me" mini notebooks to find their favorite drawings and words or thoughts. Have them share their completed mini notebooks with partners or in small groups.

7. **Gallery Walk and Reflection**

   Have students unfold their "Defining Me" mini notebooks to reveal the larger arting and writing piece, the many smaller drawings and observations put together as a whole (see Figures 11.18 and 11.19). Display these pieces in a gallery walk. Encourage the students to observe and think more deeply about their own mini notebooks, their peers' notebooks, and their notebooks together as a group:
   - What do you notice about the drawings?
   - Do you see similarities?
   - What do you notice about what your peers have written?
   - Has anyone drawn or written something similar to your work?
   - What is interesting to you in the drawings and writings of others?

8. **Assessment**

   (These assessments are formative and performance-based.)

   These initial drawings and quickwrites will inform you about the students' depth of thought (literal, metaphoric, symbolic) and understanding of their identity.

   (a) Observe students, noting the many ways in which your students are approaching the arting and writing work. Which students art/draw first? Which students are reluctant artists/writers? Notice which students are using innovative arting and writing techniques? Have these students share their arting and writing processes.

   (b) Conduct informal conferences to: (1) understand what students are wanting to communicate through their drawings and writing, and offer suggestions or arting and writing tips they may want to try as they continue their work independently; (2) provide more support to students who are struggling with generating ideas, drawings, or writing; and (3) extend students' thinking.

Figure 11.18. When the mini notebook is unfolded it reveals a larger arting and writing piece. The composite drawings reveal multiple aspects of the subject studied, in this case, her identity as a young Hawaiian.

Figure 11.19. This example of a mini notebook was done in pencil. It reveals personal and cultural symbols important to the artist–writer. These symbols tell a visual story that will inspire her writing piece.

LESSON 3: *'O WAI KOU INOA?* WHAT DOES YOUR NAME TELL ABOUT YOU?

Creating my Name Piece

(Home project and 12–15 class periods)

OVERVIEW

Part 1 of this lesson is a home project engaging the students in researching the origin of their names by interviewing family members. It also includes prewriting (in-class exploration) and envisioning with mentor texts.

Part 2 of this lesson takes students through one entire cycle of the writing process. Students use their prewriting and home project information to create a poem or narrative writing piece. Students envision, compose, and develop a writing piece about their name and identity (see Figures 11.31, 11.32, and 11.33 are completed student examples).

OBJECTIVES

- Explain orally and/or in writing the origin/significance of at least one name (first, middle, last).
- Analyze various mentor texts for meaning, structure, and writer's craft.
- Intentionally use selected writer's craft elements while composing a writing piece (poem, narrative, or other).
- Complete a writing piece (poem, narrative, or other), explaining the significance of one's personal name.

MATERIALS

- My Name Interview sheet (Appendix I).
- Stories/books with the significance of a name or naming as the main idea (starter list included at the end of this lesson).
- Mentor poem: "Choosing My Name" by Puanani Burgess. An audio version is available on the Bamboo Ridge website (http://www.bambooridge.com/ edpisode.aspx?eid=63) and at a website (http://apiwomenfaithaction.blogspot. com/2010/10/puanani-burgess.html – scroll down to the bottom of Puanani Burgess' biography to locate the poem) that includes her biography by Lee (2010). The poem has been published in *Growing Up Local*, edited by Eric Chock, James Harstad, Darrell Lum, and Bill Teter (Chock *et al.*, 1998: 278), and also in *Ho'omānoa: An Anthropology of Contemporary Hawaiian Literature*, edited by Joseph B. Balaz (Balaz, 1989: 40–41).

- Mentor text: "My Name" by Sandra Cisneros from *The House on Mango Street* (Cisneros, 1984); available online at: http://theliterarylink.com/mangostreet.html
- Teacher's completed example of a prearting/prewriting brainstorm (for Part 2, Step 6).
- Teacher's draft of personal name story as an example (for Part 2, Step 7).
- Drawing pencils and erasers.
- Crayons, color pencils.
- Markers.

LESSON PROCEDURES

Part 1: Home Project on Name Origins

1. **Teacher Creating Connections through Story** (2–3 class periods)
   Read aloud poems, stories, and books about names and naming. A list of resources we used is included at the end of this lesson. Follow up on these readings by encouraging students to share thoughts about the importance and significance of a name and what they know about the origins of their own names.

2. **Student Home Project on Name Research**
   Students interview parents and/or other family members on the origin of their names. Depending on the age of the students, the interview sheet can be created by the teacher or can be co-created with older students (see Appendix I, My Name Interview sheet, for an example).

3. **Teacher-Guided Prewriting and Envisioning with Mentor Texts**
   Conduct this step while students are working on their home project.
   (a) Provide students with copies of "Choosing My Name" by Puanani Burgess.
   (b) Read aloud, twice. It is important that you read aloud the poem so students can hear the rhythm, cadence, and sound of the words.
   (c) Meaning-making: Provide time for students to work independently and then with a partner or small group. Have students analyze and annotate the poem for meaning, using the following guiding questions:
      1. What is this author saying about her name?
      2. What words or phrases support your thinking?
      3. Why do you think she wrote this piece? Who might her audience be?
      4. What is the tone of the piece? What words and phrases support your interpretation?
   (d) Each student selects an important word or phrase from the text to share aloud in quick succession, or "popcorn" style.
   (e) Follow the share-aloud with a whole class conversation on students' thoughts about the meaning of the piece:
      1. Were there any words or phrases that recurred during the popcorn reading? Why are these specific words or phrases important in understanding the meaning of the poem?
      2. Did the share-aloud change or affirm their understanding of the poem? Why or why not?

(f) Analyzing Text Structure and Writing Craft: Have students go back into the poem to notice its structure and identify craft elements. This is an opportunity to informally assess which structural aspects and writing craft elements students are able to identify and which elements need further teaching. What are students noticing or not? Add to the conversation by pointing out some techniques or ideas they may have overlooked.

Guiding Questions:

1. How did the author organize the poem (sequence or group ideas)? Why do you think she organized it this way?
2. How did the organization enhance the meaning of the poem?
3. What writing craft elements do you notice that the author used: simile, metaphor, word choice, sensory details, repetition, or others?

Next class period:

• Repeat the process with "My Name" by Sandra Cisneros, either reading the narrative aloud for younger students or having older students do independent and partner reading, reading first for meaning and then for text structure and writing craft analysis. (A video of the author reading the text is available on Vimeo at https://vimeo.com/105508553.)
• Following the analysis of both texts, have students compare and contrast the two "My Name" texts using the following guiding questions:
    1. In what ways are they similar? Different?
    2. Why do you think Burgess chose to write a poem instead of a narrative?
    3. Why do you think Cisneros chose to write a narrative rather than a poem?
    4. What are the advantages of poetic structure? Or narrative structure?

4. **Reflection**
    (a) Students identify at least 1–3 writing craft elements from the mentor texts that they would like to use in their own writing piece.
    (b) Optional: Students write a short opinion piece in response to one of the mentor texts, supporting their point of view with reasons and information from the text.

Part 2: Creating a Name Piece

(upon completion of Part 1: Home Project)

1. **Making Connections**
    Students informally share the origins and stories of their own names (in small groups or with the whole class).

2. **Prearting/Prewriting Teacher Demonstration**
    A completed teacher example should be used as a model, along with Figures 11.20 and 11.21.
    (a) Inform students that for the next part of this lesson, they will compose a writing piece, similar to the writing of Burgess and Cisneros, about their name. They will do a name brainstorm to generate feelings and ideas about their names and who they are. They will also be using information from their name research.

(b) Share your completed prearting and prewriting brainstorm in your artist and writer's notebook. Explain your thinking behind the lettering of your name and the reasons for the surrounding pictures and symbols. Read aloud some of your phrases and words. Provide a variety of examples and multiple levels of thought (literal, metaphoric, and symbolic) to encourage the students to think more deeply about their names and personal characteristics. Figures 11.20 and 11.21 are examples of what the prearting/prewriting might look like.

3. **Directions for the Prearting/Prewriting Activity**

The purpose of this activity is for students to generate, explore, and experiment with ideas gathered during their name research and the mentor text study.

(a) Students draw/write their whole name in the middle of the page. Artists might choose to draw some letters of their name as paint brushes; sports players might make a letter *o* in their name a soccer ball, basketball, or football; people who enjoy the beach may choose to have shells or waves represent letters in their name.

(b) Students then use the name drawings as a way to brainstorm significant symbols, sketches, words, and phrases about themselves (see Figures 11. 20 and 11.21).

(c) Have students reread their "Defining Me" mini notebook and their name research. Students add further words, thoughts, and phrases to their name drawings.

Figure 11.20. This teacher-created example of a name brainstorm uses images to create the letter shapes of her name. The teacher then elaborated on each letter image, explaining its significance to family, place, and identity.

Figure 11.21. This variation of the name brainstorm was done as a series of thumbnails. Each successive drawing shows the evolution of this artist–writer's thinking. The pictures in the final thumbnail (lower right) represent important family relationships and favorite activities.

4. **Writing Teacher Demonstration – Envisioning and Composing**

   (a) Demonstrate to your students the process (rereading, highlighting, and circling important ideas and information) they will go through to review the prewriting they have done thus far in this unit: family tree and genealogy, "Defining Me" mini notebook, name research, study on the two name pieces, and name brainstorm. Share any new insights you have gained about your family and yourself through these activities.

   (b) Share aloud some ideas you are considering for your name piece. Include some of the information and insights gained in earlier lessons along with ideas generated in the mini notebook. Share some of the specific ideas you would like to include in your new writing piece and where they came from: a physical feature from the identity notebook or a sentence from the mini notebook.

   (b) Select a genre for your name writing piece: poetry, narrative, or other. Explain your reasons for selecting this genre:

   (c) Think aloud about what you are envisioning. For example:
   - Which mentor text are you using as a model? Burgess or Cisneros?
   - What are you envisioning about the text's structure?
   - What will be the tone of your piece?
   - What new writing craft element(s) are you thinking of including?

   (d) Model composing the initial draft or its beginning. Think aloud as you compose. Model the following strategies to help students anticipate and get through some of the challenges they might encounter:

- Not knowing how to begin – just write down what you are thinking, even though it is not quite what you want. This is just the first draft.
- Not knowing the specific word – put a blank line as a place holder and come back to it later.
- Using general words that need specificity – circle words that aren't precise enough and revisit during revisioning.
- Spelling – underline words that may be misspelled and need to be edited.

5. **Independent Student Writing – Envisioning and Composing**
   (a) Students gather all of their prearting and prewriting to reread, and to highlight or circle important ideas and information they would like to include in their writing composition.
   (b) Students select a genre: poetry, narrative, or other. If they select a genre other than poetry or narrative used in the mentor text study, they may need support to review other mentor text examples as possible models.
   (c) Students select 1–3 new writing craft element(s) they would like to explore and include in their piece.
   (d) Students begin to compose.

6. **Writing Teacher Demonstration – Composing**
   Over the next day or two, use the writing you are doing on your piece as a model. Discuss which information from your prewriting is included in the piece, the basic structure envisioned, and the blank lines you left from the earlier demonstration that have now been filled in with words. Some of the words may still be circled or underlined to be left for the revisioning and editing stages. You may also want to have a few students share their work as models.

7. **Independent Student Writing – Composing**
   Students write until they feel they have gone as far as they can and have a completed first draft. Allow several class periods for composing and set a reasonable deadline for them to work toward.

8. **Writing Teacher Demonstration – Revisioning**
   (a) Demonstrate revisioning your first draft in front of the class. Begin by explaining that you feel your first draft is finished because you have taken the piece as far as you can and are ready for feedback from others. Explain that your draft includes most of the ideas and writing techniques envisioned. If an idea or writing technique was abandoned, explain why you changed your mind and made the decision not to include it.
   (b) Read your piece aloud to the class, indicate the parts of the piece you like with a star, and then point out some of the things you are not quite happy with. For example, "I think I may be missing information here" or "I think I need to go back and clarify this by including more details." Demonstrate how to go back into the piece to add words or information using a caret; a single line strikethrough or a proofreading squiggle symbol to delete unnecessary information; or arrows to indicate where a word, sentence, or paragraph will be moved. During revisioning, although many changes are made, emphasize that there should be no erasing because it is a work in progress. It is helpful when changes remain visible. This allows the writer to return to previous threads of thought as the writing is viewed as a working

draft. In this stage of the process, the focus is on fine-tuning ideas through considerations such as those below. (Creating and posting a large chart listing the considerations below can support the students in thinking through their revisions independently.)

- Organization: Do ideas flow, one to the next, or do some need to be reordered? Use arrows to indicate where sentences and paragraphs need to be moved.
- Word choice: Is this word specific enough to convey the meaning I want the reader to understand or is there a better word? Use a single line strikethrough or proofreading squiggle symbol to indicate deleting a word and a caret to insert the preferred word.
- Adding information: Is there something missing that needs to be added? Use a caret to indicate additional information.
- Deleting information: Is the information unnecessary, that is, can you conclude that it does not contribute to moving the ideas or story forward? Use a single line strikethrough or proofreading squiggle symbol to indicate a deletion.
- Clarifying information: Is this confusing to the reader and do I need to explain or include more details? Use a single line strikethrough or proofreading squiggle symbol to indicate a deletion and a caret to insert the rewritten phrase or sentence.

9. **Independent Student Writing – Revisioning**
   (a) Have students review their own pieces, starring the parts they are pleased with and circling the parts they would like to continue to work on during revisioning.
   (b) Students engage in informal sharing with writing partners or small groups to allow the writers an opportunity to read their pieces aloud to hear how they sound. If some students are not finished with the first draft, have them share whatever they have completed or feel ready to share. If students are accustomed to providing positive feedback and asking clarifying questions, then peer feedback/conferring may be included as part of the sharing.
   (c) Students revision their pieces, thinking through the considerations. Confer with those students who are finished with independent revisioning in small groups or one-to-one.

10. **Share – Revisioning**
    Select several students to share their revisioning work with the class as models.

11. **Writing Teacher Demonstration – Editing**
    To demonstrate how a writer intentionally uses punctuation to assist a reader in reading and comprehending a text, read your piece aloud. By hearing a piece read aloud, students develop a sense of how punctuation assists a reader in understanding a text, and also how lack of punctuation makes reading more challenging and misplaced punctuation can cause confusion. Demonstrate grade-level appropriate grammar and punctuation corrections you expect your students to be able to make independently. Or work with one student as the rest of the class observes and assists in editing the student's piece. Check if the student is comfortable sharing her/his work with the class. Assure that the environment is

a safe one where the student's work will be honored and seen as a contribution to the group's learning and where the child will not be embarrassed.

12. Independent Student Writing – Editing
Students edit their pieces for appropriate grammar and punctuation.

13. Exhibiting and Publishing
Students type or rewrite neatly a clean copy for exhibition with the completed arting piece.

14. Sharing
Students read aloud their final pieces in small groups or with the whole class.

15. Assessment and Critique
(This assessment is summative and performance-based on the written product.)
(a) Analyze student writing pieces for application of the following:
  - Writer's craft elements from mentor texts in personal name piece
  - Genre-specific text structures and selected writer's craft elements in their writing piece (poem, narrative, or other)
  - Capturing the significance of at least one personal name (first, middle, or last)
(b) Older students may critique their work and that of others for the use of genre-specific text structures and/or the use of writer's craft elements.

Stories/Books with Name/Naming as a Central Theme
- Ada, Alma Flor (1993) *My Name is Maria Isabel* (Illus. K. Dyble Thompson). New York: Atheneum.
- Choi, Yangsook (2003) *The Name Jar*. New York: Random House Children's Books.
- Fosberry, Jennifer (2010) *My Name is Not Isabella: Just How Big Can a Little Girl Dream?* (illus. Mike Litwin). Naperville, Illinois: Sourcebooks, Inc.
- Fosberry, Jennifer (2011) *My Name is Not Alexander* (illus. Mike Litwin). Naperville, Illinois: Sourcebooks, Inc.
- Henkes, Kevin (1996) *Chrysanthemum*. New York: Harpercollins Children's Books.
- Recorvits, Helen (2003) *My Name is Yoon* (illus. Gabi Swiatkowska). New York: Frances Foster Books.

LESSON 4: WHERE I'M FROM

The Significance of Home

(7–10 class periods)

OVERVIEW

This lesson takes students through one entire cycle of the writing process. It includes reading and analyzing several texts with a similar "Where I'm From" theme in the prewriting stage. Students then envision, compose, and develop their own "Where I'm From" piece to provide inspiration for the background of their self-portrait (Lesson 5). This written piece may be included as part of the final arting and writing project of this unit.

OBJECTIVES

- Analyze several mentor texts ("Where I'm From" poems) for meaning, poetic text structure, and specific writing craft techniques used.
- Intentionally use selected writer's craft elements while composing a "Where I'm From" poem.
- Complete a "Where I'm From" poem explaining the significance of one's place, family, culture, and/or identity.

MATERIALS

- An assortment of "Where I'm From" poems (A variety of mentor poems are available on the internet).
- Mentor poem: "When I Was Young On An Island" by Diane Kahanu. An audio version is available on the Bamboo Ridge website (http://www.bambooridge. com/episode.aspx?eid=71), and the poem has been published in *Growing Up Local* (Chock *et al.* 1998: 5–53).
- Mentor text: *When I Was Young in the Mountains* by Cynthia Rylant (Rylant, 1982).

LESSON PROCEDURES

1. **Creating Connections**
   Have students share the second spread of their "Defining Me" mini notebook (Lesson 2) with a partner or in small groups first; then with the whole class. Ask them to share about the place they chose as their home, its geographical features and any significant landmarks. This is the place they call home and will be writing about in this lesson. Some students may want to change their place. Allow them to do so, asking them to complete a prearting and prewriting on this place indicating at least 3 geographical features and/or significant landmarks.

2. **Teacher-Guided Prewriting and Envisioning with Mentor Texts**
   ("Where I'm From" poems)
   (a) Optional: Read aloud one of the "Where I'm From" poems so students can hear the rhythm, cadence, and sound of the words.
   (b) Meaning-making: Provide time for students to work independently and then with a partner or small group. Have students analyze and annotate the poem for meaning, using the following guiding questions:
   - What is this author saying about where s/he is from?
   - How do you think s/he feels about where s/he is from?
   - What is the tone of the piece?
   - What words and phrases support your interpretation?
   (c) Analyzing Text Structure and Writing Craft: Have students go back into the poem to notice its structure and identify craft elements. (This is an opportunity to informally assess which structural aspects and writing craft elements students are able to identify and which elements need further teaching. What are students noticing or not?) Add to the conversation by pointing out some techniques or ideas they may have overlooked. Some guiding questions might be:
   - How did the author decide to organize the poem? Why do you think s/he organized it this way?
   - How did the text structure enhance the meaning of the poem?
   - What writing craft elements do you notice the author used: simile, metaphor, word choice, sensory details, repetition, others?
   (d) Have the students repeat the process with a different "Where I'm From" poem. With older students, give each small group a different poem to analyze and share with the rest of the class. Guide the students to read first for meaning and then for text structure and writing craft analysis. Some guiding questions might be:
   - How did the author decide to organize the poem? Why do you think s/he organized it this way?
   - How did the text structure enhance the meaning of the poem?
   - What writing craft elements do you notice the author used: simile, metaphor, word choice, sensory details, repetition, others?
   (e) Guide the students to compare and contrast the two (or more) texts. In what ways are the two pieces similar? Different? Which poems do you like? Why? Which of the poems were most effective in conveying their message? Why?

3. **Reflection**
   (a) Students identify at least 1–3 writing craft element/s they would like to explore in their own writing piece.
   (b) Optional: Students may write a short opinion piece in response to one of the mentor texts, supporting their point of view with reasons and information from the text.

4. **Writing Teacher Demonstration – Envisioning and Composing**
   Review the prewriting work you and the students have done: family tree and genealogy, "Defining Me" mini notebook, study on "Where I'm From" poems.
   (a) Share aloud some of the ideas you are considering for your "Where I'm From" poem. Share some of the specific ideas you would like to include and where they came from (e.g. from the "Defining Me" mini notebook or from a specific "Where I'm From" poem).

(b) Think aloud about what you are envisioning. Which mentor text will you use as a model? What are you thinking about the text structure? Tone? What new writing craft element(s) are you thinking of including?

(c) Model composing the initial draft or its beginning. Think aloud as you compose. Model the following strategies to help students anticipate and get through some of the challenges they might encounter:

- Not knowing how to begin – just write down what you are thinking, even though it is not quite what you want. This is just the first draft.
- Not knowing the specific word – put a blank line as a place holder and come back to it later.
- Using general words that need specificity – circle words that aren't precise enough and revisit during revisioning.
- Spelling – underline words that may be misspelled and need to be edited.

5. Independent Student Writing – Envisioning and Composing

(a) Students gather their prearting and prewriting to reread, highlighting or circling important ideas and information to include in their new composition.

(b) Students select a mentor text to use as a model and choose at least one new writing craft element they would like to try out.

(c) Students begin to compose. Students write until they feel they have gone as far as they can and have a completed first draft.

6. Writing Teacher Demonstration – Revisioning

(a) Demonstrate revisioning your first draft in front of the class. Begin by explaining that you feel your first draft is finished because you have taken the piece as far as you can and are ready for feedback from others. Explain that your draft includes most of the ideas and writing techniques envisioned. If an idea or writing technique was abandoned, explain why you changed your mind and made the decision not to include it.

(b) Read your piece aloud to the class, indicate the parts of the piece you like with a star and point out some of the things you are not quite happy with. For example, "I think I may be missing information here" or "I think I need to go back and clarify this by including more details." Demonstrate how to go back into the piece to add words or information using a caret; a single line strikethrough or proofreading squiggle symbol to delete unnecessary information; or arrows to indicate where a word, sentence, or paragraph will be moved. During revisioning, although many changes are made, emphasize that there should be no erasing because it is a work in progress. It is helpful when changes remain visible. This allows the writer to return to previous threads of thought as the writing is viewed as a working draft. In this stage of the process, the focus is on fine-tuning ideas through considerations such as those below.

- Organization: Do ideas flow, one to the next, or do some need to be reordered? Use arrows to indicate where sentences and paragraphs need to be moved.
- Word choice: Is this word specific enough to convey the meaning I want the reader to understand or is there a better word? Use a single line strikethrough or proofreading squiggle symbol to indicate deleting a word and a caret to insert the preferred word.
- Adding information: Is there something missing that needs to be added? Use a caret to indicate additional information.

- Deleting information: Is the information unnecessary, that is, can you conclude that it doesn't contribute to moving the ideas or story forward? Use a single line strikethrough or proofreading squiggle symbol to indicate a deletion.
- Clarifying information: Is this confusing to the reader and do I need to explain or include more details? Use a single line strikethrough or proofreading squiggle symbol to indicate a deletion and a caret to insert the rewritten phrase or sentence.

7. **Independent Student Writing – Revisioning**
    (a) Students review their pieces, starring the parts they are pleased with and circling the parts they would like to continue to work on during revisioning.
    (b) Students engage in informal sharing with writing partners or small groups to allow the writers an opportunity to read their pieces aloud to hear how they sound. If some students are not finished with the first draft, have them share whatever they have completed or feel ready to share. If students are accustomed to providing positive feedback and asking clarifying questions, then peer feedback/conferring may be included as part of the sharing. If students are not accustomed to providing feedback, this is an opportunity to teach them the skill of conferring as a "critical friend" or as a part of a writing group.
    (c) Students revision their pieces. Confer with those students who are finished with their independent revisioning in small groups or one-to-one.

8. **Share – Revisioning**
    Select several students to share their revisioning work with the class as models.

9. **Writing Teacher Demonstration – Editing**
    To demonstrate how a writer intentionally uses punctuation to assist a reader in reading and comprehending a text, read your piece aloud. By hearing a piece read aloud, students develop a sense of how punctuation assists a reader in understanding a text, and also how lack of punctuation makes reading more challenging and misplaced punctuation can cause confusion. Demonstrate grade-level appropriate grammar and punctuation corrections you expect your students to be able to make independently. Or work with one student as the rest of the class observes and assists in editing the student's piece. Check if the student is comfortable sharing her/his work with the class. Assure that the environment is a safe one where the student's work will be honored and seen as a contribution to the group's learning and where the child will not be embarrassed.

10. **Independent Student Writing – Editing**
    Students edit their pieces for appropriate grammar and punctuation.

11. **Sharing**
    Students share their final pieces.

12. **Assessment**
    (This assessment is summative and performance-based on the written product.)
    Analyze student writing pieces for application of the following:
    - Writer's craft elements from mentor texts in "Where I'm From" piece.
    - Poetic text structure and selected writer's craft elements in their writing piece.
    - Capturing the significance of one's place, family, culture, and/or identity.

LESSON 5: PORTRAITURE

Arting and Writing Come Together

(10–14 class periods)

OVERVIEW

We are a reflection of those who have come before us. Cultural heritage, relations, and personal identity are reflected upon, internalized, and realized through creating one's own image, a self-portrait.

There are a wide variety of self-portrait possibilities, ranging from full-body portraits to the more common portrait bust. This lesson focuses on students creating their own self-portrait to sit alongside their written piece(s). They will observe their physical features in a mirror and draw themselves. They will then create a background scene, a significant place, as a context for their portrait to inhabit.

OBJECTIVES

- Create a self-portrait.
- Place significant objects in relationship to foreground, middle ground, and background within the composition.
- Create a background scene of a significant place. For example, Samantha loves to surf and creates an ocean background including waves, surfers, and a sun. Kawika's favorite place is next to his grandpa on the porch steps learning to play chords on his *'ukulele*, so he draws the front porch steps of Grandpa's house and an *'ukulele*.

MATERIALS

- A variety of self-portraits (exemplars); images can be found online as Google Images at http://bit.ly/1BS1Tzs.
- Drawing pencils (4b–6b recommended because b-type drawing pencils are softer and create a darker line).
- 2–3 sheets of drawing paper (12" × 18") per student.
- Small upright mirror for each student.
- Magic rub erasers.
- Blending sticks, or tissues or paper towels, for smudging and blending graphite.
- Oil pastels, color pencils, watercolor sets (preferably Prang brand because of the quality of both brush and paint).
- Scratch paper for experimenting.

Figure 11.22. This 3rd grader from Koko Head Elementary School on Oʻahu shares her portrait drawn before instruction, right side, and her final portrait after instruction and practice, left side.

LESSON PROCEDURES

Part 1: Portrait

1. **Creating Connections**
   Share/display a variety of self-portraits by master artists and other students. Ask students to reflect on what they notice about the portraits and create a working definition of self-portrait. Analyze the similarities and differences in the self-portraits. Although there are a wide variety of self-portrait styles, this lesson focuses on the more common portrait bust. If working with older students, you may want to give them a choice of portrait type.
   (a) Fold the 12" × 18" sheet of drawing paper in half like a book.
   (b) Demonstrate drawing your self-portrait, what you think you look like on the cover. No mirrors or phones are allowed! This is just practice.
   (c) Students draw themselves, what they think they look like, on their covers. 20 minutes is usually sufficient time, less with the younger students. (see Figure 11.22.)
   (d) Students share with a partner about the experience of drawing themselves.

2. **Prearting Teacher Demonstration**
   Think of this prearting exercise as practice, similar to practicing letter formation in handwriting.
   (a) On the left inside page of the spread, draw two intersecting lines dividing the half sheet into four equal rectangles (see Figure 11.23). Explain to the students that they are going to observe their facial features in a mirror and

practice drawing what they observe. Verbalize the observations you are making of your own facial features (head shape, eyes, nose, mouth, and other features).

(b) Demonstrate drawing each feature several times, one feature per quadrant: (1) head shapes: circle, oval, almond; (2) eyes: include eyelids, eyebrows, eyelashes, pupil, and iris; (3) nose: include bridge and nostrils; (4) mouth: include the upper and lower lip. Think of this visual exercise as practice, similar to practicing letter formation in handwriting.

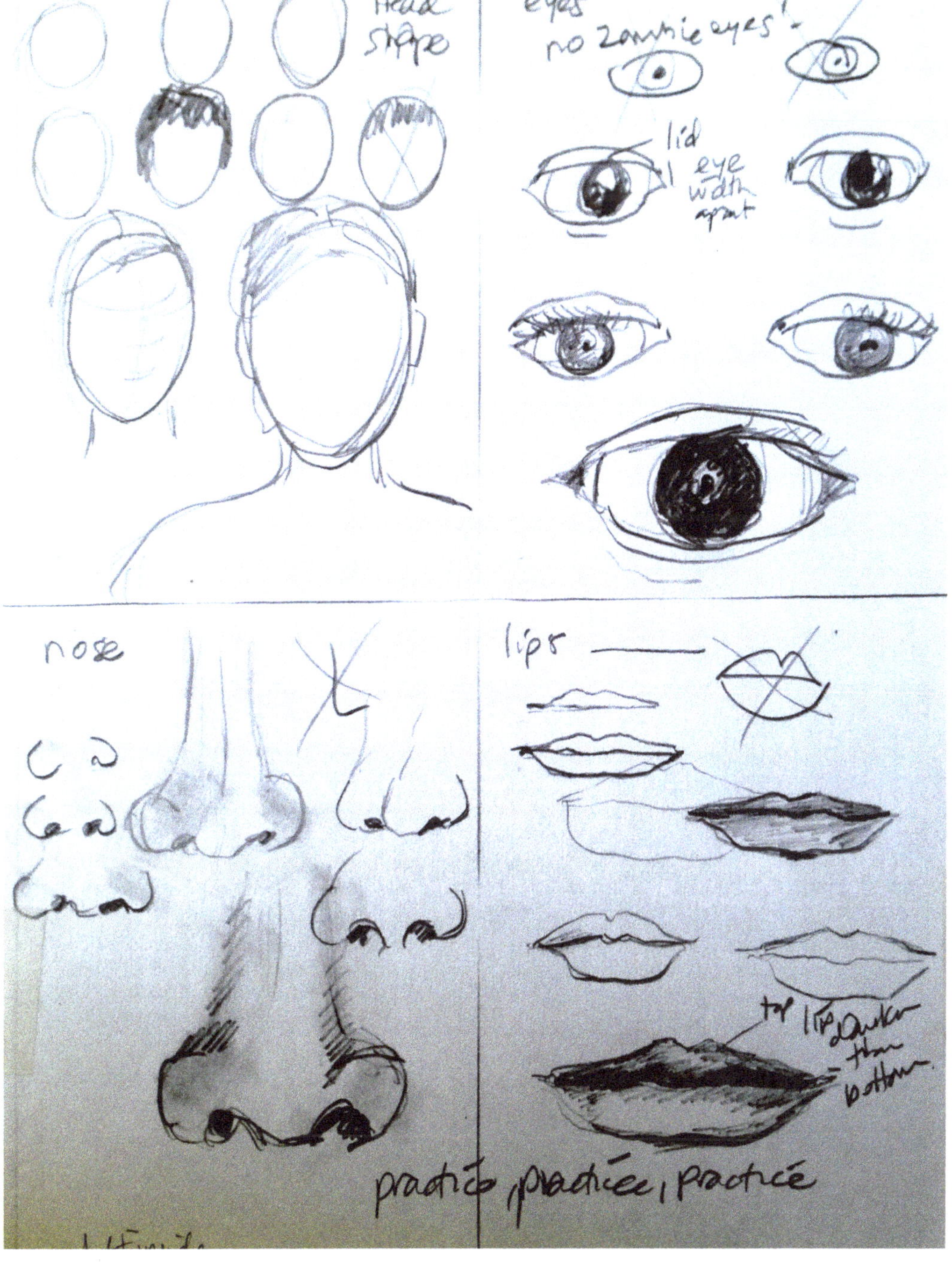

Figure 11.23. Students practice drawing their facial features using a mirror.

3. **Independent Student Prearting**

   (a) Students work on the left inside page of the spread, and draw two intersecting lines dividing the half sheet into four equal rectangles (teachers may want to do this for the youngest students).

   (b) Students study the details of the facial features of their peers and draw practice sketches of each feature within a quadrant (20 minutes of practice should be sufficient): (1) head shapes: circle, oval, almond; (2) eyes: include eyelids, eyebrows, eyelashes, pupil, and iris; (3) nose: include bridge and nostrils; (4) mouth: include the upper and lower lips.

4. **Arting Teacher Demonstration – Envisioning and Composing**

   On right inside page of the spread, demonstrate studying your own facial features in a mirror and drawing your self-portrait. Don't be afraid to give it a go! Feel free to use an eraser to make corrections as needed. This is a draft; therefore, pencil marks left on the paper after erasures are fine and expected at this point in the process.

   (a) Begin by lightly marking in the head shape. Bring attention to the chin area. One's chin must be thinner, similar to the narrow part of an egg. Add neck and shoulders. Mark in facial features to get an overall sense of composition and placement.

   > Marking, in art, has to do with drawing lightly in order to establish the beginning of a composition. There is a tentative nature to this part of composing. It is like rehearsing steps of a dance or practicing notes on a musical instrument.

   (b) Outline features with attention to scale, proportion, and placement (see Figure 11.24).

   > Eyes should be placed halfway down the face from the top of the head; nose should be approximately halfway between eyes and chin. Mouth is roughly halfway between nose and chin. Eyes are an eye width apart. Don't forget the eyebrows. Ears should be placed on side of head between eyes and mouth. Include neck and shoulders. Pay attention to proportion when drawing the neck (see Figure 11.24). Children tend to draw skinny bird-like necks and want to include their entire body, in miniature, as part of the portrait.

   (c) Add details and appropriate shading: iris and pupils of eyes, nostrils, lips, hair quality (wavy, curly, thick, coarse) and shade of hair, and skin coloring.

   > Darker brown eyes should be shaded more darkly than blue eyes. Shade in nostrils and lip color. Capture the quality and character of hair by following the directionality of the hair strands. Shading skin color to match complexion is important to bring authenticity to the work.

Figure 11.24. This is an example of a self-portrait in process.

5. **Independent Student Arting – Envisioning and Composing**
   (a) Students work independently on right inside page of the spread to draw their own portraits using mirrors. Circulate among the students to offer encouragement, model technique, and give feedback. Always ask permission if you would like to demonstrate further or make corrections directly on a child's work.
   (b) Upon completion of the first draft of the self-portrait, students dialogue in pairs and/or small groups to self-assess their own drawings, sharing one or two things that they like or are proud of in their self-portrait and also what they would like to improve on in their next practice draft. As in writing, students also complete more than one draft in arting.
   (c) Students complete their final draft portrait on the back cover (see Figure 11.25).

6. **Informal Exhibition**
   Create a portrait gallery by placing the self-portraits on student desk tops. Open up the 12" × 18" sheet of drawing paper so that each student's initial drawing (without the mirror) and second draft sit side-by-side, allowing students to notice improvements in likeness and the specificity of detail in the second drawing (see Figure 11.22). Viewing each other's work for inspiration and ideas will offer them the opportunity to give constructive feedback on what they noticed in each other's work.

Figure 11.25. This is a completed self-portrait done in pencil.

7. **Reflection**

Have students share informally about creating their portrait, what they learned from viewing the work of others, and the next steps for revisioning for their final portrait.

Part 2: Background Scene

The final portrait piece will successfully integrate the self-portrait within the context of a background scene or significant place from the "Defining Me" mini notebook. This background scene may also incorporate culturally significant elements from the third spread of the "Defining Me" mini notebook. The finished portrait should present a visually compelling story such as Samantha loves to surf and creates an ocean background including waves, surfers, and a sun; Kawika's favorite place is next to his grandpa on the porch steps learning to play chords on his *'ukulele*, and so he draws the front porch steps of Grandpa's house and an *'ukulele*.

1. **Creating Connections**

Students share with a partner or in small groups the second spread of their "Defining Me" mini notebook from Lesson 2, about the place they chose as their home. Some students may decide to choose a different place as a context for their portrait. If so, we recommend showing various scapes (land, sea, sky, urban) from master artists as examples to inspire students to begin to think of their background drawings in storied ways.

2. **Prearting Teacher Demonstration**

Using ideas from your "Defining Me" mini notebook, demonstrate thumbnail sketching (remember that these are small sketches done quickly) of geographical features, landmarks, time of day, and/or weather conditions of your chosen place. In addition, consider incorporating things that are culturally important and represent you, your family, and/or your culture from the third spread of the "Defining Me" mini notebook of Lesson 2 (see Figure 11.26). Cultural examples might include the basket woven by aunty; a fishing spear or hunting bow; reindeer for the Sámi; corn, beans, and squash for the Iroquois; or *kalo* for Hawaiians.

Figure 11.26. These thumbnail sketches were created using elements from the "Defining Me" mini notebook, with additional ideas being added during the envisioning stage.

3. **Independent Student Prearting**

    Students generate thumbnail sketches of a background scape in their notebooks or practice papers integrating geographical features or landmarks.

4. **Arting Teacher Demonstration – Envisioning**

    On drawing paper, demonstrate creating a working sketch with ideas chosen from your thumbnail sketches. Think aloud as you demonstrate selecting various elements and/or objects from your thumbnail sketches to provide direction and a theme for the final background composition. The scale of those objects in relationship to foreground, middleground, background, and placement of those objects should also be considered (see Figure 11.27).

Figure 11.27. This working sketch of a background scape was created during envisioning after prearting the thumbnail sketches.

5. **Independent Student Arting – Envisioning**

    On drawing paper, students create a working sketch, using ideas from the thumbnail sketches.

6. **Arting Teacher Demonstration – Composing a Final Background**

    On 12" × 18" drawing paper oriented either horizontally or vertically, lightly draw in the background. Use arting elements and principles of design – line, color, shape, space, perspective, texture, pattern, movement and rhythm, scale and proportion, emphasis, contrast, balance, and unity (see Appendix D, Elements and Principles of Design) – to develop the overall composition of the piece (see Figure 11.28). Complete the background in full color using one or a combination of the following media: color pencils, watercolor paints, and/or oil pastels.

Figure 11.28. This is an example of a background scape.

7. **Independent Student Arting – Composing a Final Background**
Using 12” × 18” drawing paper, students compose their final background. Students use arting elements and principles of design to develop their overall composition. They may want to experiment beforehand on their working sketch, using one or a combination of media (color pencils, watercolor paints, and/or oil pastels) to try out and then complete the background in full color.

Part 3: Bringing Portrait and Place Together

1. **Final Composition**
   (a) Students cut out their portrait. If students want to add adornment to their portrait (e.g. hat, goggles, necklace), they should complete the adornment before cutting out the portrait.
   (b) The students position their portrait onto the background, experimenting with placement on the page.
   (c) The portrait is then glued onto background to complete the piece.

2. *Hō‘ike*: **Exhibiting and Publishing**
The student places the final 12” × 18” background with portrait and writing piece(s) onto a larger colored poster board as a frame for the final arting and writing work.

Figure 11.29. This artist added goggles and a snorkel to her self-portrait because she will be swimming in her background scape, the ocean.

Figure 11.30 This is an example of a completed self-portrait on background scape.

Figure 11.31 A portrait and poem, about her last name, created by a 6th grader.

<u>Ae'a</u>
By Kayce Ae'a

What is my name?
Kayce Aiko Puanani Ae'a
It is my deep desired soul that speaks out
It is my heart
The stone that is the foundation of my 'ohana …
Kayce Aiko Puanani Ae'a.
These different names have meaning
One is so very special and unique
Ae'a.
The foundation on which my family is built
The one name my whole family shares
Ae'a, the flowing waters
I see a waterfall constantly moving
So peaceful and alive
It stays strong.
Just like my family
My foundation
My love
My family's name
Ae'a.

Figure 11.32 A 6th grader writes a narrative about her last name and family members to sit beside her self-portrait.

Aluli, My Last Name

Aloha, my name is Puali'imaikalani Brook Aluli, but I usually go by Maikalani. My last name, Aluli, is special to me and is a big part of my life. Almost all of my family that lives here on O'ahu are Alulis and we are all very close. This name is known throughout the Hawaiian Islands. My grandma, Irmgard, is a famous musician and composer. She has composed over 300 songs. She has just recently been recognized for being the first living legend to be included in the Hawaiian Hall of Fame. Music runs in the family and everyone has beautiful voices and talents in playing instruments. My brothers and cousins have just started to play in a band together and they want to become popular.

My Uncle, Emmet Aluli, is known for being a doctor on the island of Molokai. He also participates in the Protect Kaho'olawe 'Ohana, a group that helps to save the land.

Aluli, this name really has special meaning for me and it makes me proud to be in this family. I hope it stays this way forever.

I AM PROUD TO BE HAWAIIAN!

Figure 11.33 In this poem displayed next to his self-portrait, a 6th grader tells about his Hawaiian names.

My Hawaiian Name
By Keahemakaniokalaniku Nuʻuhiwa

My Hawaiian name is Keahemakaniokalaniku
It's also my first name
It means softly blowing wind of Kalaniku
It was given to me by my mom and dad
Kalaniku is part of my dad's name.

My second Hawaiian name is Nuʻuhiwa
It is also my last name
Like in the stories of Lono Nuʻuhiwa who ruled Molokai
But never had a son.
So he declared that the boy that's born
With an eel mark on his body will be the next ruler
And a baby was born with an eel mark.

I like my Hawaiian names
They are important to me
I'm Hawaiian
Keahemakaniokalaniku Nuʻuhiwa.

POSSIBLE PORTRAIT VARIATIONS

Instead of completing a traditional self-portrait as in the preceding lessons, portrait variations – such as those given below – are a fun option.

Figure 11.34 Portraits can be created in a variety of forms. In this example, a high school student contemplates his ethnic identity.

Figure 11.35 In this portrait variation, a kindergartener imagines interests she will have as a grown-up.

1. **Heart Map and Recipe of Me**

    Arting: Heart Map
    Students create a "Map of My Heart"
    Resource*: My Map Book* by Sara Fanelli (Fanelli, 1995).
    Students create a shape for their heart, as in Figures 2.12 and 11.36; or, following a study of the heart, students create an anatomically correct drawing of their heart, as in Figures 11.37 and 11.38. All of the things they love are located inside their heart: family, pets, things they like to do. Things they dislike or are afraid of are located outside their heart.

    Writing: Recipe of Me / I Love ... Poetry
    Students study recipes as a genre – the purpose, elements, and types of words used in a recipe – to create their own whimsical "Recipe of Me" (see Figures 2.12 and 11.36). Or students research the heart to create anatomically accurate drawings and write poems about the people, places, and things closest to them (see Figures 11.37 and 11.38).

Figure 11.36. This heart map and "Recipe of My Heart" was created by a 3rd grader following a genre study on recipes.

Translation:

Recipe of my Heart
By Kalau Marasco-Ayau

Ingredients (clockwise): 5,000 gallons of Molokai (the island his family is from); 4 cups of sunshine; 80 cups of the ocean; 20 gallons of alertness; 5 cups of the volcano; 200 cups of my family guardians.

Directions: 1) Get a bowl and put in the alertness with 1 cup of family guardians and mix well. 2) Combine Molokai with the ocean and mix until smooth. 3) Pour the dough into a baking dish and bake in the oven at 450 degrees. 4) When ready, spread the sun with the volcano to make it more delicious. The result is a happy heart second to none.

Figure 11.37. This heart map drawing was created by a 2nd grader as part of an interdisciplinary unit of study on the heart.

Translation:

I Love …
By Makaliʻi West

I love Bunny
Because she is super cute
She has lots of fur
And she is a playmate for me
I give her food and water

My brother and my friends
play dodgeball

We're good
And it's fun

I really love to surf
Because when I surf
it calms my *naʻau*

I love my dog Boomer
Because he is cute
And very furry

Figure 11.38. This heart map and poem shows and explains things this second grader loves.

Translation:

I Have Love
By Hiʻiaka Foster

I have so much love for
my great grandpa.
He's a wrestler.
He won all his rounds.

I love playing softball.
It's a game that's close to my family.
My dad helps me in softball.

I love cooking
with Kuʻuipo, my older sister.
One day we made
dessert. It was so much fun.
I want to do it again.

My family is very important to me.
I love my family a lot.
I have no other needs.

I love my dog.
Ruby is very important to me,
She's my dog.

2. The Future Me

Arting: Life-Size Portrait of Future Me

Students create a life-size portrait of themselves by lying down on a large sheet of paper and having a friend trace around their body. They craft their visual story by drawing/painting clothing and objects to represent their future occupation or who they will become (e.g. a future fireman could include a helmet, jacket, boots, and a fire hose; an astronaut might include a spacesuit, helmet, radio transponder, and jet propulsion tanks).

Writing: Recipe of Future Me

Students study recipes as a genre – the purpose, elements, and types of words used in a recipe – to create their own recipes of what it will take for them to become their future selves.

Figure 11.39. In his-life size portrait, this student envisions himself as a clown when he grows up because he wants to make people laugh. The "Recipe of Future Me" is written in large lettering as a background.

Figure 11.40. In his life-size portrait, this artist–writer portrays himself as an artist because he loves to draw.

3. My Personal Constellation

Arting: Mapping My Personal Constellation
On a large map of the world, students mark the places their ancestors are from. (If ancestors are from a single country, state, or city, a map of that country, state, or city can be enlarged to locate the various places). Then, ledger-sized tracing paper is used to mark dots of these places, creating a dot matrix drawing similar to a dot-to-dot drawing or star constellation (see Figure 11.41). Students use the dot matrix to envision a personal constellation, an object that symbolizes an important aspect of their cultural identity or family background. For example, a child might see a *'ukulele* in the dot matrix that represents her/his family's musical traditions. Another child may see a dragon in the dot matrix as a way to represent her/his Chinese heritage. The dot matrix can be compared to the constellations people on Earth see as pictures in the sky. The final constellation is placed into its context, the sky, as part of the final arting composition (see Figures 11.42 and 11.43).

Writing: Where I'm From (see Lesson 4)
Students use their constellation image as a springboard for creating a "Where I'm From" writing piece that explains the significance of the drawing to their family and to their own personal and cultural identity.

Figure 11.41. This is an example of a dot matrix drawing. The larger stars on the drawing indicate where this student's parents are from. He imagined the stars as the backbone of a lizard and formed his constellation to show this shape.

Figure 11.42. This student imagines himself as a benevolent dragon.

Figure 11.43. The *'āweoweo*, or "Hawaiian Bigeye" fish, symbolizes this student's connection to the ocean.

4. **Cultural Collage**

Arting: My Cultural Identity

This arting and writing project follows Lesson 2: Defining Me (completion of Lesson 1 first is not necessary). From their "Defining Me" mini notebooks, students choose 1–2 objects from each spread as a part of this collage. They are to compose a draft integrating at least 3 of the most important aspects of their identity into a collage drawing, creating a monochromatic piece using one color with black and white. They can then use the same color pencil and watercolor paint, considering the transparent and opaque qualities of color.

Writing: Incorporating Text with Image

Students compose short statements, poems, or descriptions of the objects, explaining the importance or significance of each. During composing, students write directly onto the paper, integrating the text into the collage and adding to the visual story. Trace over the penciled writing with a fine marker so that the writing is darker, more visible, and easier to read.

Figure 11.44. This 3rd grader uses her arting to direct and inspire her writing. On this draft, she envisions how her writing will be placed onto her final arting piece as she composes.

Figure 11.45. A 5th grader uses his working composition to compose his final arting and writing piece. The objects represent aspects of himself and his cultures.

Nānā i ke kumu.
Look to the source.

References

Ada, Alma Flor (1993) *My Name is Maria Isabel*. New York: Atheneum Books.

Ada, Alma Flor (1994) *Where the Flame Trees Bloom*. New York: Atheneum Books.

Ada, Alma Flor (2002) *I Love Saturdays y Domingos*. New York: Atheneum Books.

Arnheim, Rudolf (1969) *Visual Thinking*. Berkeley: University of California Press.

Balaz, Joseph B. (ed.) (1989) *Hoʻomānoa: An Anthropology of Contemporary Hawaiian Literature*. Honolulu: Ku Paʻa.

Bamboo Ridge Press and Hawaiʻi Public Radio (2010) Aloha shorts. http://www.bambooridge.com/episode.aspx?eid=71 and http://www.bambooridge.com/episode.aspx?eid=63

Barnes, Douglas and Shemilt, Denis (1974) Transmission and interpretation. *Educational Review* 26(3): 213–228. https://doi.org/10.1080/0013191740260305

Benham, Maenette K. P. and Heck, Ronald H. (1998) *Culture and Educational Policy in Hawaiʻi: The Silencing of Native Voices*. Mahwah, New Jersey: Lawrence Erlbaum.

Banyai, Istvan (1995) *ZOOM*. New York: Penguin.

Burgess, Puanani (1989) Choosing my name. In Balaz (1989: 40–41) and Chock *et al*. (1998: 278). Audio versions available at http://apiwomenfaithaction.blogspot.com/2010/10/puanani-burgess.html (Lee, 2010) and at http://www.bambooridge.com/edpisode.aspx?eid=63

Calkins, Lucy and Harwayne, Shelley (1990) *Living Between the Lines*. Portsmouth, New Hampshire: Heinemann.

Caruana, Wally (2003) *Aboriginal Art*. London: Thames & Hudson.

Chock, Eric, Harstad, James, Lum, Darrell and Teter, Bill (eds.) (1998) *Growing Up Local: An Anthology of Poetry and Prose from Hawaiʻi*. Honolulu: Bamboo Ridge Press.

Choi, Yangsook (2003) *The Name Jar*. New York: Random House Children's Books.

Chun, Malcolm Nāea (2011) *No Nā Mamo*. Honolulu: Curriculum Research and Development Group, College of Education, University of Hawaiʻi, and University of Hawaiʻi Press.

Cisneros, Sandra (1984) My name. In *The House on Mango Street* 10–11. New York: Vintage Books. Available online at http://theliterarylink.com/mangostreet.html. Video of the author reading the text is available at https://vimeo.com/105508553

Common Core State Standards Initiative (2010) *Read the Standards*. National Governors Association Center for Best Practices & Council of Chief State School Officers. Washington D.C.: Authors. http://www.corestandards.org/read-the-standards/

Csikszentmihalyi, Mihaly (1990) *The Psychology of Optimal Experience*. New York: Harper and Row.

Demmert, William and Towner, J. C. (2003) *A Review of the Research Literature on the Influences of Culturally Based Education on the Academic Performance of Native American Students*. Educational Resources Information Center (ERIC), U.S. Department of Education. Portland, Oregon: Northwest Regional Educational Laboratory.

Eisner, Elliot W. (2002) What can education learn from the arts about the practice of education? *The Encyclopedia of Informal Education*. http://www.infed.org/biblio/eisner_arts_and_the_practice_of_education.htm

Fanelli, Sara (1995) *My Map Book*. London: ABC, All Books for Children.

Fletcher, Ralph (1996) *A Writer's Notebook: Unlocking the Writer within You*. New York: Harper Collins.

Fletcher, Ralph (2011) *Mentor Author, Mentor Texts*. Portsmouth, New Hampshire: Heinemann.

Fosberry, Jennifer (2010) *My Name is Not Isabella: Just How Big Can a Little Girl Dream?* (illus. Mike Litwin). Naperville, Illinois: Sourcebooks, Inc.

Fosberry, Jennifer (2011) *My Name is Not Alexander* (illus. Mike Litwin). Naperville, Illinois: Sourcebooks, Inc.

Freire, Paulo (1970) *Pedagogy of the Oppressed*. New York: Continuum.

Fullan, Michael (2001) *Leading in a Culture of Change*. San Francisco: Jossey-Bass.

Fuller, Buckminster R. with E. J. Applewhite (1975) *Synergetics: Explorations in the Geometry of Thinking*. New York: Macmillan.

Fuller, Buckminster R. with E. J. Applewhite (1979) *Synergetics 2: Further Explorations in the Geometry of Thinking*. New York: Macmillan.

Gay, Geneva (2010) *Culturally Responsive Teaching: Theory, Research, and Practice* (2nd edition). New York: Teachers College Press.

Genealogical Tree of The Queen and Her Descendants. http://www.americanancestors.info/wp-content/uploads/2010/11/victoria_family_tree_1901.jpg

González, Norma, Moll, Luis C. and Amanti, Cathy (2005) *Funds of Knowledge: Theorizing Practices in Households, Communities, and Classrooms*. Mahwah, New Jersey: Lawrence Erlbaum.

Google Images: Self portrait. http://bit.ly/1BS1Tzs

Graves, Donald (1983) *Writing: Teachers and Children at Work*. Portsmouth, New Hampshire: Heinemann.

Henkes, Kevin (1996) *Chrysanthemum*. New York: Harpercollins Children's Books.

Hesse, Karen (1997) *Out of the Dust: A Novel*. New York: Scholastic Press.

James, Van (2001) *Spirit and Art: Pictures of the Transformation of Consciousness*. Great Barrington, Massachusetts: Anthroposophic Press.

Kana'iaupuni, Shawn, Ledward, Brandon, and Jensen, Umi (2010) *Culture-Based Education and Its Relationship to Student Outcomes*. Honolulu: Kamehameha Schools Research & Evaluation.

Kawai'ae'a, Kekauleleanae'ole (2010) *Kohala Kuamo'o: Nae'ole's Race to Save a King*. Honolulu: Kamehameha Publishing.

Ke Aloha Aina (1912, July 27). http://www.nupepa.org

Ke Kula 'O Samuel M. Kamakau (2008) *He Ka'ao no Hauwahine lāua 'o Meheanu: A Bilingual Tale of Hauwahine and Meheanu*. Honolulu: Kamehameha Publishing.

Kahanu, Diane (1998) When I was young on an island. In Chock *et al.* (1998: 5–53).

Kent, Corita and Steward, Jan (2008) *Learning by Heart: Teachings to Free the Creative Spirit*. New York: Allworth Press.

Krishnamurti, J. (1969) *Freedom from the Known* (ed. Mary Lutyens). Krishnamurti Foundation Trust Ltd. San Francisco: HarperCollins.

Ladson-Billings, Gloria (2009) *The Dreamkeepers: Successful Teachers of African-American Students*. San Francisco: Jossey-Bass.

Lamott, Anne (1994) *Bird by Bird*. New York: Pantheon Books.

Langcaon, Jeff (2005) *Grandpa's Magic Banyan Tree*. Honolulu: Mutual Publishing.

Lee, Deborah (2010) Interview with Rev. Wako Puanani Burgess. API Women, Faith & Action: Fourteen oral histories of Asian Pacific Islander women and their faith-based activism. http://apiwomenfaithaction.blogspot.com/2010/10/puanani-burgess.html

Leland, Christine and Harste, Jerome (1994) Multiple ways of knowing: Curriculum in a new key. *Language Arts* 71(5): 337–345.

Luke, Rebekah and Meyer, Meleanna Aluli (eds.) (2008) *'Umeke Writings: An Anthology*. Hau'ula: Nā Kamalei Ko'olauloa Early Education Program.

Martin, Bill (1967) *Brown Bear, Brown Bear What Do You See?* New York: Henry Holt.

McGilchrist, Iain (2009) *The Master and His Emissary: The Divided Brain and the Making of the Western World*. New Haven and London: Yale University Press.

Meyer, Manulani (2003) *Ho'oulu: Our Time of Becoming*. Honolulu: 'Ai Pohaku Press.

Miller, John P. (2007) *The Holistic Curriculum* (2nd edition). Toronto: University of Toronto Press.

Mower, Nancy Alpert (1984) *I Visit My Tūtū and Grandma*. Kailua, Hawai'i: Press Pacifica.

Mower, Nancy Alpert (1988) *My Tūtū Kāne and Grandpa*. Mililani, Hawai'i: Booklines Hawaii.

Murray, Donald (1990) *Shoptalk: Learning to Write with Writers*. Portsmouth, New Hampshire: Boynton/Cook.

Murray, Donald (1996) *Crafting a Life in Essay, Story, Poem*. Portsmouth, New Hampshire: Boynton/Cook.

Nogelmeir, Puakea (2010) *Mai Pa'a I Ka Leo: Historical Voices in Hawaiian Primary Materials*. Honolulu: University of Hawai'i Press.

Peterson, Ralph and Eeds, Maryann (1990) *Grand Conversations: Literature Groups in Action*. Broadway, New York: Scholastic.

Powell, Kimberly (2014) Family History – *Fifty Questions for Family History Interviews: What to Ask the Relatives*. http://genealogy.about.com/cs/oralhistory/a/interview.htm

Pukui, Mary Kawena (1983) *'Ōlelo No'eau: Hawaiian Proverbs & Poetical Sayings*. Honolulu: Bishop Museum Press.

Ray, Katie Wood (2006) *Study Driven: A Framework for Planning Units of Study in the Writing Workshop*. Portsmouth, New Hampshire: Heinemann.

Recorvits, Helen (2003) *My Name is Yoon* (illus. Gabi Swiatkowska). New York: Frances Foster Books.

Republic of Hawai'i (1896) *Laws of the Republic of Hawai'i Passed by the Legislative Assembly, Special Session 1895*, Section 30 of *Act 57*, Honolulu: Robert Grieve, Steam Book and Job Printer.

Rockstrom, Johan (2010, July) Let the Environment Guide Our Development. Presented at the T.E.D. Global conference, Oxford, U.K. http://www.ted.com/talks/lang/eng/johan_rockstrom_let_the_environment_guide_our_development.html

Rosenblatt, Louise (1978) *The Reader, the Text, and the Poem: The Transactional Theory of the Literary Work*. Carbondale: Southern Illinois University Press.

Rylant, Cynthia (1982) *When I Was Young in the Mountains*. New York: E. P. Dutton.

Rylant, Cynthia (1985) *The Relatives Came*. New York: Scholastic.

Say, Allen (1993) *Grandfather's Journey*. Boston: Houghton Mifflin.

Siegel, Marjorie (1995) More than words: The generative power of transmediation for learning. *Canadian Journal of Education* 20(4): 455–475. https://doi.org/10.2307/1495082

Short, Kathy and Pierce, Kathryn M. (1990) *Talking about Books: Creating Literate Communities*. Portsmouth, New Hampshire: Heinemann.

Spandel, Vicki (2011) *Creating Young Writers: Using the Six Traits to Enrich Writing Process in Primary Classrooms* (3rd edition). Boston: Pearson.

Spivak, Gayatri C. (1988) Can the subaltern speak? In Cary Nelson and Lawrence Grosserg (eds.) *Marxism and the Interpretation of Culture* 271–316. Basingstoke, U.K.: Macmillan Education. https://doi.org/10.1007/978-1-349-19059-1_20

Standing Bear, Luther (2006) *Land of the Spotted Eagle* (new edition). Lincoln: University of Nebraska Press.

Swink, Floyd and Wilhelm, Gerould (1994) *Plants of the Chicago region* (4th edition). Indianapolis: Indiana Academy of Science.

Tangaro, Taupuri (2009) *Lele Kawa: Fire Rituals of Pele*. Honolulu: Kamehameha Schools Press.

Taylor, Sheryl V. and Sobel, Donna M. (2011) *Culturally Responsive Pedagogy: Teaching like Our Students' Lives Matter*. Leiden and Boston: Brill. https://doi.org/10.1163/9781780520315

Vygotsky, Lev S. (1978) *Mind in Society: The Development of Higher Psychological Processes* (eds. Michael Cole, Vera John-Steiner, Sylvia Scribner, and Ellen Souberman). Cambridge, Massachusetts: Harvard University Press.

Webster's New World College Dictionary (4th edition) (1999). New York: Macmillan.

Wong, Janet, S. (2000) *The Trip Back Home*. San Diego: Harcourt.

Appendix A

Cultures: Home, Host/Indigenous, Local, Global

The word "culture" derives from Latin, *cultus*, meaning to care, cultivate, to till: see cycle. (*Webster's New World College Dictionary*, 1999)

Home Culture

Home is a place of familial and ancestral relationships, sometimes a blending of multiple cultural influences. Here, identity is formed and shaped. This circle of caring relationships includes: mother, father, grandparents, sisters, brothers, cousins, aunties, uncles, and *hanai* (extended) family members. Home culture sets an emotional and psychological barometer for relationships beyond home long before children arrive at the doorway of a classroom. Home culture supports the assertion that children come to school enabled and affirmed by their cultural identity. Home culture answers the questions: What is my genealogy? Who do I belong to? Where do I come from? What are my strengths?

Host/Indigenous Culture

Every geographic locale has a host/indigenous culture: Native Americans of North America, First Nations peoples of Canada, Hawaiians of Hawai'i, Maori of New Zealand, Aboriginals of Australia, etc. Host/indigenous culture is nurtured by an intimate and valued relationship with its particular land, air, and water as kin – as family, not as a commodity. Host culture answers the questions: Who first settled here? How has the land been cared for? What are the names of the significant land forms and waters? What are the stories of this place? It sets into motion a relationship of respect, responsibility, permission, protocol, and sustainable reciprocity to the natural and social resources of that locale.

Local Culture

Local culture is an intersection of communities of diverse and shifting groups of people. It is dynamic, fluid, and malleable, allowing for constellations of interdependent and ever-evolving relationships that make up local culture. It answers the questions: Who are your neighbors? Who do you work with? Who are your school mates? Who do you play with? What clubs, groups, or other social networks do you belong to? Participants in this circle of caring relationships are friends at school, church, workplace, sport activities, clubs, etc. In Hawai'i, as in many other places, there is a local, multiracial, cultural mix that is rich and unique.

Global Culture

Global culture is the largest possible grouping that encompasses everyone as a member of the culture of humanity. It is an ever changing and evolving system of economic, political and social inter- and intra-dependence with one another, orchestrated on the largest cultural scale. "*Isola* earth," the notion of earth as an island, summons us to acknowledge that humankind is indigenous to the planet. It positions humankind as a part of nature, not dominant over it. It admonishes us to recognize that our natural resources are finite and that we have a responsibility to care for the earth as it cares for us. Global culture asks the questions: What is our relationship with the earth and others? How do we sustain a healthy relationship with planet? How do we cultivate a just and equitable society for all?

Appendix B

"Any-Kind": An Explanation

Particularity is quintessential to the artist (and the writer) in accurately representing or capturing the essence of a person, place, or thing. The drawing on the left can be a cloud, a piece of popcorn, a bush, flower, or a mud puddle. It is meant to be a hibiscus flower; however, it lacks details. When one draws what she thinks she knows, without attention to the particularities, it is what we call an "any-kind" drawing. It does not provide the viewer with enough information. The drawing on the right, however, is clearly a hibiscus flower with the particular petal shape and detailed pistil with the stamen and stigma.

The idea of not drawing "any-kind" challenges students to study, do close observation of the actual object, models, video or photographs. It involves capturing details, minutia, colors, textures, patterns, scale, and proportion. A well-crafted piece can move and inspire the viewer to respond to the work.

Appendix C

An Indigenous Color Palette

A western primary palette of blue, red, and yellow differs from an Indigenous palette which uses pigments from natural materials of the earth. Indigenous cultural orientations, whether in dying fibers for weaving, coloring totem images, or painting traditional pottery are inspired by the colors found in nature. Four earth tones seem to prevail: black, white, red and yellow. Black, made from soot, charcoal, or plant pigment; white, made from coral or chalk; red, made from blood, berries, or soil; and yellow, made from turmeric, ochre, or flowers.

The blending of these earth tones also creates a range of color tones from dark to light, transparent to opaque. Browns are made from blending pigments and often worked into the color palette to augment the existing range of colors being used.

Find out more about what the native peoples of your area traditionally used for coloring and decorative applications.

Appendix D

Arting Elements and Principles of Design

Elements and principles of design are the essential tools in a visual artist's tool box. Elements of design are the ABCs or building blocks of a visual artist working from a western orientation. Principles of design build on the elements to create the voice of a visual composition. The list below is not intended to be exhaustive, but these are terms that our artist member, Meleanna, considers foundational to arting.

Elements of Design

Line: Line is the most basic element for a visual artist. Lines are used to create outlines, contours, and shapes. There are many types of lines: straight, wavy, broad, thin, vertical, horizontal, jagged, diagonal, curved, patterned, repetitive, calligraphic, expressive, sharp and precise, blurred and exploratory, gestural. The quality of a line often expresses an artist's emotions; flamboyant and intense, or muted and demure. Mark-making with a line can be multi-directional and begins with a point moving through space and time.

Color: Color is another basic art element. There are all kinds of colors to know about: primary colors (red, yellow, blue); secondary colors (green, purple, orange); and tertiary colors (created when a primary color is blended with a secondary color). Hue refers to the twelve common colors: three primaries, three secondaries, and six tertiaries. Complementary colors appear opposite each other on the color wheel (red and green, yellow and purple, blue and orange). Analogous colors appear adjacent to each other on the color wheel.

Value measures the brightness of a color. Value includes tints, shades, and tones. A tint is a color mixed with white; a shade is a color mixed with black; and a tone is a color mixed with white and black. These categories allow for an infinite range of color possibilities.

Saturation has to do with the purity or intensity of a color. High saturation colors are vibrant; low saturation colors are dull.

Shape: Shapes are created when lines intersect or cross to form an enclosed space. They are two-dimensional, having length and width. Geometric shapes include squares, rectangles, triangles, and circles. Forms are three-dimensional, having length, width, and depth. In three dimensions, squares become cubes, circles become spheres, and triangles become pyramids. Shading two-dimensional shapes adds depth, creating the illusion of a three-dimensional form. A circle becomes a sphere. Details added to a form create a specific object; for example, a sphere becomes a moon (see Chapter 3,

Figure 3.7 and Table 3.1). Organic shapes are those found in nature, and these naturally occurring shapes are less well-defined, such as the shape of a mud puddle, a tree, a flower, a cloud, or a fish.

Space: Space can be defined as the area around, above, below, between, and within an object. Positive space is the area an object occupies; negative space, or ground, is the area surrounding an object.

Perspective: Perspective creates the illusion of depth on a two-dimensional surface (see Figure 11.30). There are several kinds of perspectives: linear, overlapping, aerial and atmospheric. Linear perspective is most common. It includes foreground, realized as the lower third of the picture plane, which appears closest to the viewer; middle ground, the center third of the picture plane; and background, the top third of the picture plane, which appears farthest from the viewer. Overlapping perspective is when one object overlaps another, giving the appearance of dimensional space with one object in front of the other. Aerial perspective is when the artist takes a bird's-eye view and looks down upon a landscape. An atmospheric perspective refers to the use of color and space to create the appearance of depth and distance. Objects in the foreground are more saturated, having greater contrast and detail. Objects in the distance appear paler, less detailed, and less defined or hazier.

Texture: Texture is a valuable element because it engages another sense besides sight – our sense of touch. It describes the tactile quality of a three-dimensional object, how it feels when touched. When drawing or painting, art techniques such as cross-hatching, stippling, and mottling create a tactile sense of texture for the viewer.

Principles of Design
Pattern: Pattern refers to the repetition of an element of design. Patterns assist in creating a kind of visual beat or movement in the work. It focuses attention on a recurring element or elements that can be viewed as regular, irregular, or varied.

Movement and Rhythm: Movement and rhythm create the visual energy of a composition. The way in which the artist uses pattern contributes to the overall movement and rhythm one experiences when viewing a work. The visual look of a piece and how it moves can give a lyrical or discordant quality to a composition. A piece can be static or dynamic, symmetrical or asymmetrical.

Scale and Proportion: Scale refers to the overall size of an object in relation to another. Proportion refers to relative size of an object and has to do with the relationship between the parts and the whole. Proportion gives weight and balance to different parts of a composition, resulting in its overall visual quality and aesthetic impact.

Emphasis: Emphasis refers to the center of attention or the dominance of a particular part of the composition. It draws a viewer to a focal point or place to enter into the work. It also helps guide the viewer through the composition.

Contrast: Contrast utilizes the range between two opposites: light and dark, large and small, soft and hard, young and old. It is the juxtaposition of elements of a given type in different forms: thin and thick lines, organic and inorganic shapes, or light and dark colors. It is a dynamic principle that adds variety to a composition, creating interest, excitement, or tension within the whole.

Point of View (POV): POV is the orientation from which an artist creates and a viewer observes an artwork. Being aware of the multiplicity of points-of-view allows an artist the flexibility to create from a wide range of possible vantage points: upside-down, inside-out, front, rear, top, bottom, or side.

Balance and Unity: Balance and unity refer to the reading of a composition as a whole. The most common ways of creating or viewing balance in a work are through considerations of symmetry or asymmetry. Unity in a composition refers to the coherence of a piece and is achieved through the effective and integrated use of the elements and principles of design. Balance and unity give a work a sense of wholeness and resolution.

Composing: Composing determines what an artist considers important and includes in a work, and how one part relates to another. It focuses on the relationship of figure to ground, emphasis of color and lighting, and depth of field. It establishes the coherence of a work, how it holds together visually and aesthetically. Framing is a technique used when composing that defines the limits of a composition, what gets included and excluded. Framing also considers point of view.

Appendix E

How to make a Mini Notebook

Create a simple mini notebook with any 11 × 17 or 8.5 × 11 sheet of paper. Each mini notebook will have a cover, three spreads and a back cover.

(1) 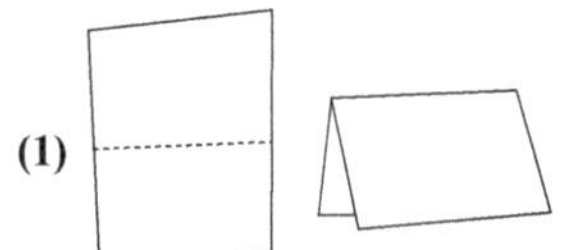

Start by folding a 11" × 17" or 8.5" × 11" sheet of paper in half.

(2) 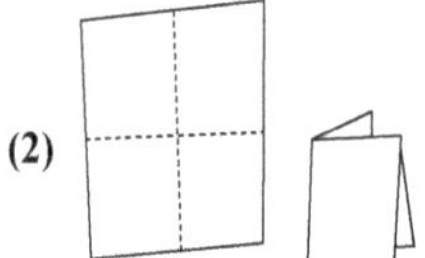

Fold in half again.

(3) 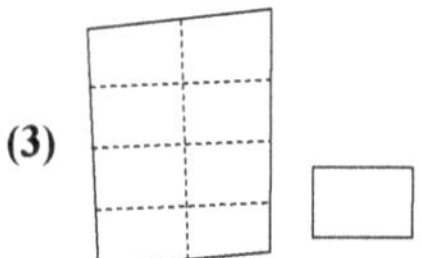

Fold in half again, creating 8 sections.

(4) 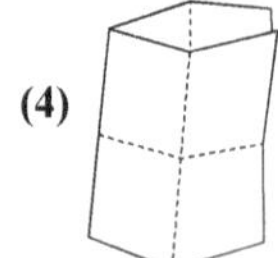

Open up the folded paper and fold in half, width-wise.

(5) 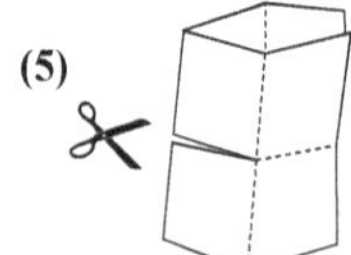

Make a cut or tear perpendicular to the half-fold. Cut only to the first intersecting crease.

(6) 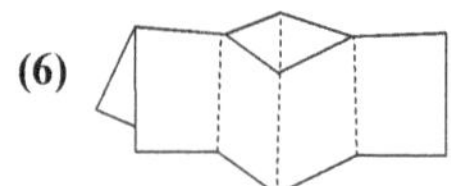

Fold length-wise, leaving the slit open.

(7) 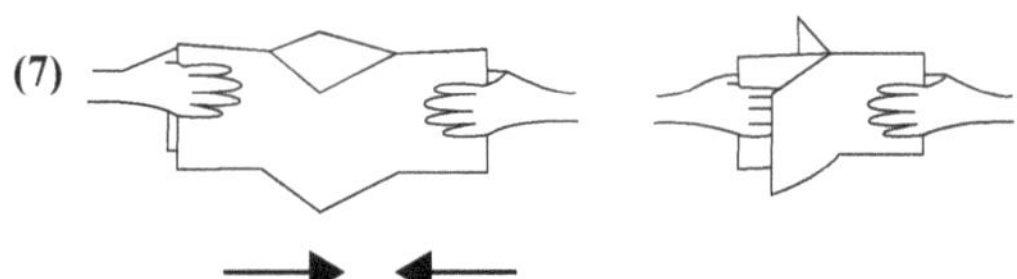

Holding both ends, push towards the center.

(8) 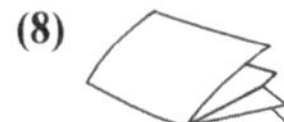

Flatten, crease, and begin drawing in your new mini-notebook.

Appendix F

Sample Letter to Families for the Family Tree and Genealogy Project

Aloha Parents,

Your child will be researching her/his *mo'okū'auhau*, family genealogy, as part of a family tree arting and writing project. Attached is a family research template example and an interview sheet. Please review and complete, as much as possible, the family research template and the interview with your child. If additional information is needed and/or grandparents are available, assist your child in scheduling and conducting the grandparent interviews.

Please provide photographs of the family members listed on your family research template. I will photocopy them to be used for the project and return the originals to you. If photographs are not available, your child will create a drawing of that family member.

Once the family information has been collected, your child will be asked to select and research a tree or plant that has significance to your family, cultural background, or place where your family is from. Your child will be asked to explain the significance of the tree/plant and what it represents to her/him and your family.

Please return the completed family research template and interview sheets by ___________________________. Feel free to write or call if you have any questions.

Mahalo nui,

Kumu ____________________

Appendix G

Genealogy Template

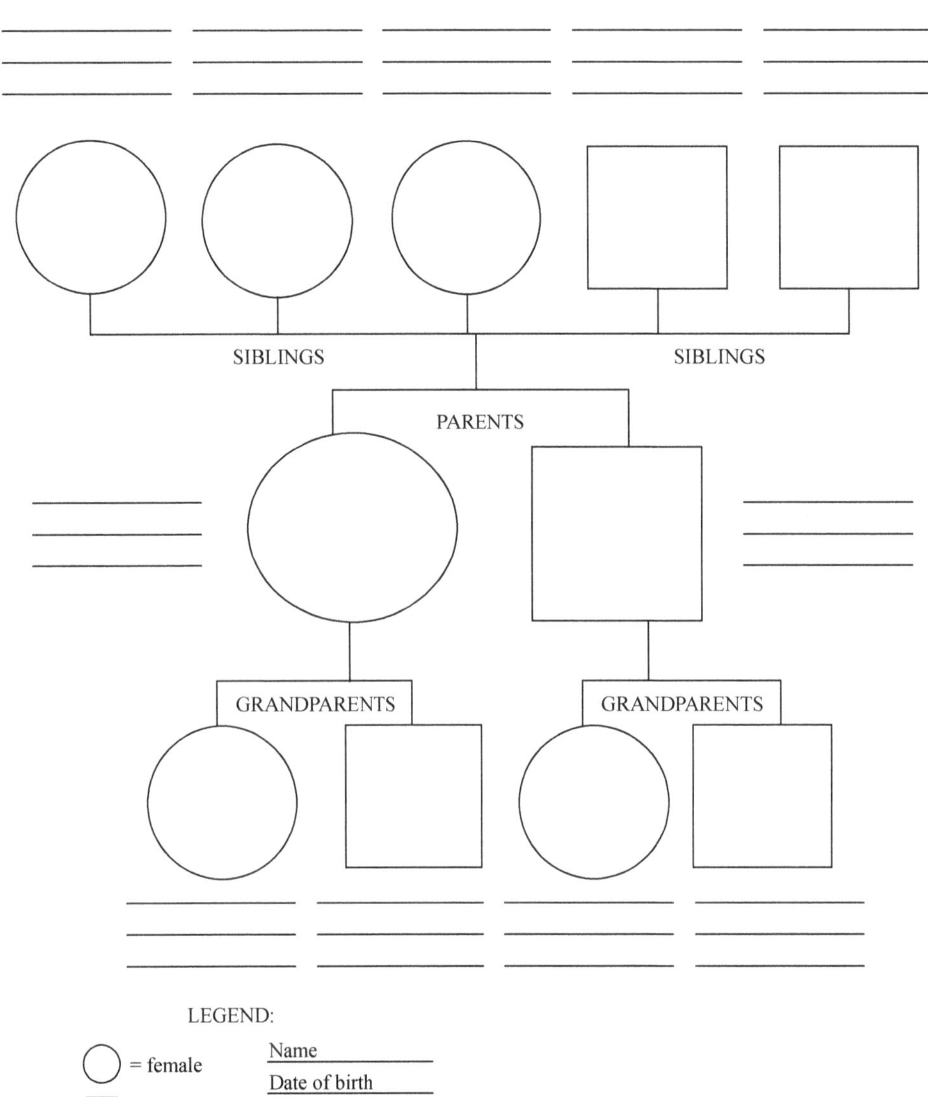

Appendix H

Family History Interview Sheet

Name ____

Family relationship _______________________________________

1) What is your full name? _______________________________

2) How did your parents select this name for you? ______________

____

____

____

____

3) Did you have a nickname? How did you get your nickname?

____

____

____

____

4) When and where were you born? _______________________

____

5) How were holidays (birthdays, Christmas, etc.) celebrated?

____

____

____

____

6) What are some of the family traditions you remember?

7) What are some of the naming traditions in your family, like naming the firstborn son after his paternal grandfather?

8) What are some of the physical characteristics that run in your family?

____

____

____

____

9) What are some family heirlooms or memorabilia that have been passed down in your family?

____

____

____

____

Questions adapted from: Powell, Kimberly (2014) Fifty Questions for Family History Interviews. http://genealogy.about.com/cs/oralhistory/a/interview.htm.

Your Own Additional Questions:

10)

____

____

____

____

11)

____

____

____

12)

13)

14)

15)

Appendix I

My Name Interview Sheet

My full name is ____

1) What is the story of your name? How did your parents or other family members select this name for you?

____

____

____

____

____

____

2) Do you have a nickname? How did you get your nickname?

____

____

____

____

____

____

3) What are some of the naming traditions in your family, like naming the firstborn son after his paternal grandfather?

Questions adapted from: Powell, Kimberly (2014) Fifty Questions for Family History Interviews. http://genealogy.about.com/cs/oralhistory/a/interview.htm.

List of Contributors

The tables on the following pages list all of the contributing organizations and people who participated in our work and have given written permission to use their images, photos, or artwork in this book. We are eternally grateful for their generous participation and contribution.

Contributing Organizations

Name	Person/Place	Figure
Bishop Museum	Blair Collis	5.15
Camp Mokulē'ia, O'ahu Kua Ke Ahu Community Mural	Rev. David Turner	1.2, 4.6
Hau'ula Elementary School	Hawaiian Language Immersion Program	See list of individual contributors
Hau'ula Elementary School	Hau'ula, O'ahu (3rd grade)	6.9
Hawai'i State Foundation on Culture and the Arts (HiSAM)		1.10
Honolulu Museum of Art	Linekona Art Center	2.11
Kahalu'u Elementary School	Naomi Matsuzaki, Principal Carl Okamoto, Vice Principal	2.4
Kaiao Community Garden Mural Project	Hilo, Hawai'i	1.1
Kalihi Ahupua'a Ulu Pono Ahahui (KAUPA)	Barbara Natale, Executive Director	2.15
Kamehameha Schools		5.5
Ke Kula 'o Samuel M. Kamakau	Ivy K. Kelling, Principal/ Kāne'ohe, O'ahu	1.4, 1.11, 2.7, 2.18, 5.16, 5.17, 7.6, 7.7, 7.8, 8.3, 9.2, 11.42, 11.43
KEEP Project "Stories Told by Us"	Heitiare Kawehi Kammerer in 'Umeke Writings	2.16, 2.17
Koko Head Elementary School	Honolulu, O'ahu	See list of individual contributors
Na Lima Mili Hulu No'eau, LLC	Paulette Kahalepuna	3.6
Pu'uhonua Society	Maile Meyer (Hawai'i Kākou Mural Project at Hawaii Convention Center)	1.5, 1.16, 2.19, 3.2, 4.14, 6.2
Waiau Elementary School	Hawaiian Language Immersion Program	1.7

Individual Contributors

Last Name	First Name	School/Organization/Occupation	Figure
Aea	Kayce	Kamehameha Elementary School, Kapālama, Oʻahu	4.13, 11.31
Ayau-Odom	Heona	Ke Kula ʻo Samuel M. Kamakau	2.14, 5.8, 5.9, 6.5, 9.11
Baker	Kai Mālie	Kamehameha Elementary School, Kapālama, Oʻahu	1.6
Baker	Kaneikoliakawahineikaʻiukapuomua	Ke Kula ʻo Samuel M. Kamakau	I.3, 11.35
Ching	Kahi	Artist	4.15
Chung	Andy	UAchieve Hawaii	Discussions regarding dimensional drawings
Cleghorn	Faith Kuʻuleiokalani	Waiau Elementary School	1.7
del Rey	Kailani	Hauʻula Elementary School	9.4, 10.21, 10.26
Domingo	Kahikinaokalā	Ke Kula ʻo Samuel M. Kamakau	1.3, 9.3, 10.20
Domingo	Claire Ann Kalaunuola	Ke Kula ʻo Samuel M. Kamakau	4.1, 7.2
Enos	Solomon	Professional Cultural Artist	I.5
Enos	Cyan		5.7
Fermantez	Kialoa	Hauʻula Elementary School	1.9, 1.13, 7.4
Fermantez	Konaʻaihele	Hauʻula Elementary School	1.9, 6.10, 10.12
Fifita	Robin	Artist apprentice	11.1, 11.2
Foster	Hiʻiaka	Hauʻula Elementary School	11.38
Getz	Nichole Kamalani	Waiau Elementary School	1.7
Glassco	Kaʻio	Ke Kula ʻo Samuel M. Kamakau	10.13, 10.24, 10.25
Goodhue	Heua	Ke Kula ʻo Samuel M. Kamakau	6.3
Goodhue	Ioane	Ke Kula ʻo Samuel M. Kamakau	11.34
Goodhue	Kauʻi	Ke Kula ʻo Samuel M. Kamakau	1.19, 9.11, 11.44
Graham	Ron	Punahou School	Discussions regarding dimensional drawings
Graycochea	Keʻalohi	Hauʻula Elementary School	9.12
Graycochea	Noʻeau	Hauʻula Elementary School	4.2, 10.27
Harbottle	Kawena	Kamehameha Elementary School, Kapālama, Oʻahu	1.6
Hee	Dustin	Kamehameha Elementary School, Kapālama, Oʻahu	8.1
Horswill	Kamila	Waiau Elementary School	1.7
Kaea	Paige	Kamehameha Schools Scholars program	6.4
Kahana	Maikalani Aluli	Kamehameha Elementary School, Kapālama, Oʻahu	11.32
Kaleo	Kupaʻaikeolaaloha	Waiau Elementary School	1.7
Kamaka	Kalei	Ke Kula ʻo Samuel M. Kamakau	1.20
Kammerer	Heitiare Kawehi	Teacher, Hauʻula Elementary School	2.17, 10.15
Kanaʻiaupuni	Malialani	Ke Kula ʻo Samuel M. Kamakau	4.3, 4.7
Kawaiaea	Kekaulele	Kamehameha Elementary School, Kapālama, Oʻahu	9.9

Kawasaki	Wehi	Waiau Elementary School Hawaiian Immersion	1.7
Lagunero	Al	Artist	6.1, 7.1
La Pierre	Lance Genson Mahi	Papahana Kuaola, He'eia, O'ahu	2.23
Lehano	Kamalama	Camp Mokulē'ia Community Mural	1.3
McGough	Cameron	Kamehameha Elementary School, Kapālama, O'ahu	6.6
McKee	Patricia Louise Allison Lei Roselani	Hau'ula Elementary School	8.2, 10.11
Medeiros	Kendra		5.1, 5.2
Medeiros	Lamakūikealapono	Ke Kula 'o Samuel M. Kamakau	4.21, 6.8, 7.3
Morasco-Ayau	Noah Kalau	Ke Kula 'o Samuel M. Kamakau	11.36, 11.45
Napoleon	'Aiku'e	Ke Kula 'o Samuel M. Kamakau	6.12, 6.13, 6.14
Napoleon	'Onipa'a	Ke Kula 'o Samuel M. Kamakau	5.4, 6.11, 9.3
Napoleon	Ōpu'u	Ke Kula 'o Samuel M. Kamakau	4.9, 5.4, 6.12, 6.13, 6.14, 8.5
Navarro	Keira	Kamehameha Elementary School, Kapālama, O'ahu	7.5
Nu'uhiwa	Keahemakaniokalaniku	Kamehameha Elementary School, Kapālama, O'ahu	11.33
Orme	Harinani	Professional Cultural Artist	2.22
Phillips	Makana	Ke Kula 'o Samuel M. Kamakau	3.9, 4.9, 9.3
Pilila'au	Makau	Kamehameha Elementary School, Kapālama, O'ahu	9.7, 9.8
Sai-Dudoit	Heua	Ke Kula 'o Samuel M. Kamakau	6.3
Seymour	Joe	Artist	2.21
Shizuru	Matea	Kamehameha Elementary School, Kapālama, O'ahu	4.8
Takata	Julia	Kokohead Elementary School, Honolulu, O'ahu	11.22
Walker	Kahia	Hau'ula Elementary School	11.39
Walker	Makani	Hau'ula Elementary School	1.13
West	Aokeaokalani	Hau'ula Elementary School	11.40
West	Makali'i	Hau'ula Elementary School	10.22, 10.23, 11.37
Wilhelm	Māhie	Ke Kula 'o Samuel M. Kamakau	8.4, 9.11
Wilhelm	Makanaokalani	Ke Kula 'o Samuel M. Kamakau	2.12, 4.9, 5.4, 9.11
Wilhelm	Meakala	Ke Kula 'o Samuel M. Kamakau	1.19
Wright	Kamalei	Hau'ula Elementary School	1.13
Wright	Kia'ipono	Hau'ula Elementary School	1.13, 4.20
Yun	Kathreen	Kokohead Elementary School, Honolulu, O'ahu	9.1
Zidek	Puali'i Ann	Kamehameha Elementary School, Kapālama, O'ahu	1.6

Meleanna Meyer Artistic Photos

Figure	Title/Subject	Place
I.2	Kūkaniloko	Wahiawa, Oʻahu
I.4	Arting, Writing Journal	
I.8	Treasures from the Sea	Mokulēʻia, Oʻahu, Hawaiʻi
I.9	My Back Yard	Waimānalo, Oʻahu, Hawaiʻi
I.11	Heart Speaks	
I.12	Coming into Being	San Francisco, California
2.1	Gratitude to Our Ancestors	Oʻahu, Hawaiʻi
2.3	Mural with Eyes	San Francisco, California
2.6	A Child Expresses…	Kailua, Oʻahu, Hawaiʻi
2.9	Native American Carving	Helendale, California
2.10	Totem in Skagway	Skagway, Alaska
2.13	Pōhaku Aloha ʻĀina	Honolulu, Oʻahu, Hawaiʻi
2.20	We Are Family	San Francisco, California
3.1	Elegance of a Seed Pod	Honolulu, Oʻahu, Hawaiʻi
3.4	As Above, So Below	Puakō, Hawaiʻi
3.5	Lei Haku	Waikikī, Oʻahu, Hawaiʻi
4.4	A Bulldozer	Honolulu, Oʻahu, Hawaiʻi
4.18	Contemplation of a Turkey Wishbone	
4.19	Nā Lonoa	
5.3	A Metaphor of Needles and Threads	
5.15	Hoʻohuli	
PART III (Section divider illustration)		Hilo Garden Mural Project
10.4	Elder Brother, Hā-loa-na-ka-lau-ka-pa-li-li	

Meleanna Meyer Artwork

Figure	Title/Subject	Medium
INTRO I.1	Na Piko Ekolu – (Three Power Centers)	Acrylic painting
PART I (Section divider illustration)	Nā Kaula Akua (Prayer Cords)	Acrylic painting
2.5	The Nested Nature of Culture	Pencil drawing
PART II (Section divider illustration)	Arting and Writing	Pencil & watercolor drawing
3.7	Illustration as Story	Pen and ink
3.8	Close Observations	Arting and writing
4.12	Mini Notebook	Pencil drawings

4.16, 4.17	Any Kind Drawings	Color pencil and watercolor
4.18	Notebook Entry	Pen drawing
4.19	Mini Notebook Entry	Pen drawing
5.3	Pre Arting and Writing Metaphor	Pen and watercolor
5.6	Masterwork	Oil pastel and watercolor
10.8	Leaf Shapes	Pen drawings
10.18, 10.19	Kalo Mini Notebook	Pen drawings
11.3, 11.4, 11.6, 11.7, 11.8, 11.9, 11.10, 11.11, 11.12	Sample Family Tree	
11.13, 11.14, 11.15, 11.16, 11.17, 11.18	Sample Mini Notebook	
11.23, 11.24, 11.25, 11.26, 11.27, 11.28, 11.29, 11.30	Sample Self-Portrait Project	
11.41	Sample of Personal Constellation Map	

Miki Maeshiro Artistic Photos, Artwork, and Written Work

Figure	*Title/Subject*	*Medium*
I.13	Koʻolau, Oʻahu	Photo
I.14	Lanihuli, Kāneʻohe, Oʻahu	Photo
4.12	Mini Notebook	Pencil drawings
5.10	Pueo	Prewriting in notebook
5.12	Self-Portrait	Pencil drawing
5.13	Self-Portrait and Memoir	
5.14	The Kentucky Hills	Completed composition
10.2, 10.3	Kahana, ʻOahu	Photo
10.9	Teacher Writing and Arting Example of Ti Leaf	Pencil drawing
10.14	Diagram of the Kalo Plant	Oil pastel drawing
10.16	Demonstration Drawing	Pencil drawing
11.20	Mini Notebook	Prearting & prewriting

Anna Sumida Artwork

Figure	*Title/Subject*	*Medium*
11.19	Mini Notebook	Pencil drawings
11.21	Prearting and Prewriting	Pencil and pen

Index

Printed in the USA
CPSIA information can be obtained
at www.ICGtesting.com
JSHW071514131023
49863JS00012B/118